SO YOU'RE GOING TO BE A DAD

*This book is dedicated to my wonderful children,
whom I ignored for six months while I wrote
a book on how to be a good father.*

So You're Going to Be a Dad

PETER DOWNEY

Illustrations by Nik Scott

Da Capo
LIFE
LONG

A Member of the Perseus Books Group

First published in Australasia in 1994 by Simon & Schuster Australia, 20 Barcoo Street, East Roseville NSW 2069

Viacom International
Sydney New York London Toronto Tokyo Singapore

Credits:
Quotes from *Parenthood* on pages 9, 35 and 178 copyright © Universal City Studios, Inc. Courtesy of MCA Publishing Rights, a division of MCA Inc.

Library of Congress Cataloging-in-Publication Data
Downey, Peter, 1964-
    So you're going to be a dad / Peter Downey ; illustrations by Nik Scott.
    p. cm.
    Includes index.
    ISBN 1-55561-241-5   ISBN-13 978-1-55561-241-2
    1. Fatherhood. I. Title.

HQ756 .D59 2000
306.874'2—dc21   00-025709

Da Capo Press is a member of the Perseus Books Group.

Find us on the World Wide Web at http://www.dacapopress.com

Da Capo Press books are available at special discounts for bulk purchases in the U.S. by corporations, institutions, and other organizations. For more information, please contact the Special Markets Department at the Perseus Books Group, 11 Cambridge Center, Cambridge, MA 02142, or call (617) 252-5200.

EBC 40 39 38 37 36 35

Contents

Chapter 4: Surviving the Hospital

Chapter 5: Surviving at Home

Acknowledgments

Thanks to

MEREDITH, my companion and wife, for her love, patience and total devotion to me and our children. It's easy to be a good dad when you've got a good mom by your side. I hope she remains as loving, patient and totally devoted when she discovers that I've published lots of personal stuff about her.

RACHAEL, GEORGIA and MATILDA, my adorable girls. I couldn't have been a dad without you.

HILDA and STAN, my parents and role models, for always letting me know I was important.

RAY FARLEY, fellow author and father, for his coaching and rope-showing.

SUE WILLIAMSON, cousin and lactation consultant, who taught me all I know about breast milk and baked goods.

DR. STEWART MONTANO, friend since elementary school, for setting me straight about medical stuff and letting me join his Inventors Club when we were in third grade.

DR. KEITH HARTMAN, obstetrician and Alfa driver, for his impressive professional skill and personal touch.

PASCALE BEARD, for suggesting that *So You're Going to Be a Dad* is a catchier title than *Becoming a Dad—The Real Man's Guide to Fatherhood*.

NOEL from the local video store for keeping me stocked during the film-research stage.

My publishing team: SUSAN MORRIS-YATES, executive editor, for taking a chance with a new boy; STEPHANIE FUNNYWALK ... no, FENNINGWORM ... no, PFENNIGWERTH, my trusty editor, for the spit and polish in turning my scrawl into a fluent read; and SIMON SCHUSTER, publisher and all-around great guy, for letting me use his chalet.

And all my PATERNAL COMRADES for their advice, anecdotes and fellowship as we walk the road together.

Author's Note

————— ❧ —————

You know, when I was nineteen, Grandpa took me on the roller coaster . . . up . . . down . . . up . . . down . . . Oh, what a ride! Some didn't like it. They went on the merry-go-round. That just goes around . . . nothing. I like the roller coaster. You get more out of it.

Helen Shaw (Grandma), *Parenthood*

It is impossible to avoid generalizing in a book like this. Every pregnancy is different. No labor experience is the same. Each baby is unique. Doctors' views differ. Hospital policies vary. Averages are just that—averages.

Some of the items I have covered here in a casual aside are the topics of three-hundred-page books. So whatever you do, don't memorize this book as if it were a detailed, Sinai-delivered blueprint customized for your particular situation. You can't use this book for fathering by numbers. It won't work. I have written it simply to give you a little information, raise some issues for you to discuss with your wife, and stimulate thought regarding what it means to be a dad.

In talking about the female person who will form the other half of the parenting team in your family, I have used the word "wife" instead of "partner." Yeah, yeah, I know that not every guy who reads these words will be a "husband," but I had to choose one of them and I like the sound of "wife" rather than "partner." It sounds more relation-y, if you know what I mean. And anyway, it's my book so I can do anything I darn well please.

In referring to the baby in the book, I alternate between *he* and *she*, *him* and *her*. I know it sounds wishy-washy, but I just couldn't make up my mind. So there.

Preface

Being a dad has advantages and disadvantages. The advantages are

- You get a tax deduction.
- You can hang out in toy stores without embarrassment.
- Nice people let you cut to the front of lines.
- You can drive a minivan, which looks like the *Lost in Space* buggy.
- You can break wind in a crowded room and blame it on the baby.

The disadvantages are

- It wrecks your life.

This is a book about being a dad. I've written it for three reasons.

First of all, I want to become a rich and famous author. I hope this book ends up with one of those "Three Million Now in Print!" stickers on it. This will mean that I can do the talk-show circuit, dress in black and consume cappuccinos in inner-city cafés while chatting on a cell phone. I will jet-set around the international author scene and retire to a villa in Portugal.

Second, I'm writing this book to warn you: Becoming a dad is life changing. Somebody needs to prepare you. It might as well be me.

My wife, Meredith, and I are the proud parents of three daughters: Rachael, Georgia and Matilda. And I do mean proud. I love my kids. I love being their dad.

I loved it that time Rachael brought home some clay from preschool and thought she'd help me cook the evening meal by throwing a few chunks into my simmering pot of chicken stew. Of course, I didn't realize it until my guests started eating.

I loved it that time I left Georgia unsupervised for ten seconds and she knocked the receiver off the phone while simultaneously pressing the preset auto-dial of friends in Morocco, which then connected with their answering machine. Of course, I didn't realize this for well over an hour.

And I loved it that time I was dressed in a formal suit because I was going to a wedding in ten minutes and I went in for a final check on the kids and I picked up Matilda, and the chunky stuff from her diaper leaped out onto my suit but I didn't have another one so I just had to wipe it off, but all night during the reception people kept asking me, "What's that funny smell?"

Yep, there's nothing quite like being a dad. I consider myself a full-fledged family man. Being a dad is really important to me. I wouldn't swap my spot in life with anyone, except maybe Mel Gibson. But I haven't always felt so strongly, and I certainly wouldn't say I have enjoyed every minute of it. As a new dad, I remember crawling into bed each night mumbling inanely to myself, *Why didn't anybody tell me about this? Why wasn't I warned? Can I change my mind about this whole dad thing?*

I remember feeling angry that I had been sold an ideal that being a dad was easy and fun and full of warmth and wonder all the time. I felt vaguely annoyed that the male species had failed to prepare me adequately and truthfully for my new station in life. But then again . . . I should have expected it. It was the same male species that brought me up believing that bachelor parties were loads of fun, strip-clubs were elegant and sophisticated and that getting blind drunk was a great way to spend an evening.

Becoming a father is a shock to the system. It's not like getting a new car or a new dog. So I'm writing to give you the lowdown, the scoop, the big picture, the man-in-the-street view.

Third, I have a strong conviction about the importance of dadhood as an institution. The world needs good dads. Our kids need good dads. What more noble cause can a man be involved in than playing a primary role in getting members of the next generation ready to play their part in the world? And for too long we dads have taken a back seat in the parenting game!

It makes me happy that many "millennium men" are pretty good at taking an active and involved role in their family life. Unfortunately, many males in our society still view parenting as a maternal thing. They see their role as breadwinner and beer-drinker. This is a tragedy. As far as I can make out, the only parenting things that men can't do are

- get pregnant in the first place
- carry the baby for nine months
- give birth
- breastfeed
- change a diaper without sticking a pin in their finger or getting that same finger stuck to the disposable sticky tab

Unfortunately, as a high school teacher, I have met dads who are "not into family stuff," dads who seem permanently away on business, dads who are perpetually busy and are so wrapped up in their own lives that they and their children pass like ships in the night. They are men with no time for family.

I was leafing through a stack of old magazines the other day and came across an article on the new breed of workaholics—men who seem to live for their work and have little or no time for their own kids. But as any sociologist will tell you, one day these men will wake up and look around at the children who don't know them . . . and they will wonder that surely, there must be something more.

So in writing this book, I hope that I help some other guys out there realize how important and how enjoyable it is to be called "Dad."

But how exactly do you "be a dad"?

Good question, but I'm not going to give away the secret here in the Preface or you might not read the rest of the book.

Unfortunately, we males can't go to night school to get a Certificate of Fathering and, as far as I know, universities don't offer bachelor degrees in Paternity. And an apprenticeship with the guy down the road who has a three-month-old is probably out of the question.

So how do we, as aspiring fathers-to-be, learn the ropes of fathering without hanging ourselves, so to speak?

When my wife, Meredith, was pregnant with our first child, Rachael, I had a thousand questions that needed answering. We had plans to make and things to do and I knew nothing about kids. I needed information. I needed *lots* of information. And the best source of information was, of course, the guys who had trail-blazed the fathering path ahead of me. I would corner some poor unsuspecting new father at work or at a party and grill him about all the intricacies of pregnancy, labor, diapers, feeding and fatherhood.

I haunted bookstores looking for decent books that would prepare me for dadhood. Unfortunately, most seem to be written exclusively for women. You can tell because the covers are soft-focus photos of models, silhouetted against frosted windows, or they show a ridiculously well-groomed dad on the cover. I did find a few books written just for dads, but they were either so dry or thick that they scared me off, or they were written by authors with sideburns.

That's when I decided to write this.

The question you may be asking at this moment is, *Who exactly is Pete Downey to be telling me about all this stuff, anyway?*

Yet another good question.

Well, I'm not a medical doctor or a researcher. I'm not a child psychologist or a professional author. I'm not a learned obstetrician or pediatrician. My qualification is that I'm an ordinary guy, probably just like you. I live in the suburbs, work five days a week, wash the car on the weekend and occasionally wear cowboy boots and listen to old records.

Then one day I became a dad.

One day I was a normal, carefree guy, just like you. The next day I was driving a minivan and wearing sandals with socks.

So here I am, a few years down the road, ready to share my joys, frustrations, ideas and mistakes. If that isn't enough, I've also watched plenty of movies and TV shows with dads and babies in them.

My basic message in this book is that being a dad takes energy, commitment and involvement. It takes a lot of time and effort. You can't do it half-heartedly. You can't do it in your spare time. This is very important for you to understand, so I'm going to write it again.

Being a dad takes energy, commitment and involvement. It takes a lot of time and effort. You can't do it half-heartedly. You can't do it in your spare time.

It means being active and involved in the daily life of your baby. It means getting your hands dirty and participating in all aspects of family life. It means sharing the parenting and rejecting stereotypes that say parenting is for women only. If you still haven't gotten the message, read this paragraph again.

And before I come under attack from any women for the inherent sexism in the pages that follow, let me say that this book is for guys. It's not designed for couples, nor is it designed for women. I wrote it with the male in mind, the male who knows little or nothing about fatherhood but who is eager to give it a try.

But in concentrating almost exclusively on the dad, let me just say that by no means do I consider men to have a more important role than women in the rearing of children. Parenting is a team sport. Moms are just as important as dads. I have nothing against women. In fact, I like women.

I even married one.

So welcome to the wonderful world of fatherhood. You have a long road ahead of you. A hard road. A road fraught with obstacles and tribulations. But it is also a rewarding road, peppered with great experiences and golden moments that you wouldn't have thought possible. And once you walk the road, you'll never be the same again.

So, good luck on your journey.

You'll need it.

CHAPTER 1

Beginnings

*If only I could have seen the writing on the wall. It
would have said, "Your wife's pregnant! Run away!
Run away!"*

Sex and Its Side Effects

WARNING: The Surgeon General advises that sex may cause children.

Sex is an appropriate starting point for us to ponder the wonder
of fatherhood. After all, this is where the journey begins.

Because you are actually reading this page, I can safely
assume that you have already passed this first crucial test. With
flying colors. For this reason, and in the interest of good taste,
I shall refrain at this point from elaborating any further on how
much fun you had in the process and "was it good for you too,
baby?" and all that.

But we know what happened. While you were sitting in bed,
sighing in post-passion euphoria—an armada of about 300
million of your sperm set off from Port Penis on the first leg of
their six-inch (or so) marathon swim through all that female
plumbing, the names of which I can never quite remember.

(I will probably never come to terms with all those bits and
pieces of the female anatomy. As a teenager, sitting in a health
class at an all-boys school, I was always perplexed by the
textbook cross-sections of women's insides. You know the picture
I mean? That's right, the diagram of the one-legged woman. I
could never follow all the bulbous squiggles and channels with
the funny names. In fact, it was only years later that I discovered

that the cross-section diagram was in fact a *side* view, not a top view. Maybe I should have paid more attention, instead of cutting up at the back of the classroom with Paul Brinkman, trying to put diaphragms on our heads like swim caps.)

Cross-section of women's insides

Anyway, while nothing to you, those inches are a veritable New York Harbor to these little tadpoles. Like salmon swimming upstream, they have to swim from the vagina, north through the uterus (or womb) and climb one of the two Fallopian tubes, where an egg is hiding. And there can be only one winner! There are no consolation prizes. If they don't win the victor's trophy (the "egg" or "ovum"), they're out of the picture for good. And with odds like 300 million to one—much worse than any lottery played in the history of humankind—the competition is fierce.

An hour or so later, with the swim mostly over (probably while you were snoring loudly, totally oblivious to the creative energies you had unleashed upon the world), only a few thousand of the strongest sperm had survived the journey. The finalists had navigated the obstacles and the plumbing with the complicated names and had located the prize—the golden egg.

Now, this is not an egg in the chicken-type, hard-boiled, fried or sunny-side-up sense of the word. It is more like a dot. A cell. A little pinprick. A dot on the back of a cell sitting in the middle of a pinprick. The point is, it is very, very tiny. It makes the period at the end of this sentence look like a beach ball.

Like the sperm, the egg too has undergone a journey. Women have about half a million of these ova stored in their ovaries. Each month during ovulation, the mature or "ripe" ovum leaves its sisters and bobs on down one of the Fallopian tubes, like a little planet waiting for the strange aliens with the tails to come and visit.

So it sits there, waiting.

Waiting.

Waiting.

Time is critical, because this ovum has a "use-by" date of about 24 hours. So for the next couple hours after their journey, all the remaining spermatic contenders go into Stage Two of their biathlon, which is basically a head-butting competition. The sperm all find a spot on the ovum they can call their own, stick their heads down and start spinning around and around like fence-post diggers. The winner is the one who breaks the ovum wall and gets in first.

The instant this happens, the ovum gets all coy and undergoes a chemical change, which shuts out all the other contenders. It's disappointing for them, probably, getting all that way, only to be locked out at the last minute just because they couldn't dig fast enough. But hey, it's a jungle out there. They probably get depressed and swim around until they die.

Sad.

Anyway, what you have now is a fertilized egg sitting in its own little dark, warm universe. You can almost imagine the *Starship Enterprise* zooming past through this microscopic universe with Spock at the viewscreen musing, "It's life, Jim . . . but not as we know it."

So there you have it. The egg is officially fertilized. The wheels of fate have spun and, although you don't know it yet, you're going to be a dad.

This is the miracle of life. The miracle of sex. And it *is* a miracle.

God really was clever to have thought it up.

And this child of yours is unique in the universe. You and your wife are the only combination in history who could have created him. Think of it this way: Your wife has about half a million ova. You have about 300 million sperm per ejaculation. Let us assume, for the sake of argument, that you have sex once a week over a ten-year potential parenting period. Your child could be *any combination* of any single sperm and any single ovum. So if my mathematics serves me correctly (which it might not, considering I got only 42 percent correct on my math final in my senior year), then that makes your child one of 78,000,000,000,000,000 (78 quadrillion) possible people combinations.

God really was clever to have thought it up.

This is a humbling thing for a father to think about. Without getting into a philosophical debate, it's kind of awesome to think about the infinitesimal beginnings of human life—the beginnings of the life of your child. What is at this point an indistinct speck will grow to be a person whom you will know and love intimately—a person, I might add, who will change your life.

You will see this infinitesimally small spot learn to crawl, walk and talk. It will create bizarre drawings for you to stick on your refrigerator and say great stuff like, "I love you, Dad." It will get dressed up as a bear for school-play night. You will worry when it goes out on its first date and you will lie awake at night because it borrowed your car and is two hours late getting home. And then one day that microscopic cell will *leave* home and you'll wonder what you ever did before it came along.

Morning Sickness

Of course, at this stage, you are probably still unaware you are traveling down the road to dadhood. The thing is, you don't turn on the evening news and hear

> *"This bulletin just in . . . Mr. Peter Downey's wife became pregnant yesterday in what some have referred to as a nocturnal orgy of sex. Early reports state that both mother and father are in stable condition."*

Similarly, the stork doesn't wake you up in the morning by tapping on your bedroom window and squawking, "YOUR WIFE'S PREGNANT! BRAAA! YOUR WIFE'S PREGNANT! BRAAA!"

But there is a telltale sign. An early warning system, if you like. It's called *morning sickness.*

One day a few years ago (in our glory days, when we were DINKs—Double Income, No Kids), Meredith accompanied me to get a haircut. The "salon" was half-full of women getting perms and rinses and other things out of my experience and beyond my comprehension. Everything was going fine until my wife unexpectedly leaped up and staggered into the bathroom at the back of the salon. For the next few minutes we all sat there perplexed by the cacophony of gurgling and gagging, beautifully amplified by the tiled walls and floor.

At the time, I simply assumed this sudden and violent illness was due to my failed attempt at Thai cooking the previous evening. I don't think I'd even heard of morning sickness before. But that sickness was the trumpet blast that heralded the beginning of a new stage in my life: dadhood.

If only I could have seen the writing on the wall. It would have said, "Your wife's pregnant! Run away! Run away!" But back then I was naïve and ignorant about such things. You see, on the *outside* my wife looked fine and normal. I had learned from TV that pregnant women were huge and ugly, waddled when they walked, and dressed in tents. But my wife was slim and attractive, she sauntered when she walked and she was wearing jeans; therefore, she was not pregnant.

But on the *inside*, that sperm and ovum combination was hard at work on its human cocktail. And you can't have another person starting to grow within your own personal body space without certain side effects on your own well-being. The little dynamic duo was busily producing a nasty hormone potion called *beta hCG*. Meredith's blood and major body systems had gone into overdrive. One "small" side effect was that she felt nauseated.

They call this *morning sickness*. It's like being carsick, except that it keeps going even after you get out of the car. It's probably the same sensation you get when you scarf down a seafood platter, a dozen raw eggs, a large chocolate sundae and a few mugs of beer before going for a spin on a roller coaster. It usually lasts for three months, but in some cases it can last the entire pregnancy. The term *morning sickness* was obviously thought up by a man, because in fact it can happen all day long, not just in the morning.

To be accurate, it should be called *morning, afternoon and night sickness*, but this doesn't really roll off the tongue as well.

Confirming the Obvious

Some women know they are pregnant within a few weeks of conception. Their biological systems start ringing alarms and they soon put two and two together. But you also hear stories about women who go to their doctor with a suspected gallstone problem only to find their gallstone has eyes, hands and a heartbeat and is already eight months old. Obviously, their biological alarms did not ring loud enough. They put two and two together, but ended up with five.

However, quite a few moms I know assure me that most women know when they are pregnant. "It's just one of those instinctive things," they say. Being a guy, I'm not sure about the validity of this comment, but I guess there must come a point in every woman's pregnancy when she begins to suspect that something is going on down in the engine room. It might be because of a missed period. It might be because her breasts have become sore or because she is suddenly moody or tired. It might be because of her unexpected tendency to vomit, even when you didn't cook the night before. It might even be "women's intuition."

Once the woman reaches this point, however, things really start to heat up. She can go to the drugstore or the doctor to have her suspicions confirmed with a pregnancy test.

The Test

Ah, the marvels of modern medical science! This urine test is really quite amazing. If you can, it's worth seeing. It's called a *beta hCG* test and it measures the hormone level in the woman's urine secreted by the suspected internal intruder.

A couple of different tests are available on the market. One looks like a swimming pool chlorine tester and the other looks like a credit card. Meredith used the latter. Four or five drops of urine were dripped onto one corner of the card. The urine then seeped across to the other corner, passing through a little view window en route. Then she sat and watched as a little cross appeared in the window, which meant, *Welcome to the world of parenthood.*

You can even carry around this little card with you! Don't worry about the smell—show your friends!

And Now, the News

As far as I can make out, there are two distinct types of fathers. First, there are the fathers *who have been trying* to become fathers. This word "trying" is a great example of a euphemism. What it basically means is that they have been having sex a lot. They have talked it over with their wife and have both been "trying" for a long time to get it all happening. For some, this is a long, complicated and frustrating process, perhaps involving thermometers, calendars and visits to the doctor—maybe even a visit to that special doctor in the city who gives you a glass jar and says, "Third cubicle on the right, sir."

Anyway, the bottom line is that this type of father and his wife have been working hard at getting pregnant, at becoming parents, mother and father, mom and dad. He is expectant and is anxiously waiting, planning and preparing for the missed period and those magically whispered words, "Honey, I'm pregnant."

Then there is the second type of father. He is the one who has *not* been trying to become a father. This doesn't necessarily mean he hasn't been having sex a lot. Perhaps in the heat of passion he and his wife brushed aside the security of contraception. Perhaps the contraception failed. Maybe he simply forgot that sex causes children. Perhaps he just wanted to see what would happen. Of course, he could be just plain stupid. Anyway, the bottom line is that this type of father enjoyed sex largely for relational purposes, as opposed to specifically "extending the family tree" purposes.

He is *not* expectant and is *not* anxiously waiting, planning and preparing for the missed period and those magically whispered words, "Honey, I'm pregnant."

Now, both of these guys have two things in common:

1. In just a few months, they will both become fathers.

2. The day will come soon when this important fact is revealed to them.

At this point, they will probably have pretty distinct and different responses to the actual news that fatherhood is on the horizon. Let's examine the different scenarios:

Father Type I—the one who has been *trying*—may experience the standard middle-class television scenario. Coming home from a busy day at work, he will throw his stuff into a corner and yell, "Damn corporate headquarters! That contract I've just spent months on won't be ready till November. As if I don't have enough work around Christmas as it is."

To which his wife, coming down the stairs, will say, "Well, don't make too many plans for the end of the year."

(At this point wafting violins will start to swell in the background. He will eye her hopefully.)

"You mean . . ."

"Yes, honey, I saw Dr. Lloyd this afternoon."

(Crescendo of violins. Counter-melody subtly and harmoniously introduced by cellos and violas.)

"You mean . . ."

"Yes, my love. The tests were positive."

(Massive crescendo. Entire symphony joins in.)

"You mean . . ."

"Yes, my honey blossom pancake . . . You're going to be . . . (and then the magical words as the whole room starts to spin uncontrollably, accompanied by beautiful orchestral themes) A DAD."

He will experience a sensation of being lifted off the ground. He will soar above the trees and spin around among the clouds. Clutching his wife to him, he will feel a deep inner warmth and fulfillment. It is a beautiful moment, full of music and fireworks.

Now for Father Type II—the one who has *not* been trying. Coming home from a busy day at work, he will throw his stuff into a corner and yell, "Damn corporate headquarters! That contract I've just spent months on won't be ready till November. As if I don't have enough work around Christmas as it is."

To which his wife, coming down the stairs, will say, "Well, don't make too many plans for the end of the year."

(At this point he will hear the theme from *Jaws* waft menacingly through the air. He will eye her suspiciously.)

"What are you talking about?"

"Darling, I saw Dr. Lloyd this afternoon."

(Crescendo of *Jaws* theme. Aggressive counter-melody suddenly introduced à lá staccato stabs from *Psycho*.)

"Yeah, and?"

"I had some tests. They were positive."

(Massive crescendo of timpani and other nastily percussive instruments.)

"You mean . . ."

"I'm pregnant. You're going to be . . . (and then the room will spin sickeningly to the deafening chorus of cannons, breaking glass and sirens) A DAD."

He will experience the curious sensation of being clubbed across the forehead with a baseball bat while toppling backward over a huge cliff. His head will swim and his knees will buckle. He will clutch his wife to him so he doesn't fall over. He may even experience inner warmth as his bladder malfunctions. His jaw will flop around and, in a feeble attempt at speech, he will produce only pathetic squeaks and gurgles.

In this situation, it is important to handle the moment delicately. For example, there are certain things that a Father Type II should *not* say:

- "How did that happen?"
- "I've got football practice."
- "So what?"
- "We can't afford it."
- "What's for dinner?"

All of these comments are things that males might have said back in the insensitive seventies. But come on, this is the new millennium. We're all Sensitive New-Age Guys.

Aren't we?

By the way, when your wife says she's pregnant, DON'T— whatever you do, DON'T—say, "Oh, you'd better sit down." They only say that on TV.

If you're a Father Type I, you probably feel pretty good. If you're a Father Type II, don't feel too bad. I've been a Father Type II three times now and it hasn't done me any harm. Not that my wife and I were irresponsible or stupid or anything like that. Meredith had been on the pill for a while. For various and personal reasons, which are frankly none of your business, we both decided that she should "come off" the pill. Our basic idea was that nature would take its course and she would get pregnant eventually (that is, in a few years) and whenever that happened would be just fine.

It happened the next day.

Call me naíve, call me stupid, but I thought that pregnancy was actually a pretty difficult thing to achieve and that our "nature's course" method would take a while. We have since discovered that we are as fertile as the Nile Delta and only need to drink from the same coffee cup for Meredith to start feeling sick in the morning.

I clearly remember the day I found out my life was about to take off in a new and radical direction. I had been sitting at my desk waiting for Meredith to pick me up. It was a Thursday in March.

She'd needed the car that day because she was going to the doctor. She hadn't been her usual self since that emergency at the hairdresser's. We were a little concerned.

She waltzed in, said hi, looked totally cool and normal. We engaged briefly in some light chat and then headed out through the drizzle that had plagued our city for the past few months. My mind was filled with thoughts of what we were going to have for dinner. Pizza? No, a chicken dish . . . or those Mexican things. What are they called?

"Pete, what are you doing on October twenty-fourth?" she asked.

"Nothing," I replied, eyeing her sideways. "Why, what have you got in mind?"

Of course! *Tacos.*

"Parenthood," she said, with a mischievous grin.

Or are they *nachos?*

Parenthood.

Nachos.

Parenthood.

The word spun inside my head for a few seconds, trying desperately to find something to grasp on to, but all it found were mental cookbooks. Toasted sandwiches, perhaps?

"Excuse me?" I'm sure this is what I meant to say, but for some reason my mouth said something along the lines of, "E bed du plarnd?"

"Parenthood" came the word again. "I'm pregnant. We're going to be parents. You're going to be a dad."

She smiled. Cool. Collected.

I wobbled. Shocked. Flushed.

Time seemed to stand still. My mind scrambled.

A father.

The words slowly sank in.

A *father?* Aren't they the guys who drive minivans and spend a hundred bucks on junk at the mall?

A *FATHER?* Aren't they the ragged-looking men who wear socks and sandals and go to bed at 8:30 P.M.?

A father? Me? My father is a father! *His* father was a father! I'm only a son. Worse, I'm just a boy, a child. I've only just left home. I can't even iron my shirts right. Panic! Changing diapers? Me?

Mayday . . . Mayday . . . I'm going down! What about sleep? What about our mortgage? What about that overseas trip we were planning?

And what about dinner?

At this moment, one of my students went by. "Hey, Mr. Downey. How you doing?"

If only you knew, boy, I thought. *If only you knew.*

By the way, we had leftovers for dinner.

How Do Ya Feel?

This was my introduction to the wonderful world of fatherhood. One minute I was coasting along through life at a happy pace. I was in control, closely following "the plan." Our young married lives were progressing nicely and the bank balance told us we were gradually finding our feet. The next minute, my life was spinning madly out of control on a bizarre and completely unexpected tangent.

Our future was suddenly plunged into the abyss of new and unexplored terrain.

Some men are thrilled and excited to hear the news of their impending dadhood. Some feel delirious and "over the top." I felt a whole lot of emotions at once.

The main one was guilt. I felt guilty that I wasn't ecstatic. I felt guilty that I didn't rush forward and grab my wife and say, "I love you," or something like that. It wasn't like in the movies at all. Why didn't I feel all paternal? Where was the symphony orchestra? To be blunt, it took me a little while to warm to the idea.

In a way, I also felt excited. I didn't really know what lay ahead of me, but the news brought the kind of expectant, nervous thrill you get when something really big is about to happen. It was the same sensation I experienced as a child, lining up for a ride at the carnival while listening to the screams of fear from those already inside. I was struck dumb by the total awesomeness of the moment and felt that some philosophical and momentous words were in order. In a kind of slow-motion haze, I put my hand on Meredith's stomach and mumbled something grandiose about how just inches away, under the skin, a new life was forming.

"No," she said, moving my hand, "just inches away under the skin is my bladder. The baby is *here*."

Another feeling I had was fear. I felt it in the pit of my stomach and tasted it in my mouth. I was scared of this great big thing called "fatherhood" now rushing inevitably toward me like a freight train. I was scared of the unknown. I knew absolutely nothing about babies. And I do mean *nothing*. I never even liked holding other people's babies. Come to think of it, I still don't.

It wasn't that I was opposed to the idea of becoming a father. It just took me by surprise, that's all. I mean, I didn't even suspect that Meredith was pregnant. To my mind there were no subtle hints at what was to come. So I felt shocked and awkward that this was not another of our carefully laid, middle-class-young-upwardly-mobile-couple plans. I could not even begin to comprehend what the words "you're going to be a dad" meant. I knew how to teach *Hamlet* and how to cook a reasonable stir-fry. But a baby? You must be kidding! It all seemed so big and scary.

So *life changing*.

Since then, I have noticed that my reaction is not that uncommon. I've now realized that it's all right to feel shock and guilt and the burden of responsibility. It's all right to feel inadequate and scared. Fatherhood is a big and scary prospect. It's not something that can be digested and dealt with in a few minutes, or learned by glancing through cute anecdotes from the *Reader's Digest* left in your doctor's waiting room.

Remember, there's comfort in numbers. Don't be so self-indulgent that you forget that your wife is also having the baby. Oh yes . . . You remember now. She may be feeling the same way you are. On top of which, she has the added anxiety of disruption to her work and nine months of increasing bodily discomfort, only to be topped off by incredible physical pain during the birth and months of sheer exhaustion afterward.

So talk it over. Discuss your fears, feelings and concerns. Share your expectations and ideas. Communicating and sorting out your feelings is a great way to establish the team philosophy of parenting, even at this early stage.

Also remember that nobody expects you to be an instant parent. You're not supposed to be an expert in the blink of an eye. Even if you are totally stupid and extremely ignorant and hopeless with kids, it doesn't matter. You'll learn.

I did.

You'll be surprised at how little time it takes you to get used to the idea of fatherhood. And once you've recovered from the shock, it's time to start taking action.

There's much to be done and only a few months to go.

Let's Go Public

So where does that leave you now? To summarize, you have

- had child-producing sex
- found out that your baby will enter the world in less than a year
- recovered from the initial shock

The next stage can be pleasant or frightening, depending on

- how you handle it
- whether your wife's family and friends actually like you

I'm talking about *breaking the news* to people.

Watching the various reactions of family and friends—screams, fainting, hysterical laughter, weeping, muscle failure, casual nonchalance and so on—can be a source of great amusement and the topic of dinnertime storytelling for years to come. But before you reach for the phone, keep a few things in mind.

First, don't go public too early. It is important for you and your wife to have a little time to get used to the idea of becoming parents before you go telling everybody. Wait a couple of days. Wait a couple of *weeks*. There's no rush. Once the cat's out of the bag, everybody will want to give you advice and ask about parenting and have you over for dinner and start knitting little jackets and so on. Your conversation will be dominated by annoying questions and lengthy anecdotes. Your friends and relatives will cease to look at you as "a couple"; you will become "parents-to-be."

So you and your wife should stew over it a while first to get more comfortable with the whole idea. Treasure your last moments together as "a couple."

Second, news about impending parenthood spreads faster than the bubonic plague. Research statistics have shown that from the time you break the news to the first person, it takes on average only forty-five seconds for every single person you have ever met in your entire life to find out you're going to be a dad.

This is particularly the case if you have one of those friends who loves to act like the town reporter. You know the type I mean. As soon as they hear any news of a vaguely gossipy or topical nature (such as engagements, births, pregnancies, divorces, socially awkward medical-test results and so on), they see it as their destiny in life to spread the word to everybody in their address book. This person can dial a phone number in the time it takes you to blink.

Tell this person last.

If you want to tell people yourself instead of letting them hear it through the grapevine, you have to time the announcement with the precision of a military operation. And once you go public, you have to do it *quickly*. If you don't, the surprise will be spoiled and everyone will know.

Third, there are familial and peer politics to consider. Some families have a "pecking order" and if you don't pay attention to it, you may end up paying the price for the rest of your life. You know what I'm talking about. If you tell your neighbor before you tell your mother-in-law, there will be hell to pay. Like an elephant, she will never forget. (Just let me make it clear at this point that in no way do I consider my mother-in-law to be in any way like an elephant.)

Anyway, one of the best things about good news is telling other people, so that's just what we did.

First, my parents: We sat them down on the couch. Not knowing how to broach the subject subtly, I jabbed my finger at Meredith and blurted, "She's pregnant!"

My mother's legs did a little involuntary dance and her frame shuddered slightly. Father, repeating his performance from the day we announced our engagement, sat there flapping his jaw with a glazed expression on his face. When he stirred himself into action, several moments later, he pulled Meredith onto his knee and mumbled, "You'd better sit down."

Then we told my ninety-year-old great-aunt. "WE ARE HAVING A BABY!" I yelled into her hearing aid.

"No, no gravy for me, thank you," she replied with a smile.

My mother-in-law was pretty cool about the whole thing. We told her in the hallway of her apartment as she came home from work one afternoon laden with groceries. I was hoping she'd drop them, but I was disappointed.

Then there were our friends. One leaped screaming across a table at us while her husband had a small seizure. Another group of friends immediately broke out warm champagne. One friend suddenly developed lockjaw—his mouth didn't function for several seconds—and another went into shock—all he could do was constantly repeat sounds like "Wwwoaaaahhhh" and "Woooooow." Meanwhile some of my less intellectual male friends nudged me in the ribs and leered as if to say, "We know what you two have been up to!" Smart thinking, guys.

Lots of people we told over the phone just went silent. Maybe they fainted.

Myth Busting

Before we go any further with our exploration of fatherhood, I would like to explode some myths. Many of the expectations that I had as a new father turned out to be pure fiction. As a consequence, discovering paternal reality turned out to be a rude awakening. And why? Because for many of us, our main source of information about many facets of the universe is that hideous creation of the twentieth century—the television.

Unfortunately, television has proven to be an unreliable teacher across a whole range of human endeavor. The main problem is that a lot of what you see on television regarding life only takes place on *Fantasy Island*. Most of it is the creation of a screenwriter—and I would lay money on the fact that most of the screenwriters responsible have never experienced what they are writing about. To be blunt, you will be in trouble if you believe that what you see on the screen is reality.

For example, regarding sex. Turn on the TV at any time of the day or night and there it is. When I got married, I carried with me the adolescent expectation that when I got home after a hard day's work, my negligee-clad wife would greet me at the door with a glass of champagne in her hand and a rose clamped between her teeth. Each night would herald a candle-lit feast, followed by nocturnal pleasures on an epic scale.

It wasn't like this. The TV lied.

The same applies to violence. The TV says that a gang of muscular, martial-arts thugs can bash you in the face and ribs with big lumps of wood and you can get away with only disheveled hair. The TV says that when you get shot, you can grimace and get up again with all guns blazing. And I must have seen a hundred bottles smashed over a hundred heads in TV dramas. In real life, it's not the bottle that smashes.

Television also paints a different picture of reality where pregnancy, birth and, of course, fatherhood are concerned. Real-life pregnant women don't always stagger around groaning with their hands on their hips, and they don't need to sink awkwardly into a chair after every step they take. They don't usually wake you up in the middle of the night and send you on an errand to the local convenience store to satisfy their craving for a can of tuna, a giant chocolate bar and a few pickles. They don't always give birth with their feet up in stirrups and, I'm sorry to disappoint you about this, but you probably won't get to wear a gown and surgical mask during the labor. I haven't yet been to a hospital that lines up their newborns behind a plate-glass window for all the relatives to stare at, either. And if you try to light a celebratory cigar in a hospital waiting room, you'll probably be beaten by nurses with bedpans.

If you're hoping the TV will supply you with a paternal role model, don't bother. Dads on the idiot box fall into one of two categories, both of which are equally ineffectual and pathetic.

On one hand, there is the Superfather. He is the one with an understanding smile and incredible wisdom. He solves all problems with a few paternal clichés and the family is better again. He is always in control and is always selfless and giving. He has no life apart from his kids. Just watch any modern American sitcom or check out the classics like *The Brady Bunch*, *Happy Days*, *My Three Sons* or, one of my favorites, *Lost in Space*, and you'll see what I'm talking about. Of course, you never see these dads make a bed, change a diaper, set the table or lose their temper.

On the other hand, there is the Antifather. These dads are ridiculously hopeless and inept at fathering. They have terrible relationships with their kids and treat them either as cuddly toys or with a sense of vague detachment. If you've ever seen *Married with Children*, *The Simpsons* or *Roseanne*, you'll know what I'm talking about.

But television isn't entirely to blame for this constant stream of lies, damn lies and statistics. The same applies to a lot of books on parenting, particularly the big ones with lots of glossy photos. I'm not sure where they take these photos exactly, but it sure isn't planet Earth. It must be that fantasy world known as *Bookland*, a place of perpetual political correctness and saccharine soft focus.

In Bookland, pregnant women float about in flattering pastel outfits. They spend their days with their hands resting meaningfully on their abdomens and soft, warm, contemplative expressions on their faces. Their Bookland husbands (who are well-presented, clean-cut professionals wearing comfortable but socially acceptable casual-Friday wear) hold their wives tenderly and stare deeply into their eyes. Bookland dads are especially good at assembling cribs and car seats without losing their tempers or putting out their backs.

In Bookland, laboring women don't sweat—they merely look determined. Their serious but competent husbands support them by knowing exactly what they want and then giving it to them. The women give birth to remarkably clean babies on crisp sheets without blood or other fluids. All is laughter and tears of joy and sincerity dripping from the intravenous bag.

Of course the stars of the Bookland fantasy are the superbabies—babies that perpetually smile, gurgle and cock their heads cutely, like puppies. Their eyes are alert, their skin is perfect and their heads are the way heads should be. Incredibly, their diapers are totally devoid of any unsightly substances.

It isn't like this, either. The books lied, too.

So, as you walk the parental road, try not to think about what happens on the TV or in books—in some books, anyway.

That will only get you into trouble.

Congratulations

So, you're going to be a dad.

Congratulations! Have a cigar. Take the day off work. But (and I don't mean to spoil the moment here) exactly why should you be congratulated? No offense, but what exactly have you done that is worthy of all this back-patting, pal? To be blunt, you had sex. That's all you've done. Chipped in a few sperm. A roll in the hay. This is why one columnist described fatherhood as "a moment of male pleasure followed by nine months of female agony."

This idea was conveyed quite succinctly in a bizarre foreign film I saw late one night a few years ago on TV—the title of which has now disappeared from memory, along with the content of most of my secondary education. In one particular scene, an angry woman yells at her husband in brash Portuguese:

> *"What does being a father mean to you? But one second!"*

No, she wasn't criticizing him for being a premature ejaculator. She was saying that to the husband, fatherhood was merely a side effect of a brief moment of sexual pleasure. Ron Howard's perceptive and terrific film *Parenthood* makes a similar comment. In it, Keanu Reeves says brashly to Dianne Wiest:

> *"You know . . . You need a license to buy a dog or*
> *drive a car. Hell, you need a license to catch a fish.*
> *But they'll let any . . . assh—e be a father."*

A razor-sharp truism like this hits you right between the eyes.
To become a teacher, it took me four years of university study.
To drive a car, I took lessons and had to pass written and road
tests. To be a father, however, all I needed was an erection, my
wife and a few glasses of wine.

This logic seems backward to me, considering that becoming
a dad is infinitely more important and significant than learning
about verbs or knowing how far away from a stop sign you can
park your car. Any man with a working appendage can become
a biological parent. But becoming a good dad takes considerably
more time and effort than a simple sperm donation. That was
the easy part, the fun part. All the hard work lies ahead of you.

You don't suddenly start wearing the "dad cap" on the day
your child is born. Don't wait that long to start working on
becoming a father. If you keep waiting for the "right time," it
will never come. You'll end up like the guy in that ad from
late-night television:

> *"Do you remember last week how you said that next*
> *week you'd play with your kids? It's next week."*

Even worse, you could end up like the dad in the classic
Harry Chapin song *Cat's in the Cradle*, who was always too busy
to spend time with his son. One day, he woke up and realized
that his son had grown up, but by then it was too late. This is a
great song, which constantly inspires me to spend time with my
children. I must admit, though, that I have never quite
understood exactly what the cat was doing in the cradle in the
first place.

Anyway, I'm getting sidetracked. Back to the heavy stuff.

Being a dad—being a *good* dad—is really important. It is a
huge responsibility and a mammoth commitment. And it

doesn't start tomorrow. It starts the moment you find out your wife is pregnant. It starts while your baby is still an indistinct cell division in the womb. It's vital that you get your head together early in the game and establish good patterns in fathering. So if you want to be a good dad—an involved dad—start now.

Congratulations on having the privilege and responsibility of becoming a father. But if you want to smoke the cigar, earn the right.

CHAPTER 2
Pregnancy

*They have to go from being a single cell with only a
touch of DNA for good luck to being a whole person
complete with a full set of functioning body parts.
Now that's what I call an achievement.*

Sugar and Spice

Have you ever noticed that a lot of the questions people ask you
are really dumb? They're the kind of questions people ask when
they actually have nothing to say but are just using their vocal
chords to kill time.

For example, on your birthday, when people ask you if you feel
any older. Or on the return from your honeymoon, when people
ask you if you are enjoying married life. Or on Christmas Day,
when someone asks you if you like the present they gave you.

Like I said . . . dumb.

Being in the baby-making game does not exclude you from
such unrelenting conversational stupidity. For example, the
question that I am constantly asked during every pregnancy is,
"What do you want . . . a boy or a girl?" This is asked with the
same casualness as, "What do you want on your sandwich . . .
mayo or mustard?"

Some people obviously consider this a critical question. I
think it is a dumb question. For goodness sake, we're talking
about a baby here, not a sandwich. You get what you get and
you should be grateful that you've got something at all. What
I wanted was a human being and, quite frankly, I didn't give a
darn what sex it was. But few people actually believed me.

For some fathers-to-be, however—and maybe for you—the
sex of their child is a big deal. It seems to me that a lot of dads

desperately want a son. I don't know why. Maybe it's because they want to vicariously live out their wasted youth. Maybe they want to do macho father-and-son stuff, like chopping down trees.

But remember, we're not talking about buying a dog or ordering fast food. What if you don't get what you want? What if you really want a son and you get a daughter? What if you really want a daughter and you get a son? You can't send them back, you know. The way I look at it, it's better not to spend nine months thinking about the sex of your child because then you get a nice surprise when they're born and there are no disappointments. I guess most people have a preference, which is fine. But don't get too obsessive about it. If your baby is even vaguely human, just be glad that you are able to be a dad.

People still say to me that as the father of three daughters, I must be desperate for a son. Well, I'm not. I like having girls. At least they don't urinate on your face while you're changing their diaper. Besides, everyone knows that girls are made of sugar and spice and everything nice, whereas boys are made of frogs and snails and puppy dog tails, which is really disgusting when you stop to think about it.

I love being the dad of three girls and only foresee a few problems arising from this situation. One such problem is a potentially lethal phenomenon, described in sociology textbooks, in which women living in the same household get together and coordinate their cycles. No, I'm not talking about bikes all painted in complementary colors. I'm talking about one week of PMS each month. Can you imagine what this is going to be like for me in a few years' time? The only male in a house of moody women! And I know they'll make me pay for being a guy, because it's so unfair that guys don't get PMS and guys don't suffer the pain of childbirth and guys' jeans are usually ten dollars cheaper than women's.

This week of PMS will inevitably cost me a lot of money because I'll have to move into a nearby hotel until it's all over.

The other problem I foresee is that when my young, precious, naïve, innocent girls start to go out on dates with pimply, hormonal boys with surfer vans, I will have heartburn because I will remember what I used to do when I went out on dates with young, precious, naíve, innocent girls.

I may also end up in jail because I will sit in front of my house with a rifle and shoot any boys who bring my daughters home late.

And I hope that by the time my daughters want to get married, our society will have lost its medieval assumption that the father of the bride has to pay for the wedding. Because if it hasn't, the only wedding presents my daughters will get from me will be a ladder and a suitcase each.

On the other hand, I wouldn't have minded having a boy, either. We could have done macho stuff together, like chopping down trees and painting murals on the side of his surfer van. And I would have looked forward to the day of his marriage because it surely wouldn't have been me paying for it. Everyone knows that's the father of the bride's responsibility.

Internal Growth

Much of the hoopla surrounding this whole *childbirth thang* is directed at the moms and, to a lesser extent, us dads. Much thought, the pages of many books and hours of videotape are directed at all the emotional, social, physical and psychological changes that we parents will need to make as we take on our destined roles in life. This is to say nothing of all the parental— and if you're really unlucky, *grand*parental—advice that will be coming your way.

You will be busy trying to adjust mentally to fatherhood, you will be racing around trying to baby-proof your home, and you will be exhausted from shopping for all the necessities. But in the midst of all this business and self-indulgence, we can sometimes begin to forget the star of the show—the baby.

Oh yes, you remember now. The baby.

If you think *you've* got problems getting it all together in only nine months, imagine how the baby feels. She has to grow from a single cell with only a touch of DNA for good luck into a whole person complete with a full set of functioning body parts. Now that's what I call an achievement.

So let's put things back in perspective. The last time we mentioned the baby, the sperm had just connected with the ovum up there in the Fallopian tube and it had started its nine-month journey toward birth into the outside world. But what happens in the interim? How does it grow? When does it grow? What does it look like?

I had no idea about any of this at first. When I was a nonfather, I really knew very little about what actually went on in the uterus, or "womb" (a word for some reason I have always disliked). Nor did I really care. When you're studying biology in high school, things like that seem pretty low on the agenda.

Years later I consulted a few textbooks from my college human anatomy courses, but the big words were enough to drive me back into ignorance. The same applied to the hand-drawn sketches on the overhead projector screen in the childbirth-education classes my wife and I took together. Then, only two months before the birth of my daughter Rachael, *Life* magazine published an article called "The First Days of Creation." This is an absolutely awe-inspiring photo essay revealing the previously hidden world of the womb. Suddenly, a great light bulb flashed somewhere above my head. The veil of ignorance was lifted and the miracle of life became clear at last.

So for all of you unversed in the biological intricacies of pregnancy, here is the layman's version:

Mr. Tadpole swims down the tunnel and . . . no, no, just kidding.

As soon as the sperm and ovum have combined, the sex of your child has been determined, depending on whether the sperm was an X sperm (girl) or a Y sperm (boy). The chromosomes and genes within the sperm and ovum have also determined all the genetic information. Even at this initial stage, the length of your child's fingers, the shape of his eyes, the arrangement of his teeth and the color of his nasal hair have all been decided and programmed into the growth sequence of the cells. This genetic program can be dominated by the features and traits of you or your wife or any of your ancestors. However, this does not explain why most babies look like Winston Churchill when they are born.

About eight days after fertilization, the nucleus will split, and continue to split again and again in the beginning of an exponential growth process. This microscopic dot at this point is called an *embryo*. It will begin to move south down the Fallopian tube on a three-day journey to the uterus, where it will spend the next nine months growing into the little person who is your child.

When it arrives in the uterus, the embryo will bob around for a while looking for a cozy spot to "dig in." Once it implants, conception has officially occurred. The embryo will then continue to split and grow until about the one-week mark, when it will closely resemble a tiny leathery sea anemone. Then it will sprout and mutate in many different directions before it begins to look even vaguely human. Two weeks later it will look like a reject from a seafood platter from your favorite coastal restaurant, and at about the one-month mark, it will look like that hideous beast from the movie *Alien,* complete with octopus-like tail and elongated head.

All this time, the fleshy blob will be developing a brain, nerves, arms, bones, legs, blood vessels, muscles, intestines, eyes, a heart and massive vocal chords (for late-night screaming). So by the end of the third month, it will have graduated to the dizzy heights of being a fetus. You could hold this fetus in the palm of your hand, although it would only be the weight of a few crackers. It even looks human—although I certainly wouldn't want to bump into one on a dark night.

And that's your child. Minuscule, yes. A little weird-looking, yes. But give it time. It's only two months old. It still has seven months to go.

The baby's wastes leave through a separate channel down the same cord . . .

During these months the fetus will float in warm fluid in a cocoon called the *amniotic sac,* inside the mother's uterus. However, being in an aquatic environment raises certain puzzling questions, don't you think? For example, if I lived in a fluid-filled sac, I would have several problems: First, going to the bathroom in the same fluid that was in my mouth would not be conducive to my good health. Second, have you ever tried eating underwater? It's not easy! Then again, none of these problems would matter because I'd drown after a minute anyway.

So you have to ask yourself:

- How does the fetus breathe?
- How does the fetus get food?
- How does the fetus go to the bathroom?

In actual fact, the fetus (or baby, if you like) does not use her mouth at all for oxygen or food consumption, and she doesn't use her behind for waste expulsion. This is a good thing, because if she did, labor would be very smelly. The secret lies in technology developed for the NASA space shuttle program. Astronauts walking in space use a hollow, hoselike tether called an *umbilical cord* to receive all their necessary life-support requirements from the mother ship. Women have taken this technology on board and now utilize it in their wombs.

The mother breathes air and eats food. She then absorbs into her bloodstream all the good stuff necessary for life. The nutrients are transferred to the baby through a halfway station where the amniotic sac and the uterine wall meet. This is called the *placenta*. Although there isn't much exchange of blood itself, all the life-support materials (oxygen, vitamins, carbohydrates, minerals and so on) soak through the placenta and travel down the umbilical cord straight into the baby's blood supply. Other things that can travel down the umbilical cord are nicotine, alcohol, garlic and some television frequencies. The baby's wastes leave through a separate channel down the same cord.

One interesting and exciting feature of all this growth is that as the baby gets bigger, he starts doing stuff. He sucks his thumb. He dreams. He starts to move around. He turns, he kicks, he punches, he stretches. Basically, he's looking for a way out of there.

To feel their child kick is a real thrill.

For most dads, getting to feel their child kick is a real thrill that makes them realize for the first time that there really is a little person in there. Most babies, however, have a sixth sense, so that even if they usually kick more than Jean-Claude Van Damme, they freeze up as soon as their father puts his hand out to feel them.

Here's to Her Health!

Since the baby is developing and growing inside the mother, it's only logical that the health and general well-being of the mother will have a direct effect on the health and well-being of the baby. In short, it is important for the mother to stay healthy during the pregnancy.

Now I know this is the twenty-first century and all, so in no way do I mean to imply that you are in charge of your wife's health. She is a free spirit, an adult who makes her own decisions. But while she is responsible for her health, it's good to know things that you can do to help.

In terms of diet, a good range of fresh food is essential to provide both mother and baby with all the necessary vitamins, proteins, carbohydrates, minerals and fats. Don't try to exist on junk food or takeout all the time. If your wife eats too many burgers or chicken wings, your baby will be born looking either like a clown with big red shoes or a southern gentleman with a white beard.

And you don't want that—especially if it's a girl.

Drugs have a direct impact on the unborn. If you ever go to the drugstore for supplies of any kind of medication (including nonprescription drugs, vitamins, minerals and herbs), always tell the pharmacist that the substances are for a pregnant woman, and always read the manufacturer's directions on the side of the box. You will be surprised at how many everyday drugs, from hydrocortisone cream to cold medicines, are "not suitable for pregnant women." (And speaking of germs and things, she should also stay away from raw meat and cat and dog feces because of a disease called *toxoplasmosis*. This is not just a piece of dietary advice.)

While some consider alcohol generally conducive to good health, in terms of the unborn, it's best if the mother doesn't drink at all. Alcohol goes straight through the placenta and into the baby, and your wife probably doesn't want a drunk baby vomiting and singing sea shanties inside her. So if you and your wife are in the habit of having a drink together or are connoisseurs of fine wines, perhaps you can help by not tempting her with a bottle of Cabernet Sauvignon over dinner.

The same applies to smoking. Smoking is really bad news for the unborn because the baby can't get all the oxygen she needs. This plus all the junk in cigarettes can cause a whole raft of problems, the least of which is stunted fetal development, which in turn leads to reduced birth weight and size. Smoking also increases the potential for miscarriage, deformity and, in severe cases, the death of the baby soon after birth. Not only that, if your baby does make it through the pregnancy, she could be born with yellow-stained fingers and a hacking cough.

If you and your wife both smoke and she decides to quit, respect her decision and support her by not smoking near her. And don't forget the solid body of evidence that suggests that secondhand smoke is also dangerous. So if you smoke and your wife doesn't, don't smoke while she's trapped in the car or in an unventilated room with you. Maybe you could even quit yourself!

Then again, that's easy for me to say. I've never smoked. In fact, I'm one of those smug, self-righteous bastards who, when people say to me at a restaurant, "Do you mind if I smoke?" replies, "Go ahead . . . do you mind if I fart?"

But hey . . . that's just me.

Decisions, Decisions

The thing about pregnancy is that the baby won't stay in there forever. He has to come out some time. When he does come out, the process is called *labor*, which in my dictionary is defined as "work, especially of a hard or fatiguing kind." This is another great example of a euphemism; a word like *agony* is probably a more appropriate term for the process of childbirth, but it doesn't have that certain ring to it.

During the term of pregnancy, you and your wife will need to make some decisions about how and where the labor and birthing process will take place. This is because like many other good things in life—cruises, fancy dinners—you can't just show up on the day. You need to make a reservation.

Some couples find hospitals impersonal and disempowering, so they opt for having their babies at home. It is perhaps more comfortable to give birth in familiar surroundings, and although the birth is usually supervised by a midwife, there is less medical intervention. If you're the kind of person who can handle this, go for it.

We decided against a home-birth for three reasons:

1. We didn't like the possibility of neighbors dropping in for a visit in the middle of it all.

2. The whole idea scared me to death. We wanted the resources of a fully-equipped, multi-million-dollar hospital, complete with expert personnel and a doctor who had done it thousands of times before and had lots of impressive certificates hanging on his office wall.

3. We'd just had new carpets put down in the house.

Other people opt for birth centers, which are more "homey" than hospitals. It seems to me these centers have a more relaxed atmosphere and a less sterile décor. They are also more accepting of less traditional birthing methods. Midwives run them, but they always have additional medical support available if necessary. The centers also tend to discourage medical intervention in the labor.

The trend toward birth centers and home-births has been increasing steadily, but they still only account for about 2 percent of all births. The majority of women still go to a hospital. Ideally your hospital should be near your home, so you can reach it relatively quickly without having to break speed limits or drive on sidewalks. The most fantastic hospital in the world is no good if it is on the other side of the city. You'll only end up having the baby in the back of the car, which will be bad for the upholstery and will lower its resale value.

Part of your choice will also be dictated by your health insurance. Make no mistake: Childbirth is expensive. All you have to do is look at the contents of the *Reserved for Doctors Only* parking lot at the hospital—imported luxury coupes with speedometers that start at 200—to realize that there is a lot of money involved in this whole childbirth thing.

Your wife can go to a *public hospital* as a *public patient*, which means she gets the specialist who is on duty in the hospital at the time. As the name suggests, the facilities are public. The women there will probably share rooms and bathrooms. I have friends who wouldn't go anywhere but the local public hospital, and others who are the exact opposite. It depends on your financial situation and your expectations. Going public is probably the least expensive option, particularly if you have no private insurance coverage.

If you want to go private, you have a choice. Choosing a hospital is like most things—you need to shop around to find out what's best for you. Ask your friends for recommendations, talk to your family doctor and visit some hospitals.

After you or your wife has called the hospital to register, your wife will probably have to fill out forms giving personal details and answering a lot of questions. The hospital will also want to know if she is using her own doctor and what kind of insurance coverage she has.

So what exactly is your wife covered for? Study your policy and, if you have any doubts, just call your insurance company. The best thing is to go down to the local branch of your insurance company and cross-reference the amount your wife is covered for with how much the hospital is going to cost. The difference will tell you your debt level for the next year or so.

For the birth of Rachael, Meredith went as a *private patient* to a public hospital. This meant that because we had the coverage, we could afford Meredith's own doctor. (See below.) But we wanted the public hospital because it was closest and we were familiar with it, since we had been to birth classes there. The maternity ward had a solid reputation and the staff was great.

However, there were some things about the hospital that we weren't too happy about afterward. During the first stage of labor, Meredith had to share one bathroom with three other laboring women who were in equal need of the facility. We were all in the same large room and the curtains did little to shield us from their wailing and moaning. After the birth, the visiting hours were not strictly enforced, so Meredith was bombarded by guests almost all day and got tired quickly. She also shared a room with a woman who was always visited by at least ten relatives with loud voices. To top it off, this woman had a baby who screamed *nonstop*.

So for the births of Georgia and Matilda, Meredith went as a private patient to a private hospital. We were both more confident the second and third time around, and so we didn't mind traveling farther away to this hospital. Meredith had her own room, so she got some peace and quiet, and her own bathroom, which made things a little easier. The staff enforced the visiting hours, too. Dads could visit anytime, but if you weren't a dad and you arrived before or after visiting hours, you'd never make it past the sentry dogs and armed nurses who patrolled the corridors. In terms of cost, with our insurance, we ended up paying only about a hundred bucks. If it weren't for the insurance, however, the births would have set us back several thousand. But that's what you pay if you want a maternity ward that serves shrimp scampi and baked Alaska for dinner.

A final word of warning: If you decide to go to a private hospital, you will need to register quickly. Spaces are limited and they go faster than lottery tickets. Some women even register within minutes of conception.

I kid you not.

Some questions to consider when choosing a hospital:

- How available are toilets and showers? Are they private?

- What are the rooms like?

- How many patients to a room?

- Do they have facilities for "different" types of births, or do they stick to "traditional" methods?

- What is their attitude about pain relief?
- How long do they let mothers stay to recover after the birth?
- Are there phones available for post-birth calls?
- Do the babies sleep in the mother's room or are they in a nursery?
- What magazines do they have in the lobby?
- Do they have a nearby emergency ward, in case a father faints and splits his head open on the concrete floor and has to be taken away for stitches?

If your wife does go as a private patient—either in a private or a public hospital—she gets to have the doctor of her choice. This specialist is called an *obstetrician*. They have a lot of letters after their name and drive cars with mobile phones, CD players and probably big-screen TVs that fold out of the glove box.

Obstetricians usually don't work in every hospital, which is another factor that may limit her choice. And like a hospital, their time is finite, so she'll have to "make a reservation" with them as well, as soon as possible.

But how do you choose a doctor?

Your wife may already have one, but if she doesn't, she has to shop for one. Most of my friends chose their doctor on the recommendation of other friends or their own family doctor. But this decision is a personal thing. It is vital that your wife likes the doctor and feels comfortable with him or her. It is also important that you both find out the doctor's attitudes toward intervention, pain relief, birth positions, the role of the father and so on. You don't want to discover in the delivery room that your ideas and expectations are vastly different.

You also need to find out how much you will be charged for any procedures or tests your insurance doesn't cover. This is *very important*. Most European cars in the doctors' parking lot are expensive to run. Haven't you ever wondered where the money for this comes from? That's right . . . you.

Choosing a doctor . . .

I repeat: Check your insurance coverage. (I know of one woman who visited four obstetricians and chose the one she liked best. Shopping around like this promises to be expensive, however. Don't do it unless at least one of you is an international business tycoon.)

It is the obstetrician's job to monitor both mother and baby during the pregnancy and then to be there to supervise the birth and "deliver" the baby. Part of the monitoring process involves a series of checkups. These are usually monthly, but as the birth draws closer, your wife may go in every couple of weeks and then every few days. During these visits, your wife's blood, urine, weight and blood pressure are tested. These visits also test your wife's patience as invariably she will sit for three hours waiting for her appointment.

On several occasions I was able to go along with Meredith to her checkups. This was really beneficial, because I got to meet and know the doctor and was able to ask a number of questions. This was also a great way to share the experience of pregnancy and it helped me to prepare for what lay ahead.

On one of these occasions, the doctor put a microphoney thing (a *fetal stethoscope*) on Meredith's stomach and she and I sat in awe, listening to the rattle of our unborn baby's heart. This was a great thrill! It made me completely realize that there was a little person in there! If you can, try to go along to experience this. The doctor probably will ask your wife to have an ultrasound also. This will be at around the 18-week mark of her pregnancy (see discussion below).

The doctor will calculate the expected date of birth during the first visit. A normal pregnancy lasts roughly nine months, or forty weeks. Some babies can hold on until forty-two weeks. However, the baby doesn't have a calendar in the womb and might not want to wait until the conveniently predicted ninth month before deciding to make the grand entrance. Premature babies can be born from seven months, or twenty-eight weeks, into the pregnancy.

Personally, I think this whole "due date" thing is a professional conspiracy, a private prank among obstetricians. I can almost picture it. Many years ago, at the Annual Conference for Obstetricians with Flashy Cars, one obstetrician leaned across to some others and said, "Hey guys, I've got this really great joke that we can all play on nervous expectant couples . . ."

I'm not sure how they actually calculate the date, but I suspect it's done either with a crystal ball or a dart thrown onto a calendar.

Ultrasound

Without a doubt, we live in a wonderful age of technology. We have at our disposal all kinds of fantastic gismos and whirligigs that can do all sorts of amazing and incredible things that our parents would have believed impossible.

Sadly, some of our advancements have been a big mistake and have only served to drag humanity further into the abyss of self-destruction. These include

- spray cheese

- those things that make the water in your toilet turn blue

- ozone-depleting sprays
- karaoke machines
- talk shows
- timer functions on video recorders

But some advancements seem to be great ideas, and quite frankly I don't know why someone didn't think of them earlier. For example:

- microsurgery
- photocopiers with a collating function
- those icy drinks you get at convenience stores
- unbleached toilet paper
- microwave popcorn
- and, of course, the wonderful ultrasound machine

It used to be that Mom and Dad had to wait for the grand debut, on the day of birth, to get their first look at Junior. Those days are gone, thanks to the marvels of modern medical technology.

And here's how it works:

You and your wife go to the clinic or hospital OB/GYN department. Then you sit in the waiting room until you're called in to lie down on the ultrasound couch. This will take place at the exact moment when you're up to the climax of the "A 747 crashed into my car . . . and I survived!" story in *Reader's Digest*. At this point, make sure that your pregnant wife lies down on the couch, not you. This will save much embarrassment later on.

(Before I go on, here's a useful thing to remember. For the ultrasound to work, the woman has to drink gallons and gallons and gallons of water. This is uncomfortable at the best of times, but if she has to have an ultrasound later in the pregnancy, her bladder may be only slightly larger than a walnut. When this is the case, do not under any circumstances tickle her or attempt to give her a hug.)

Anyway, back to the couch. The radiologist will come in and probe the swollen front part of your wife (that is, where the baby lives) with a microphoney thing. This sends out high-frequency sound waves (hence "ultra-sound"), which are then reflected back and processed onto a television monitor for all to see in glorious black and white.

And there you have it.

A black screen with lots of white fuzzy wriggling squiggles.

This is your child.

The radiologist will say amazing things to you like, "There's baby's arm," "There's baby's beating heart" and "Baby's facing this way." Actually, I think radiologists are just joking around with us and that the ultrasound picture is simply a badly tuned TV station. It reminds me of "The Emperor's New Clothes." There's nothing definable on the screen, but still everybody goes, "Yeah, wow . . . I think I see . . . a hand!" Nobody wants to be the first to say, "I can't see a thing!" And so the myth is perpetuated.

When I saw the first ultrasound picture of Rachael, I thought Meredith was giving birth to a satellite photo of the Earth. There were her legs (cumulus clouds), her chest (low pressure front moving north), and her head (hurricane off the coast). It's pretty exciting stuff.

And the other exciting thing about a visit to the ultrasound lab is that not only do you get to look at the picture on the screen, but in some places you can even take home souvenirs of the event as well! There are two main types of souvenir. For starters, you can get snapshot "photos" of the monitor pictures. These look like X-rays, with body-part labels so you can identify exactly what it is you are looking at. Why not start your own baby photo album—months before the birth!

The other, and increasingly more popular, ultrasound souvenir is the video. If you supply your own tape, you can capture the entire ultrasound in laborious detail and watch it all again and again in the comfort of your own home. Imagine the fun when you surprise your son or daughter by playing their 40-minute ultrasound tape at their twenty-first birthday party! Won't their friends be impressed?

In fact, I'm sure it won't be long before we see a whole new line in ultrasound marketing. How about an ultrasound-print T-shirt? Or an ultrasound refrigerator magnet? Why not an assortment of 3-D ultrasound postcards to send to friends? And how about one of those tasteful plastic domes with a replica fetus inside? All you do is shake . . . and it snows!

Having an ultrasound achieves three things. First, your doctor gets to make sure everything is OK and all the baby's parts are where they're supposed to be.

Second, by measuring the length of one of the baby's bones, the doctor can check the estimated date of delivery. Invariably this is a totally different date than the one supplied to you originally. (And simply adds weight to my previously mentioned theory regarding "due dates" as an elaborate practical joke.)

Third, you can tell how many babies are in there waiting to come out. Odds are there's only going to be one. But if you can count four legs, either your wife is going to give birth to a horse or you're going to be the father of twins.

If you can count three or more heartbeats, LEAVE immediately. Go home, pack a small bag and go to the South Pole. Do not return. Ever.

Life's Little Changes

It may be hard to come to terms with all the little changes that will start to seep into your family life. They may be subtle and gradual at first, but as the months inexorably pass by, things around the house will start to seem "different." You will notice that your wife is beginning to . . . transform.

There are hormonal changes to consider. Her body is chock-full of progesterone and estrogen and so she may exhibit mood swings as variable as tropical weather conditions. For example, in answer to the simple and straightforward question,

"Would you like some iced tea?" you could get a simple, "Yes, please" or "No, thanks." However, you could also get a teary, "That's the most beautiful thing you've ever said to me," or an aggressive, "Don't *patronize* me! I can make my own tea!"

Most women will have at least one ride on the mood roller coaster in their pregnancy. Other side effects on the pregnancy smorgasbord may include cravings, headaches, clumsiness, heartburn, fluid retention, high blood pressure, cramps, vagueness and tiredness. Kind of makes you want to be pregnant, doesn't it?

Of course there's still the aforementioned morning sickness to consider. And what can you, as a caring modern man, do to alleviate the horrible nausea? I've heard of different remedies, such as dry toast, back rubs, glucose, ginger, steam inhalation, lots of fluids and a clove of garlic hung around the neck. Some people swear by iron supplements or saline drips, and I've even heard of one remedy involving a cat, a battery and a tube of toothpaste, but I can't go into detail. This is a family book after all.

Other than this there's not a whole lot you can do. Morning sickness will happen when it wants to and you can't stop it. However, you can help by not making it worse than it already is. For starters, don't give your wife a kiss when you have morning breath. Instead, make her a cup of tea to drink before she gets out of bed. Don't bait your fishing line in front of her. Don't watch *Days of Our Lives*. When cooking, avoid strong or aromatic herbs and, most important, if she looks green, don't stand between her and the bathroom.

One increasingly obvious change you will notice is that the baby is getting bigger and bigger and bigger inside her. Using basic dimensional mathematics, it is easy to deduce that all your wife's other internal bits and pieces have less and less and less room. This causes decreased bladder size. In short, it means that your own lengthy interludes in the bathroom reading the local paper or the latest *Phantom* comic will have to be cut short. It also means that you'll need to rethink epic car journeys. And whatever you do, *don't* say, "Can you just hang on for another half an hour?" A woman with a bladder the size of a walnut should not be toyed with.

Overall your wife will on average gain anywhere from fifteen to forty pounds, depending on her body size to begin with. Interestingly, only about a third of this gain is the weight of the baby. The other weight is from increases in fluids (blood, amniotic fluid), fat, the uterus and the placenta. The most obvious sign of this gain is that your wife won't be able to fit into those old denim jeans or her favorite dress anymore. Coincidentally, it's around this time that you notice a lot of your own clothes disappearing, particularly big and baggy sweaters, T-shirts and pullovers. It shouldn't take Sherlock Holmes to figure out who the culprit is. On top of this, you will probably need to break out the credit card and buy a range of fashion tents, also referred to as "maternity wear."

Another obvious change is the increase in size of your wife's breasts. This can begin early in her pregnancy but usually really kicks in during the last trimester. The change is caused by the mammary glands in her breasts getting ready for all the hard work ahead of them. In fact, they can increase in size by up to two cups, which according to the measuring bowl in our kitchen is about half a pint. But although your wife's breasts are swollen and inviting, they are probably quite sore. Just remember that they are like roses. They look great, but if you reach out for a handful, it's going to hurt—both her *and you,* when she hits you—so KEEP YOUR DAMN HANDS OFF!

While these physical changes can make life awkward, they are not always as paralyzing as television moms would have us believe (see chapter 1). Having said that, your wife certainly won't be as agile as she used to be. Due to the weight distribution, sore backs are common. Many everyday activities can become increasingly awkward and even painful for her. She won't be able to sleep on her stomach anymore—if she did, she'd probably roll out of bed. In fact, toward the end of the pregnancy, sleeping positions can be quite uncomfortable, so do all you can to help out. Stuff pillows in all the right places for support. Don't be a bed hog.

There are plenty of other things you can do to make your wife's life a little easier, but don't treat her as if she's a porcelain doll that you expect to sit in a corner for nine months. Instead, do more than your "fair share" of the cooking, cleaning, washing and ironing. Give her back rubs on demand. Tie her shoelaces for her. Avoid using words like "fat," "blubber" and "orca" in her presence. Treat her to breakfast in bed. Be understanding if her aching body or nausea interfere with social engagements. In short, be totally superhuman.

More on Sex

Ah yes—this is what caused all this fuss in the first place. And you want more?

When we announced to the world that Meredith was pregnant, one of our friends—a guy, I might add—sidled up to me with a sincere look on his face and said with a voice of utmost concern, "There goes your sex life for the next year, my friend."

Up to this point I had not even considered this as being a problem. But once it was brought to my attention, I broke out in the cold sweat of ignorance. Did this *really* mean that my wife and I would not be engaging in that which was normal and healthy in our marriage? This was a slight concern for me—and perhaps it is for you, too, particularly if you live up to the male stereotype, of having a libido the size of a football stadium.

What a relief it was to find that just because my wife was pregnant, she did not immediately enter sexual quarantine! In fact, far from it (but that's another story). Sex is possible and normal during pregnancy. And by the way, if you think your pregnant wife is off-limits because your whopping great fertility organ will be a physical threat to the baby, I have only one thing to say to you: *Don't flatter yourself.*

Having said that, however, there are a few commonsense things we guys need to keep in mind. As I said earlier, during pregnancy the female body goes through incredible changes. Because one of these is hormonal, you may find that your wife's previous voracious sexual appetite has dimmed somewhat. In short, she may not "feel like it." It may not be as frequent as in "the good old days." (Of course, the opposite may also apply.) It is important that you come to terms with this and understand all the changes her body is trying to cope with. She definitely does not need you throwing an "I want sex and I want it now'" tantrum.

And even when you do engage in sex or sexual play, there are physical limitations. You will find that it's not as acrobatic as it once might have been. Swinging from light fixtures, destruction of bedroom furniture, athletic Greco-Roman wrestling positions and anything to do with the *Kama Sutra* or yoga are definitely out. You will need to be a little more creative in terms of getting the pieces of the puzzle to fit together comfortably, if you get my drift. If you need some sensitivity training in this area, try strapping a bean-bag chair and a couple of cement blocks around your stomach and then see how you feel about sex.

Of course, all women are different. It's important that the two of you discuss your sexuality together and tell each other how you are feeling. It's important that you are understanding and supportive of her. Sex is a good and normal part of relationships, but pregnancy can temporarily alter the normal pattern.

Of Possums and Men

I feel sorry for the male possum. There he was, enjoying *coitus opossumatus* in a comfortable branch of his favorite tree, when only thirteen days later—that's right, count 'em—his mate gives birth to a possumette. This probably accounts for the high incidence of heart failure among male possums.

Luckily, we nonmarsupials are given a little more leeway. Nine months is a reasonable amount of time to get ready for our new role in life. But this does not mean that parents-to-be have nine months to relax and party on. Use this valuable time to work hard in preparing for the arrival of your humanette. And believe me, it is hard work. Spend your time wisely. Read chapter 3.

But don't be fooled into thinking that this time will go slowly. We're not as lucky as the African elephant, which has a gestation period of about 640 days! African-elephant dads certainly have no excuse if *they're* not ready for life on the veldt with a young pachyderm.

As I mentioned in chapter 1, it's common at this early stage for potential dads to feel a little disoriented. Already everyone who knows you're going to be a dad has started treating you differently, your sex life has entered the realm of the dinosaurs, you've nobly stood by your wife in steering clear of beer and cigarettes, you've stared in dismay at your bank balance, your wife has vomited in or in the vicinity of the bathroom—and it's only been twenty-four hours since you heard the news.

Welcome to pregnancy!

But don't worry. Unlike the possum, you have another 6,360 hours to get used to it.

CHAPTER 3
Getting Ready

A deathly silence fell over the room. We moved on,
but none of us was ever the same again.

Facing the Facts

To start you on the road of fatherhood, let me bring you down to
earth with a sobering thought. I have been trying to avoid
telling you this, and I've been toying with the right words to
use, but I can't procrastinate any longer.

Are you ready?

Take a deep breath.

OK, here it is in the next line:

Life as you have known it is over.

Finito. Ende. Kaput.

So long. Farewell. Auf Wiedersehen. Goodbye.

Gone. History. Jurassic.

Your life as a dad will be totally different from anything you
have known. It sure changed my life. It may come as a surprise
to you, but I haven't always driven a minivan and I never used
to leave parties at 10 P.M. I haven't always hung out at the
wading pool at the local community center and my idea of a
great night hasn't always been a drive-thru hamburger dinner in
front of *The Lion King*.

But that was *before*.

Get used to the fact that you can't be a CWOC (couple with
one child) or a CASK (couple and several kids) while trying to
live like a DINK (double income, no kids) or a SINK (single
income, no kids). The lifestyles, responsibilities, roles and daily
routines of CWOCs/CASKs and DINKs/SINKs are totally

different, opposed and mutually exclusive. If you try to live like a DINK when you're a CWOC, you will find it very frustrating and exhausting. If you try to live like a SINK when you're a CASK, you will find it impossible. You'll end up wishing you were still a WANKAA (without any new kids at all).

What I'm talking about is your use of time. You used to have a lot of it to throw around and enjoy. Game of golf this afternoon? *Sure!* Beer after work? *Yeah!* Knock off another novel in the hammock? *Great!* A quick surf? *Certainly!* A late movie? *Why not?* House renovations? *Nothing better to do!*

But not anymore. The responsibility of active fathering demands your time. You'll need to deliberately learn some basic time management in three distinct areas over the next twelve months. First, there are the months of pregnancy. You and your wife will be busy getting ready for the arrival of a new person in the house. This is an especially time-consuming operation, involving an almost infinite list of "things to do." But the better you prepare now, the better it will be for you later.

Second, there is the expected time of arrival, often referred to as the *due date*. You need to attack your calendars and day planners with thick black felt-tip pens in the weeks surrounding this elusive date, since babies don't usually follow adult timetables. They can come early. They can come late.

In fact, they probably will.

It is extremely important that you are available and on-call when that giant roulette wheel in the sky drops the ball and your baby starts climbing out of the womb. And you need to be around in the weeks that follow. There is hospital visiting to do, and then the big return home. This is a tumultuous time, when a heavy work-and-social schedule will not help the situation.

Block out almost everything. Let your employer know the due date and find out his or her expectations regarding your taking a few days off at zero notice. If your work allows you any flexibility, avoid loading up the weeks around the due date. (Don't plan interstate vacations, business trips or buy expensive theater seats or concert tickets around this time, either.) A lot of my friends took their vacations so they could be around during those crucial first weeks at home. Some employers are even so nonsexist as to have paternity leave.

And third, in the longer term, your new family life will be time-consuming. Coming home from work at unthinkable hours, commitments on every night of the week (classes, the gym, movies, rehearsals, beer drinking, hanging out with friends, meetings and so on), and partying on weekends until the wee hours will leave you with very little time to be a father (or a husband, for that matter).

Unfortunately, some modern men have invented a detestable expression: "quality time." The theory behind this is that your life can go on as normal and you can do whatever you like, and spend as much time away from home as you like, because you can make it up to your child in a weekly, thirty-minute intensive period of "quality time." Of course, if you really concentrated, you could probably cut this back to fifteen minutes.

I'm not suggesting that you leave your job and spend twenty-four hours a day with your family. Obviously there'll be times when things are hectic and work demands much of your attention. In some ways, it's an unavoidable part of our modern work ethic. But as a general rule, your family does have to be placed high on the priority list. *All* your time with your child should be quality time. I mean, is there such a thing as "not very good quality time"?

So sit down with your wife and talk over your weekly schedules. Basically, after the baby comes you'll need to spend a lot of time at home. This won't happen magically of its own accord. It takes deliberate thought and effort on your part to establish new time schedules, and it might mean you'll have to give up some things.

It all sounds pretty bleak, doesn't it? Well, it's not. It's just different.

At first, you'll still be able to operate pretty much the same. Newborns are portable and generally sedate, so you can take them with you to dinner parties or to stores without too much hassle. Later, when they're older and outings become more difficult, you and your wife can work as a team and take turns looking after the baby while the other goes out. Things like sports, part-time classes, social gatherings, rehearsals, clubs and so on can all be juggled in moderation. Baby-sitters, relatives and friends can also give you the opportunity to go out together.

Sure, you do lose some freedom. But there are no freebies in this world, and that's the price you pay for the privilege and pleasure of being a dad.

By the way, when I said that it's not really that bleak, I was only kidding.

Working in a Coalmine

Some jobs are just plain hard to do when there's another person living and growing inside your skin. If your wife is a coal miner, for example, she will find it increasingly difficult to fulfill her work commitments. Likewise if she is a professional volleyball player, aerobics instructor, mud-wrestler or police officer.

She may have a tough time if she works in a place where she is on her feet all day or has to run around town at top speeds. As the pregnancy progresses, she will tend to get tired more quickly. Muscles will ache with increasing regularity. Eventually a time will come when work will have to go. Most bosses don't want their employees having babies on company grounds. The carpet shampoo is just too expensive to take the risk.

When Meredith was pregnant with Rachael, she was working for a government department on the other side of the city. That meant she had a considerable rush-hour bus trip that included a transfer mid-route and then a good walk before she actually reached her workplace. Getting to work became harder and harder for her. First, there was the terror of having morning sickness on a crowded and unventilated bus. But she got over that. Then, when Meredith got physically bigger, she found that unfortunately chivalry was dead on many occasions. She often stood the entire trip with baby kicking, her bladder bursting and her back aching. Sometimes, if she was particularly uncomfortable, she would say in a loud voice to no one in particular, "Excuse me, I'm pregnant. Would you mi—" She never once had to finish her sentence. It was incredible how chivalrous people suddenly became!

Meredith toughed out the agony of work and public transport for a good seven months before deciding that enough was enough. However, there is no set time for when a pregnant woman has to leave work. It's usually up to how the woman feels, although I suspect that the dark shadow of mortgage payments puts a heavy strain on many couples these days. Some women leave work as soon as they "hear the news." Others tough it out as long as they can. However, they don't usually make it right up to the day.

The choices involved in leaving work are not extensive. Women can either leave their positions for good or they can take maternity leave. Either way, your family income will be affected, so be prepared to go without two incomes for at least a couple of months around the expected time of delivery.

No set time for when a pregnant woman has to leave work . . .

You and your wife must also discuss work arrangements for *after* the birth. A few years ago, this would not have been an issue. Social convention dictated that pregnant women left the workforce forever to be sucked into the vortex of domestic life. But then came *the revolution*. The air is still thick with the ash of burned bras, and social convention no longer dictates that a pregnant woman is doomed to premature career death.

So the dual-career couple is now commonplace in our society, but this presents another problem. What does the dual-career couple do when the baby comes along? You can't just leave a newborn in its crib for the day while you both go off to work. Apart from losing custody of your baby, you'd probably wind up in jail. Nor is it likely that either of you can tuck her under your arm and take her to work with you (unless you're one of those fortunate people who work at an office with a daycare).

That's right. Someone has to take care of the baby.

How you resolve this issue will probably be influenced by a number of factors, such as how flexible your workplaces are, how big your mortgage payments are, which of you earns the most money, your attitudes about breast- and bottlefeeding, how much cash you have in the bank, your convictions regarding full-time parenting, and which of you has the stronger will.

There are all sorts of possibilities and solutions open to you. Meredith and I take a pretty traditional approach. Despite having a university degree in Agricultural Economics and a career path, Meredith consciously decided to leave work to take up a more important career position as Mother and Domestic Manager with a new but rapidly growing business called The Downey Family. Doing it this way isn't so hot financially, but it does make for a constant home environment, which we both value. Maybe a few years down the track she'll earn her Masters and then get back into the workforce.

There are many other approaches available to you, depending on how flexible or innovative you want to be. The people across the road from us alternate between the workforce and the home for periods of roughly one year, thus giving each of them an experience of life as a full-time parent. Of course, it doesn't make for a smooth climb up the career ladder. And the other day at a party I met a couple who have worked out their jobs so that they both get to experience full-time parenting and full-time work. The mom works the day shift (8 A.M. until 4 P.M.) and the dad works the night shift (3 P.M. until 11 P.M.). A sitter watches the baby for two hours in the afternoon. It's good for them financially, but the problem is that they only see each other as husband and wife on Sundays. I hope they're still married in five years' time.

Other friends I know both hold down nine-to-five jobs and the baby's grandparents play baby-sitters during the day. The service is free and the grandparents relish the opportunity to spend time with their grandchild.

If you both want to work nine-to-five but your parents are nowhere to be found, consider family daycare or a daycare center.

Family daycare means your baby is cared for in the caregiver's home. It provides a stable environment for your baby, with closer supervision from the caregiver. Also, the caregiver is only licensed to take care of around five kids at a time (depending on the state or province), and the home is regularly inspected by the Division of Youth and Family Services to make sure it is safe and clean (again, the details of this, including frequency, depend on your state or province).

Daycare centers are larger, sometimes caring for up to forty children at a time. The advantage of these centers is that unlike in the family daycare situation, if the regular caregiver is sick, someone else is still available to take care of your baby. Often your baby can stay at the daycare for longer hours, too.

There are only two drawbacks: It's often difficult to get a place for your baby, and you have to pay for it. Waiting lists for infants can be up to eighteen months long, because they are more labor-intensive than your average semi-independent toddler. Babies can also be more expensive. In many states, daycares are required to have a crib per infant in their care, so the expense is almost the same regardless of how much of the day your baby spends there.

Family daycare is much cheaper, but it can also be hard to find a place you can trust. First, try calling Child Care Aware, a national service that will direct you to your local referral service (800-424-2246). The referral service will not only direct you to licensed daycare providers but also accredited providers. *Licensed* means they simply meet the minimum state requirements while *accredited* means they voluntarily hold themselves up to more rigorous standards and must continue to live up to these standards if they want to keep their accreditation.

Next, you'll need to check out the daycare in person to examine the facilities and interview the caregiver. Have a few options in mind because daycares (both centers and family daycares) fill up quickly. You'll want to get your baby on the waiting list as soon as possible.

If your wife does decide to go back to the paid workforce in whatever capacity, she probably won't do it right away. I mean, there's nothing stopping her from going back the day after the baby is born, if she really wanted to—that is, assuming she can still walk. However, most women returning to work usually go back around three to six months after the birth. By then they can walk without hobbling, their breast milk doesn't soak their blouses and people have stopped asking them, "When are you due?"

Nesting Urge

Science tells us that all birds have a nesting urge. In the period before they lay their eggs, they go into a frenzy of nest-making. This is due to the fact that when the eggs finally emerge, the mother wants to stay somewhere warm and safe until the chicks hatch.

All birds get the nesting urge.

All pregnant women get the nesting urge.

Now, your wife won't be up a tree making a little basket out of twigs, cotton and mud, I hope, but the nesting urge will definitely manifest itself in its own cute way. It is unavoidable.

It's some kind of biological thing. In women's brains, just under the hypothalamus, there is a small gland that secretes *nesting-urge hormone*. When this gland starts operating, you will notice some changes in your wife, such as an absence of logic, no concept of reason, and a strong desire to make major architectural changes to the infrastructure of your home.

I used to have a great teenager's bedroom. It was modeled on Greg Brady's "den." All the furniture was built in and connected at different levels: bed, cupboards, bookshelves, drawers and a desk. It was very modern (for the seventies, that is) and painted bright fire-engine red. The crowning glory was a huge rice-paper lamp shade, complete with tassels, which dangled from the ceiling.

A perfect room for a baby!

Or so I thought.

I remember the day clearly. Returning from work, I pulled into the driveway and immediately knew something was awry. This was primarily because my aforementioned bedroom lay in a large, red mountain of splintered and broken wood in the middle of the backyard.

In a daze I made my way into the house, clambering over an enormous roll of shredded carpet that I was sure wasn't there when I'd left for work that morning.

In the shell of my old room I found my excessively pregnant wife, bathed in sweat and grime, casually chiseling sheets of old paint off the walls. Half the room was already stripped back to bare, gray concrete. The floor lay deep in plaster and paint. I stood there agape for a while before I spoke.

"What are you doing?" I asked carefully, not wanting to frighten her.

"Making a nursery," she replied, with the same nonchalance as if she had just said, "Making a peanut butter sandwich."

"Oh" was all I could manage.

"I thought a nice yellow would do. We can sand back the window sills so they'll match the floorboards. Of course, we'll have to sand those back too."

At that point I felt a migraine coming on, so I went and poured myself some bourbon.

When the nesting urge comes, don't fight it. You'll only make things worse for yourself.

Equipment

If you're a skier, you know that you need a lot of equipment to maintain your habit. Skis, goggles, boots, gloves, roof racks and, if you're a total geek, a wardrobe of Après ski gear complete with fluffy boots. If you play a sport, you've probably got bags of sports clothes and various accessories such as cleats, shin-pads, sweatbands, mouthguards and the obligatory tube of nasty-smelling muscle ointment.

But to become a dad, there are only two basic items of equipment that you need:

- A bigger car
- A bigger home

And to get these, of course, you need a bigger income. Simple, huh?

Apart from these two necessities, there is a lot of stuff you could use to make fatherhood a little easier. But be warned! A quick stroll through the local baby equipment store will have you rethinking your mortgage. There is an almost infinite number of products, gismos and accessories available on the market. And if you were to say to the nice man behind the counter, "I'll have one of everything, please," then you'd better have a fleet of semis to transport all of your new purchases to your home—which would need to be the size of City Hall.

You have to be selective and wise in your stockpiling. I mean, when Adam and Eve had kids, they didn't have all the gadgets and gismos that we *have* to have now, and they seem to have gotten along all right. So before you go off on a second-mortgage-producing spree, sit down with your wife and work out what you need and what you can afford.

Also keep in mind that you may not need to *buy* everything that you want. You can rent some things. You may receive others as presents. If you're lucky, you may have friends who have just finished their own baby saga and are willing and ready to off-load some of their gear onto you. The classifieds are also great because they contain a wealth of secondhand goods. But if you're planning on having a few kids, it's probably more economical to buy.

Another thing. And this is an important one.

Avoid the trap of buying stuff simply because it matches your décor or for some other superficial reason. I know a couple who bought one of those old-style English baby carriages (or *prams*) because they thought they would look cute going for a walk in the park with it. The pram did look great but it didn't fold up, so they couldn't put it in their car, and it didn't store easily. It was also next to impossible to clean. In short, it was pretty damn useless. So, whatever you buy:

- Make sure it is strong.

- Make sure it is storable and will fit into your home somewhere.

- Make sure it doesn't fit into the baby's mouth.

- Make sure that after you buy it, you still have enough money for food for the rest of the week.

- Make sure it is washable, preferably able to withstand a hose-down in the backyard. Some products come certified with an International Radiation Symbol sticker. This means it has survived a nuclear explosion and, as such, has a good chance of making it through six months of use with a baby.

The Baby Zone

The baby needs a place to live. Preferably this should be some place where you won't be disturbed by her too much—say, for example, Brazil.

I have friends who decided their baby would live with them in their bedroom. This was fine for the first weeks because it made night feedings easy, but it also meant they didn't sleep. You need your own "adult space" as a sanctuary to escape to.

For Rachael, we were lucky to have a spare bedroom we could convert into a nursery. But if you are going to do this, whatever you do, don't look at the pictures of nurseries in baby magazines. These have been designed by architects, outfitted by interior decorators and photographed by professionals in the homes of millionaires.

Real nurseries are small, cramped and smelly.

For Georgia, we didn't have another bedroom to convert into another nursery and it wasn't practical to put her in with Rachael. So we "built" a bedroom in the hallway. (When she got older, she became roommates with Rachael, and Matilda took over the hallway spot.) Whether it's a room or a corridor, find a space you can set up as the "baby zone." Once you've found it, you need to fill it up with furniture and other necessities. A fan or heater will help control the temperature extremes. A comfortable chair with a rug and footstool will be nice for night feedings if feeding in bed is impractical.

Another necessity is one of those wind-up musical gismos, which are good for soothing babies to sleep. Unfortunately, the only tune available on the market is "Brahms' Lullaby." You know the one. It goes, *da-da-da, da-da-da, da-da daa-daa-daa daa-daa.* You will soon realize that Brahms was a sadist and his tune was written to be used in torture chambers.

Cradles and cribs

New babies also need a place to sleep. They usually go into bassinets or cradles because these are the right size and stay cozy. Some cradles rock. These are useful for swaying babies to sleep, but you should make sure they don't swing like an amusement park ride, flinging your baby across the room. Again, be careful not to get sucked into baby magazine fantasy advertising. Some cradles are colonial-style cherry wood creations with decorative carvings and lace coverings—oh, and by the way, they will cost you a fortune. But do you think that even for a moment the baby gives a hoot about the aesthetics of his crib? Not on your life. I know of one family who put their baby in a sturdy laundry basket. Now that's what I call ingenuity.

As your baby gets bigger, though, a crib will be more suitable for his nocturnal wrigglings. The crib must have tall sides so your baby won't fall or climb out. It must have a mattress that can withstand multiple rinsing in toxic bodily fluids. You'll also need a supply of sheets. Check on the current requirements regarding cribs before you accept a secondhand one. Among other things, slat spacing must be no wider than $2\frac{3}{8}$ inches apart to prevent baby from getting his head stuck between the bars.

We were given a bright red crib that Meredith immediately painted white. My smart and forward-thinking wife assured me that the paint was lead-free. This was a good thing because by the 15-month mark, Georgia had gnawed off most of it with her razorlike teeth.

Monitor
If the nursery is far from your bedroom or main living area, you should get a monitor so you can turn it off when you hear the baby scream. You especially need one if you have had the nursery soundproofed, or if you've built it in your nuclear shelter, three stories underground.

Lighting
During the first weeks, you will probably check on the baby a lot during the night. This is, of course, assuming that you can see the baby.

To a baby, a normal ceiling light is like an aircraft coming in to land on her face. It is understandable that she will not be happy about this.

A simple, inexpensive night-light will solve the problem. These are small, soft lights that usually plug into an outlet without a cord and are so low in intensity, they don't even register on your electricity meter. They allow midnight checkings without midnight awakenings.

Interior design
It's funny how the decor of your home changes once you have kids. Our place was once the domain of trendy black and white photographs and arty prints. Now the walls are covered in posters of rabbits wearing suspenders, train cabooses with stupid grins and gigantic bananas clad in striped pajamas.

No wonder our kids have nightmares.

It's nice to decorate the nursery so that it is colorful and interesting. There are literally hundreds of posters, wallpaper and ceiling borders available that contain an enormous array of cute animals, numbers, letters and nursery-rhyme characters. Try to avoid the ones depicting vampires or naked women. Also try to avoid hand-painted imported Italian originals. These will wreck your bank account and won't look so good with mashed egg smeared all over them.

I hung a *Terminator 2* poster in the nursery while Meredith was in the hospital. When she got home, she was furious.

Don't do this.

Not even as a joke.

Stuffed animals
There are many mysteries in our universe:

- The Bermuda Triangle

- Who shot JFK

- The curse of the Pharaohs

- The Colonel's eleven secret herbs and spices

None of these are as perplexing, however, as the mystery of the stuffed animals.

We have more than one hundred stuffed animals in our house. We didn't buy one of them. They were all gifts. We have fluffy bunnies, fluffy bears, fluffy ducks, fluffy cows, fluffy donkeys, fluffy monkeys, fluffy penguins, fluffy pigs, fluffy dogs, fluffy versions of every character from every PBS and Disney kids' show and every kind of fluffy marsupial imaginable. Worse still, half of them squeak or contain jingly bells.

The scary thing is that we only started with about fifty. Pretty freaky or what? So where did the others come from? Clearly they are breeding. They are planning the conquest of our house. It'll be just like a B-grade horror film called *Night of the Stuffed Animals* or something like that.

Don't buy stuffed animals. One way or another, they will get into your house anyway.

The Changing Zone

Diapers
You need a lot of little things for changing your baby, including diapers, pins and plastic pants (if diapers are cloth), lotions, creams, wipes, plastic bags, liners, tissues, gas masks and an industrial furnace to destroy any contaminants. It's best to establish a spot in a room where all this paraphernalia can be centralized and contained.

You can always use the floor or an appropriate chair as a changing table, but this means getting up and down like a jack-in-the-box all day. If you have the space, a number of free-standing changing tables are available on the market that have shelves for all the accessories and a comfortable mat on the top for the baby. If you buy one, make sure it is sturdy.

The main problem I found with changing tables is they are designed for midgets. I think the little guy from *Fantasy Island* was consulted by the manufacturers during the design process. If you stand over six feet like me, that slight stoop will give you back problems for the rest of your life. An alternative that worked well for us was a simple foam mat we put on top of the baby's chest of drawers. This was high enough for me and we didn't need to fill up the room with another piece of furniture.

A word of warning, though: New babies are pretty passive because they haven't yet figured out how to wriggle, twist and claw their way away from you while you're trying to change or dress them. But as they get older, they develop a lemminglike death wish that drives them to throw themselves off changing tables. *Never* leave a baby unattended on a changing table—*not even for a second.*

If you use cloth diapers, you need a convenient place to soak the dirty ones. The World Health Organization probably wouldn't be too happy if you used your kitchen sink. If you use your bathroom sink, shaving becomes a real problem. And your face starts to smell, too.

Buy two big buckets with lids and chuck the diapers in these. Store them in the bathroom or laundry room—somewhere near a sink or tap and where spillage won't matter. Make sure the baby can't get to them.

Clothing
When your baby comes home to live with you, you will notice something very interesting. Babies are much smaller than adults. As such, attempts to dress them in your own hand-me-downs will be a horrible failure. They need undershirts that snap between the legs, socks, hats and warm outfits. Jumpsuits, cardigans and nighties or pajamas with feet are ideal, depending on the weather. Most babies start off in a Size 000, which just shows you how small they really are—they don't even register on the scale!

As they get older, you will need to continually expand and upgrade their wardrobe at an almost bank-busting rate. Remember to buy for practical reasons instead of making a fashion statement. But don't run off to the mall right away. If you have a lot of friends or relatives, clothes tend to be a standard present for newborns. When Rachael was born, we had to use a shovel to move all the clothes she got as presents. In fact she got so many that Georgia and Matilda were set for years of hand-me-downs.

However, there is one disadvantage to hand-me-downs: Years from now, when I flip through my family photo albums, I won't be able to tell which of my kids is which, because they'll all be dressed the same.

*Remember to buy for practical reasons instead of
making a fashion statement.*

Bathtubs

Babies need to be cleaned. However, they're not very good at doing this themselves. Unlike us, they can't just hop in the shower. The best way to clean them is to give them a bath, but the one in your bathroom is like an Olympic swimming pool to them. You'll waste a lot of water on such a small person and also get a bad back from bending down all the time.

Your baby can either take a bath with you or, since they're so small, you can bathe them in a sink or laundry tub. We didn't have a suitable sink and our own bath was too big to be practical, so we bought a small plastic bath. These are readily available, inexpensive and can be put on a kitchen or bathroom bench or counter.

Odds and ends

You will need many odds and ends for bathing or changing your baby. I'm not sure what they're all for, but since everyone else seems to have them in their baby's nurseries, you don't want to seem negligent.

You need baby oil, olive oil, bath oil, engine oil, baby lotion, baby powder, an old nylon stuffed with oatmeal (don't ask), washcloths, baby shampoo, diaper cream, a soft brush, cotton balls, cotton swabs, tissues, rubbing alcohol, a comb, several jars of unidentifiable lumpy gray stuff, a colorful mobile of cute farm animals and one of those little musical gismos that plays "Brahms' Lullaby."

Feeding Equipment

Bottles and things
To feed a baby, you need

- two milk-swollen breasts; or
- milk formula and several bottles and nipples.

Later you'll need

- one thousand bibs;
- a supermarket full of powdered cereals and purées; and
- a collection of cute baby dishes and tiny plastic silverware.

Here's something I didn't know before we had children: Breast milk can be bottled, too. This raises the question: How do you get it into the bottle in the first place? You use a breast pump, of course.

When I heard the words "breast pump" for the first time, I had visions of Meredith entangled in my Uncle George's irrigation pump—a huge, greasy diesel beast that smoked and coughed noisily in the corner of his shed.

Fortunately, breast pumps aren't like this. They are small and dainty. You can get manual ones, which are like wide-mouthed syringes, or electric ones with a little motor. Once some milk has been *expressed* (pumped) it can be stored and labeled in plastic bags or ice cube trays and frozen for later use. Your wife can build up a supply over a period of time. This is very useful for the baby-sitter if you and your wife go out for the evening. Of course, as with using formula, you need to buy an assortment of bottles, nipples and a sterilizing kit or dishwasher container made for bottles. When the baby gets older, you can still use the bottles for water or juice.

Chairs

About the time babies start sitting up by themselves, they also start on more "solid" foods. However, if you try to have them join you at the dinner table, you will find they disappear through the cracks in your dining room furniture.

A highchair is therefore a good investment. The baby can join you for dinner at the table and all your dinner guests can get a good view when she dumps a plate of spaghetti on her head.

Make sure the highchair is cleanable (it will survive a dip in an aluminum smelter), strong (it won't collapse) and secure (your baby can't attempt the world's shortest freefall from it).

Getting Around

Babies can't walk.

They don't even crawl for six or seven months.

Even after they learn to crawl, they are still pretty slow. A short crawl to the corner store would take hours—to say nothing of the damage to the baby's knees. So modern baby-gear designers have come to the rescue by inventing many accessories for baby transport.

Car travel

It's hard to believe, but every once in a while, when I'm stopped at a light, I will glance at the car next to me and see a parent bouncing a baby on his knee. Or even worse, the baby will be tucked inside his own seatbelt.

Kids must be restrained in cars. Strapping them into adult seatbelts doesn't work and simply invites medical disaster and police fines. For example, if you are traveling at the speed limit with your baby unrestrained and you crash, the effect would be like dropping him from a second-story window onto concrete. I'm sure no self-respecting father would ever do that to his baby.

By law, you must have a car seat to transport your baby in your car, and for infants, this car seat must be rear-facing with a 3- or 5-point harness. The seat will be your baby's home in the car for their first few months (although seats are now available for babies up to 22 pounds, enabling you to use the seat for up to a year). The good news is that car seats are rentable from most hospitals and several secondhand stores. Also, most infant car seats detach from a base that stays in the car; thus you have a convenient baby carrier—convenient for short periods of time, anyway. When your baby gets a little older, he will graduate to the dizzy heights of a child seat, complete with racing harness.

If you do go with a used seat, make sure the seat has never been in a crash, is not more than ten years old (even better—no older than five), still has the instructions and the manufacturer's name and date of manufacture, so you can check on recalls. Check for vomit or other bodily fluid stains on the upholstery and look for cracks and other damage. If the harness is frayed, send it back to the manufacturer. Some manufacturers replace the straps and other parts free of charge.

Diaper bags

Whenever you go out with a baby, you need to take a survival kit called a *diaper bag*. We have one that we call *The Tardis*, after the craft in *Doctor Who* that is bigger on the inside than it appears on the outside. Our diaper bag holds more items than the laws of dimensional physics dictate should fit into it.

It contains everything a baby will ever need: sunscreen, diapers, plastic pants, pins, hats, pacifiers, bottles, tissues, cotton swabs, those always-wet wipey things, spare clothing, board books, soft toys, jars of slushy food, spoons, bibs, plastic bags, an orienteering compass, 120 feet of rope and a mobile phone with a direct line to Rescue 911.

Stroller

Babies may be small and light, but they get heavy after a while. You simply can't carry them all the time. You must have a stroller.

For summer, it is important to find a stroller that can provide shade for the baby. Some have extendable hoods or umbrella attachments, but you should at the very least be able to jury-rig a towel on it to provide cover.

The stroller we bought cost us more than my first car. It also has more features: eight rotating wheels, a reclining seat, four-way wheel-locks, independent steering, full reversibility, a luggage compartment, a shade-hood, a rain-hood, compression shocks, adjustable handles, a seatbelt, a running-board and Ben Hur chariot wheels that can easily shred the ankles of anyone stupid enough to get in our way.

It can go about 10 to 20 mph without getting speed-wobbles. It is light to push, comfortable for the baby, easy to clean, and we can fold it up without watching an instructional video. It also folds down and doubles as a crib on outings.

You will use your stroller a lot. Get a good one.

Backpacks

There are some places where a stroller is impractical, like on the west face of Mount St. Helens. If you go shopping by yourself, you need one hand to get things off the shelves and one hand to push the cart. Unless you have a third arm sticking out of the middle of your chest, carrying the baby or pushing a stroller *as well as* a cart invites disaster with very large displays of poorly stacked glass bottles.

So what do you do?

You can either put the car seat in the cart or strap the baby to your body, just like the natives do in *National Geographic*. This can be done in two ways: in the sling that fits snugly on the front of you for little babies, and in the backpack for bigger ones.

At first I thought we could just stuff the baby inside the backpack I took around Europe. After all, it was spacious, comfortable, had a strong frame and many colorful cloth badges from places of interest that I had visited. Oddly enough, the baby didn't like it very much and people in the street looked at me like I was some kind of weirdo.

On the other hand, slings are good because you can carry the baby and still have two arms free to do pretty much anything: hang out the laundry, clean the car, vacuum the house, rappel down cliff faces and compete in triathlons.

Slings are good.

Bouncers

As our babies grew, a bouncer was a great way to get them off the floor and sitting semi-upright so they could see what was going on in the world around them. It was also useful when they started eating their first solids.

Being a teacher, I noticed something very interesting about baby bouncers. They have exactly the same design and structure as medieval catapults, which were designed to hurl large and usually flaming objects through the air at great speed with the intent of causing much damage at the receiving end. It is very important, therefore, that you never depress and release the back of a bouncer too quickly. The results will be catastrophic.

Baby walkers

Look, to be honest, I'm not too impressed by these things. Walkers give babies the mobility they may not be ready for—kind of like giving a 10-year-old the keys to your car. In a walker a baby gains the ability to travel around your house at approximately 30 miles an hour and use her method of transportation as a battering ram. A walker also helps the baby stand upright and reach expensive and forbidden domestic equipment.

I'm from the old school who believe that babies will walk when they're good and ready and it's a little pretentious to push them. It also seems that babies in walkers get used to the support they provide and are slow in becoming independent walkers anyway. Most important, I think walkers are just plain dangerous. Houses are too full of stairs and inclines and sharp corners and electric cords to accommodate aspiring Formula One drivers.

Playpens

Whether they're put in a walker or not, when babies get a little older, they like to move around the house searching for things to destroy. It can be difficult to monitor their movements all day, so some parents put their babies in a portable jail called a *playpen*. This is an interesting piece of equipment because it's actually designed for the benefit of the frustrated parent, not the baby.

Some parents swear by their playpens but I can't personally recommend them because the only time I tried to put Rachael in one she didn't enjoy the experience. She made me aware of this by taking off her diaper and creating some interesting new patterns on the carpet with it. I haven't tried since then.

If you do want to get a playpen, use your common sense. Look for strength and stability. Watch out for splinters, toxic paint, sharp edges, finger-jamming hinges and head-squashing bars. Even then, don't assume that your baby's relative lack of mobility allows you to leave him unsupervised. Just think of our carpet.

So where exactly does all this leave you? With a house stacked to the creaking rafters with baby junk. And what exactly has all this cost you? To help you work out your monstrous debt, I have made a rough calculation of the cost of parenting three daughters during their first five years.

Lost income	$150,000
Minivan (used)	$8,000

Extensions to house	$65,000
Bedroom furniture	$3,000
Preschool	$5,000
Swimming lessons	$4,000
Ballet lessons	$3,000
Excess water bill	$2,000
Food thrown onto floor	$1,000
Stroller	$600
Car seats	$300
Diapers	$3,000
Indestructible dishes	$50
Carpet shampoo	$400
Plumber (when the diaper got stuck in the toilet)	$650
Video rentals	$100
VCR repairs	$175
Jewelry lost by inquisitive toddler	$6,500
Pony	$1,200
Food, stable, shoes, saddle, vet bills for pony	$4,000
Classified in newspaper advertising pony for sale	$10.50
Aspirin	$2,000

But before we leave the subject of shopping forever, let me give you a final word of advice. Watch out for feelers. *Feelers* are total strangers who lurk around supermarkets and baby stores and, upon spotting your pregnant wife, descend *en masse* and rub their hands all over her swollen stomach. "Having a baby?" they coo. "Oh my, he's a big one. Is he going to kick? Are you going to kick, little baby? Goodness, what a big kick!" And then they're gone.

I'm glad that this behavior seems to be a woman thing. I'm not sure I would like complete strangers putting their hands on my testicles and saying, "Having a baby?"

Get an Education!

In 1830, Sir Walter Scott wrote to a friend:

> *All men who have turned out worth anything have*
> *had the chief hand in their own education.*

This applies especially to fatherhood. My guess is that most guys are like I was in my prefather life; that is, they don't have the faintest idea about pregnancy, labor or caring for a baby. It is totally foreign to them. Completely out of their life experience.

But if you want to be an active and involved dad, you can't simply tag along for the ride, watching from the sidelines with a sense of vague detachment. You need to start asking important questions and finding out the facts. What happens during pregnancy? What happens during labor? How do you take care of a child? Did I remember to put the trash out? What happens if I faint? And how exactly did my wife get pregnant in the first place?

In short, as Scott said, if you want to be of any worth as a father, you need to start educating yourself. Self-education will achieve three things. First, it will help you understand what medical personnel are talking about. For example:

"Mr. Downey, the episiotomy caused a Cesarean epidural and I'm afraid your forceps were cervixed in the panic. As a consequence, our fetal monitor led to bonding with the cradle cap. Colostrum should do the trick, but if you're still concerned, rub the pelvic floor."

Second, self-education will help you know what to expect; for instance, what happens when you go to the hospital and how much your life and bank balance will be ruined from now on.

Third, it will help to prepare you for the visual spectacle of the birth itself.

Timothy Hopper was a boy in my health class at high school. I remember him because whenever we watched a film even remotely related to pregnancy or childbirth, his eyelids would start fluttering and eventually he would slump, then keel over and hit the floor. This would inevitably drive the class into a rabid frenzy—perhaps the reason why we never got to see one of those films in its entirety.

So this is the reason I was an ignoramus about fatherhood!

If you have delicate sensibilities, like our friend Hopper, go to your local video store and look through their stock of childbirth and parenting documentaries. Rent a video that has an explicit birth sequence in it. If it's in stereo, even better. Take it home, turn off all the lights and play it with the volume turned up full blast. Repeat this process until you can watch it without flinching. This will build up your resilience.

Aside from documentaries, there are a lot of regular movies with babies in them. Remember, though, that most of these films are terrible (see Appendix 1).

You can start learning in a number of other ways, too. The fact that you are reading these words is a sign that you have started. Way to go! However, no single book will give you all the answers, options, opinions and views on childbirth and parenting. My advice is to read—or at least browse through—as many books and magazines as you can get your hands on. Libraries and used bookstores are usually a reliable source. Try to stick to the more recent publications. Also, most newsstands have an entire shelf devoted to childbirth and parenting magazines. You can spot them because they have those soft-focus shots of mothers on the cover or lively photos of infants with perfect skin and ecstatic expressions (they are undoubtedly thrilled to be wearing the latest in Baby Gap fashion). And if you're a "nonreader," go to the library and say you want a book for your five-year-old son. These usually have lots of cartoons and are pretty easy to follow.

An important step in your education is to familiarize yourself with the place where your wife is going to have the baby. Hospitals usually run childbirth-education classes, which usually include tours of the labor and maternity wards. During these tours a nurse will run through the sequence of events, from the time you and your wife arrive at the hospital to the time mother and baby are happily recovering in the maternity ward and father is sleeping soundly on the chair in the corner. You are shown the place to report to, the waiting rooms, the delivery room and the maternity rooms. You'll see all the high-tech equipment and the low-tech equipment and get to ask any questions. You also find out where the really important things are, like the restrooms, gift shop, cafeteria and phone.

On our first tour, one young guy pointed at a large silvery bucket at the base of a bed in the delivery room. "What's that for?" he asked.

There was a pause.

"Waste," said the nurse dryly.

Several men were visibly shaken by this response. A deathly silence fell over the room. We moved on, but none of us was ever the same again.

Other than a source of stomach-churning imagery, childbirth classes offer information about the birthing process and how to prepare. Our classes ran for five or six consecutive Tuesday nights and were great in educating Meredith and myself on a whole range of things. We learned about pregnancy and labor, listened to speakers, watched videos, drew pictures, looked at overheads and stuffed plastic babies through plastic pelvic bones. We did breathing exercises and panted at each other. We took off our shoes and learned all about coping with contractions. We rolled around on the floor, screamed, slapped our thighs and swayed back and forth. We learned about back massages and options for pain relief. I learned about being a support person for Meredith. We asked questions and practiced birthing positions. We leaned into beanbags, squatted down, crawled on all fours and knelt. On the final night, one of the moms from the maternity ward came down and gave us a baby-bathing demonstration—with a real live baby and everything!

In short, it was great. So get into it! Read books, watch videos and go to classes. It's the only way you'll learn.

To Plan or Not to Plan?

In the "old days," a pregnant woman had little say in what happened during her labor. She was merely there as a baby incubator and everything was done for the convenience of the doctor. Supposedly, this is why many women gave birth in the Universal Television Position on their backs with their feet up in stirrups. It was nice and handy for the doctor, but it is in reality a lousy childbirth position because it doesn't allow the birth canal to open up fully. Also, the horse tends to get in the way.

(I know one guy who had heard that women give birth in the position the baby was conceived in. He was concerned because he didn't want his wife giving birth while doing the *Mexican starfish*. But that's another story.)

The last twenty years have seen a growing backlash against enforced compliance. Women are now encouraged to be knowledgeable about the birth and to participate in the decision-making process. But like most things, you can go too far.

A lot of couples work out a *birth plan*. They read a little, discuss the options available in the birth process and then custom-design their own "ideal" birth. The plan might consist of a series of statements, such as

- "We want a painless birth."

- "We don't want any pain relief."

- "We don't want a Cesarean."

- "Forceps are not to be used."

- "We want the labor to last only five minutes."

Birth plans are the stupidest thing I have ever heard of. The problem with birth plans is that unlike your nursery decor, you can't really pick and choose to any great degree what is going to happen when the baby comes out. You can pick a birth as much as you can pick the shape of your baby's toenails. Many couples get disappointed—some bitterly—because the birth wasn't what they ordered.

Many things can happen in the delivery room, from a medical emergency to some advised intervention from your doctor. If and when this happens there's no point in screaming out, "Hang on a second—that's not in the plan!"

It is in fact more common to hear the woman scream, "FORGET THE PLAN! I don't care what you do, get it out of me!"

So how do you balance between having no say in the birth and wanting a custom-designed birth where you decide everything?

You should know your options and discuss these as a couple with your obstetrician. It is okay to have preferences beforehand, but you both must remain flexible, depending on how the birth turns out. For example, while Meredith was not keen on the idea of having an epidural, I certainly would not have discouraged her if she screamed for one in the delivery room. As it turned out, she needed no pain relief for any of the three births. What a woman!

And if the doctor said to me, "Mr. Downey, I'm going to have to do a Cesarean section," I wouldn't have responded with, "I'm sorry, Doctor, but I'm afraid that's just not in our plan."

Following are some things you might need to be flexible about on the spur of the moment:

Induction

If labor is going too slowly or hasn't started at all when it should have, the staff may decide to "induce" the process. This may be because there is a problem with either the mother or the baby or, as was the case with us, the baby is late. We thought Rachael was never going to come out!

Induction can be done chemically, through an oxytocin drip or by rubbing prostaglandin gel into the cervix. It can also be done manually by rupturing the membrane inside the uterus with a long hook. This uncomfortable but speedy procedure is called an *amniotomy*.

But if you prefer an *au naturel* method, a brisk walk or a good swim can often get the wheels moving. Stimulation of the nipples is another tried and true method. (*Her* nipples, that is, not yours.) I don't know if it actually helped Meredith, but we sure enjoyed it.

Sex is said to be a good way of triggering the labor as well. This is because semen contains prostaglandin, which promotes uterine contraction. Sex with a nine months' pregnant woman is interesting to say the least, but it's also a lot more fun than having a drip or an injection.

Pain Relief Options

If the pain is too much to bear, there are options available to bring relief. Usually you can detect when your wife wants something for the pain because she will put her hands around your throat and scream, "DRUGS—NOW!"

In terms of pain relief, most modern hospitals no longer stock hip flasks of whiskey or bullets to bite on. Anesthetics have come a long way since then. One option is a narcotic analgesic (such as Demerol™) or tranquilizer (such as Phenergen®) or both. This form of pain relief relaxes the woman and alters her perception of the pain. It is usually not used in the later stages of the labor because it may affect the baby's breathing. Some women don't like this option because they lose some sensation and don't fully "experience" the birth—which is funny, because this is exactly why other women like it.

The option most commonly used during the later stages of labor and the actual delivery is an epidural block. A local anesthetic is injected via a catheter into the woman's spinal column, which knocks the lower half of her body unconscious. She doesn't feel a thing but remains awake to witness the event, which is probably like watching someone else give birth. Once again, some women don't like epidurals for this very reason.

Epidurals also affect a woman's ability to push, which could in turn prolong the labor.

Breech Birth

Most babies are born head-first. This is so they can see where they're going on the way out.

Do not be alarmed, however, if your baby is exceptionally ugly and has a crack down the middle of his featureless face. He's probably a breech baby, which means he has no sense of direction and is coming out bottom-first. Breech babies can be born normally, but if difficulties arise, an episiotomy or Cesarean might be necessary.

Cesarean Birth

A *Cesarean* means the baby is removed surgically. It used to involve a vertical cut from the mother's collarbone down to her knee, but advanced medical technology means that a modern Cesarean is usually only a small horizontal cut along her bikini line.

A birth like this will usually take place if there are complications with the baby—such as it being in a weird position—or with the size of the woman's pelvis, or sometimes if she's having twins. Usually the decision to perform a Cesarean is made well before she even makes it to the hospital.

But sometimes the operation needs to be done on the spur of the moment. The doctor will suddenly yell, "We gotta go C-section—NOW!" Everybody in the delivery room will start running around shouting "STAT! STAT!" and the doctor will look at you with serious eyes and say, "Get him outta here." Three burly hospital aides will drag you out while you scream your wife's name and really sad and manipulative music will begin to filter through the hospital's PA system.

Anyway, that's what happens on TV.

I was a Cesarean baby. That's why I have a big head and have trouble finding hats that fit me.

Baby-Removing Devices

Sometimes, in the middle of a delivery, the baby gets cold feet and decides not to come out. Or like a caver who's had one too many donuts, she can get stuck in the claustrophobic confines of the birth canal.

There are two main baby-removing devices to help her get out:

- *Forceps*, also known as *Gigantic Baby-Grabbing Pliers*, are used to grab the baby's head and pull it out—the whole baby that is, not just the head. They may be used if the baby is stuck, or if the anaesthetic has rendered the mother's pushing ineffective.

- If the custodian isn't busy with it, some hospitals use a vacuum cleaner with a toilet plunger attachment on the end, actually called a *vacuum extractor*, to get a good grip on the baby's skull. Always make sure the nurse checks that the dust-bag has been recently emptied. And check that the suction isn't up too high, or else it will suck your baby inside out.

Both of these options may cause some markings or bruising on your baby's head. Don't be alarmed—the bruises go away.

Incubator

Most babies have a "normal birth" and adjust to the outside world quickly. Some, however, can have complications and need to be monitored closely. This can be the case with premature babies, low-birthweight babies, babies with severe jaundice, babies with breathing irregularities and some Cesarean babies.

If your baby falls into one of these categories, he might be placed in a sealed crib, or incubator, which is hooked up to lots of machines that go "beep" and "ping." These machines help to monitor your baby's bodily functions, including body temperature, breathing and possibly feeding as well.

Many parents feel intimidated by all the tubes and gauges and flashing lights. They may also find the incubator frustrating because they are physically separated from their baby by a plastic shield. But you can still touch your baby through portholes, and spend time sitting next to him and talking to him. Often normal feeding is possible as well.

Ask the staff questions about your baby and the incubator. The staff in special-care nurseries are used to anxious parents and will help you to feel more comfortable about the situation. In any case, remember that your baby won't be in there forever.

What's in a Name?

It is a sad but true fact that the single biggest cause of marital disputes in Western society arises over the choice of names for an impending child. Actually finding a name that you like is pretty hard. Finding a name that you and your wife *both* like is next to impossible. Because it takes a lot of time and many nights perusing any one of hundreds of baby name books and websites, you should pick possible names for both sexes before the child is born. This gives you both plenty of time to fight about it.

Some parents don't put too much thought into the names they pick for their children. Some even choose on a whim. The problem here, of course, is that the kid is stuck with the name for life. This is a particular problem during the school years, because we all know that *children can be so cruel.*

So here are a few helpful hints. *Do not* choose any names from the following categories:

- *Names of incredibly famous people or characters too well known to need a surname:*
  Elvis, Elle, Madonna, Morrissey, Tarzan, Hamlet, Cher, Bono, Fabio, Goofy, Santa, Indiana, Twiggy, Roseanne, Oprah, Prince, Pele, Elmer, Darth or any person from the Bible, such as Jesus, Noah, Moses, Samson, Delilah, Maher-Shalal-Hash-Baz and so on

- *Bad persons of history:*
  Judas, Adolf, Benito, Lucifer, Attila, Imelda, Ghengis, Lucretia

- *Anything sounding vaguely British:*
  Winston, Winthrop, Bayfield, Beauchamp, Sebastian, Culthorp, Lester, Your Majesty

- *Stupid Hollywood inanimate-object names:*
  River, Skye, Storm, Leaf, Axl [sic], Shade, Thorn, Park, Summer, Moon Unit

- *Double-barrel names:*
  Peggy-Sue, Ellie-May, Billy-Ray, Sally-Jesse, Lee-Harvey, John-F, Loretta-Lynn, Sylvester-Anne

Do not name your child after bad persons of history.

- *Impossible-to-spell names:*
  Siobhan (pronounced Shuv-orn), Ymobhij (pronounced Jer-e-my)

- *"Blonde, big-breasted and brainless" names:*
  Dolly, Cindi, Barbi, Lucy, Trixie, Dixie, Pixie, Candi

- *Hall-monitor names:*
  Myron, Herman, Vernon, Sheldon, Donald, Nigel, Chester

- *Names that imply sexual ambiguity:*
  Boys: Percy, Cyril, Cecil, Julian, Terry
  Girls: Courtney, Les, Madison, Rumer

- *Checkout-girl names:*
  Cheryl, Doreen, Noreen, Kaleen, Darlene, Raylene,
  Charlene, Carlene, Sheila, Laverne, Rhonda

- *Names for twins:*
  Jack and Jill; Charles and Di; Abbott and Costello; Ernie
  and Bert; Mickey and Minnie; Patience and Prudence;
  Rocky and Bullwinkle; Barnum and Bailey; Sodom and
  Gomorrah; Captain and Tennille; Ren and Stimpy; Porgy
  and Bess; Torvill and Dean; Simon and Schuster

- *Names for higher multiples:*
  Tom, Dick and Harry; Curly, Larry and Moe; John, Paul,
  George and Ringo; Harpo, Zeppo, Groucho, Chico and
  Karl; Bobby, Peter, Greg, Marcia, Jan and Cindy; Gilligan,
  The Skipper, Mr. and Mrs. Howell, Ginger, The Professor
  and Mary Anne

- *Names that are innocent enough by themselves but make
  a lethal combination when mixed with particular surnames
  or abbreviations:*
  Dwayne Pipe, Wayne Kerr, P. Brain, A. Nuss, Phil
  McCavity, Hugo First, Mary Christmas and of course, that
  old favorite, Richard Head. (My own family, the Downeys,
  have shown a great lack of thought in this regard. Just ask
  my Uncle Sid or Aunty Ida.)

- *The least popular names of all time:*
  Boys: Altair, Faber, Aubrey, Stockton, Florian, Lyman
  Girls: Rosemede, Myra, Vaughan, Shobhana

- *Any names that appear in songs:*
  Roxanne, you don't have to put on the red light . . .
  Lucy in the sky with diamonds . . .
  Lola, Lo-lo-lo-lo-Lola . . . *or* Her name was *Lola,* she was a
      showgirl . . .
  Gloria G.L.O.R.I.A . . .

Janey's got a gun . . .
Eleanor Rigby . . .
Jolene, Jolene, Jolene, JOL-EE-EE-EENE . . .
Can you hear the drums, *Fernando* . . .
Oh we were so spaced out . . . B-B-B-Benny and the Jets . . .
Meet you all the way . . . *Rosanna*, yeah . . .
A little ditty about *Jack and Diane* . . .
My *Sharona* . . .
Nina, pretty ballerina . . .
Ziggy played guitar . . .
Well hello, *Dolly* . . .

Of course, if you follow my advice, your kids will be called Karen, Kathy, Jane, Peter, David, John or Michael, which is pretty boring, really. But you shouldn't follow my advice, because as you may have guessed, I am a complete hypocrite with one daughter called Georgia (as in "on my mind"). But it's not my fault. That was Meredith's choice.

Another problem, which I will just throw in here for the heck of it, is that even when you *do* agree on a name, as soon as the baby is born you will look at him and realize that the name is wrong.

"He just doesn't look like an *Irving*," you will say.

Then you have to start all over again.

To Cut or Not to Cut?

One thing you really should discuss before the child is born is circumcision. In short, should you circumcise your child?

This is a real source of debate and the cause of many dinner party disasters, as proponents of one view or the other express their opinion in a most narrow-minded, forceful and socially inappropriate manner. Well, I've got no particular axe to grind, but for what it's worth, here's my view. You can take it or leave it.

If it's a girl, no.

If it's a boy, no.

But I was circumcised, damn it, and it didn't do me any harm, I hear you cry. Why shouldn't I have my boy "done"?

According to my wife, it's because circumcision is cruel, unnecessary and has no medical justification.

I have less noble reasons.

When I was born, I received the cruelest cut as a matter of medical course. It was the "thing to do." I was quite happy about this, because twelve years later I looked the same as all the other semi-naked boys in my high school locker room. To have a different organ in this situation meant suffering the worst taunts.

Now that we're in a new millennium and surgeons are less inclined to cut something off the human body just because "it looks kinda funny," the scissors are coming out less and foreskins across the land are breathing easy. It is increasingly not "the thing to do"—these days the U.S. and Canadian circumcision rate has dropped to about 60 percent, as low as 40 percent in some provinces. The point is that twelve years from now, more boys in the high school locker room will be uncut and the poor kid *sans foreskin* may be the odd one out. Don't subject your son to that.

To Jab or Not to Jab?

Sometimes on talk radio you'll hear some debate about immunization, with both camps offering passionate arguments for and against. This is probably something you should also discuss with your wife and doctor before the birth of your child. (Immunization, not talk radio.)

Let me be honest with you. Although I have my CPR certificate, I do not consider myself to be in any way knowledgeable about medicine or the ethics of vaccination. Having said that, I think immunization is a good idea—a view, I might add, which is held widely by the medical profession. I have no desire to risk my kids getting polio, bacterial meningitis, whooping cough, measles, mumps, tetanus, rubella, diphtheria, bubonic plague, halitosis or dyslexia.

With the occasional exception, most kids in North America are immunized. In fact, many childcare providers refuse to accept children who are not on a regular immunization schedule. The shots take place at regular intervals primarily when your baby is between two and eighteen months of age, with a few more around five years and in adolescence. Consult your doctor or pediatrician for details.

When You Least Expect It

It's getting toward that time . . . the due date. All your preparations are now complete. The family and friends are primed and on alert. The nursery is furnished and ready for operation. You've been to classes. You've picked the names. You've read the books. You know the drill. Your wife's bag is packed and sitting by the front door. You have a pocket of coins so you can phone the news to the waiting world. The camera is loaded. The car is fuelled and pointed in the direction of the hospital. All you need now is for the baby to want to come out.

Babies come out when they want to.

The problem here is that you can't spend the final months following your wife around on the off chance that the contractions will start.

When Meredith was in her final weeks with Rachael, I must admit to being something of a concerned, some would even say obsessive-paranoid, father-to-be. Whenever I was out, I called every couple of hours just in case Meredith had gone into labor in the living room and needed me there right away.

I remember coming home from work one day during her "final week."

The house was empty.

Meredith had been rushed by ambulance to the hospital where she was giving birth at that very moment!

I panicked and called the hospital. "My wife's pregnant and her name's Meredith and she's not home. She's having a baby and I just got home and my name's Peter and she's not here and she's due this week. Is she in the labor ward? Is it a boy or a girl?"

Even as I spoke, I realized how pathetic I sounded. The nurse did her professional best not to sound too patronizing or annoyed, but I could tell she knew I was an idiot.

"She's not here. She's probably shopping. Goodbye," was all she said.

She was right. Meredith was shopping and I was an idiot.

So if you, like me, want to have a labor hotline but don't want to spend your entire life on the phone, rent a pager or cell phone for a couple of weeks.

Once you've done that, the only thing left to do is wait for the damn thing to go off.

Because when that happens . . . it's time to party.

CHAPTER 4
Surviving the Hospital

When you do actually go to the hospital, don't wear a pair of good shoes. They'll only get ruined.

A Brief History of Labor

It is certainly true to say that the labor process has changed over the course of history.

In her classic *Clan of the Cave Bear* stories, Jean M. Auel tells about life at the dawn of time. When the pregnant woman felt her first contraction, she was exiled to a dark corner of the cave with a few woman friends to writhe through the agony of childbirth on a mastodon-skin rug. Meanwhile, the "mate" and future father sat with the men of the tribe around the men-of-the-tribe fire to discuss the day's hunt. The men knew instinctively that labor was a "woman thing" and that this was not to interrupt their evening men-of-the-tribe chat around the men-of-the-tribe fire. Many hours later, after all the action, the newborn would be presented to Dad, who would grunt, scratch himself a few times and pass the kid back.

He definitely was not a modern sensitive man.

Well, times may have changed, but it's funny how some things never do. The dark and smelly cave has been replaced by a bright and smelly hospital. The ochre paintings of bison on the cave wall have been replaced by pastels of flower arrangements in the waiting room. But up until just recently, the inherent sexism of the labor process had pretty much remained with us.

A few years ago, men were still nowhere to be seen near a birth. When I was born, my father dropped my mother at the hospital and then went to work. Later he got a phone call informing him that he had a son and asking if he would like to come and visit.

You're probably familiar with the television-sitcom stereotype of labor. I was brought up on this and was almost disappointed when I discovered that birth wasn't like this anymore. You know the stereotype I mean: four or five dads-to-be anxiously pacing the waiting-room floor, eagerly expecting the door to open and the nurse to stick in her grinning head and announce, "Mr. Downey, it's a (insert appropriately) boy/girl/not sure yet!" I would then receive pats on the back while handing out cigars to all my paternal comrades. In fact, when Meredith was pregnant, I was given a new book that described exactly this scenario.

It doesn't sound too much different from the cave, does it?

Fortunately, times have changed enough so that we dads now have quite an important role to play in the labor process. No longer do we have to wait in the corner of the cave. No longer do we have to wait at work. No longer do we have to wait in the waiting room. Now, we get to participate. We are there. Point-blank range. Living color. Stereo sound. The whole nine yards. And this is lucky for us, because being present at and participating in the birth of your child is a wonderful experience.

Terrifying, yes. But wonderful.

Modern Man and the process of labor . . .

In fact, now we've gone to the other extreme and there is an increasing trend not only for fathers to be present at the birth, but for the rest of the family to be there also! Personally, I can think of nothing more likely to cause long-term psychological damage in a child, but I suppose everybody is entitled to his or her opinion. So why not also invite your parents, brothers, sisters, cousins, uncles, aunts, gym instructor, neighbors, co-workers and football team to come along? You could make a real day of it!

Remember: Your presence at the birth is primarily for one purpose and one purpose only. You are not just a spectator. And (heaven help us) you are certainly not there to be a cameraman capturing everything on your camcorder (see below). You are there solely as a support person for your wife. You are there to help her get through the ordeal that lies ahead of her. You are there to soothe her, to encourage her, to reassure her. To do this, you must be totally focused on her needs and on the labor process.

Should I Be at the Birth?

Yes.

But What's It Like?

Before we go further, I must make one point clear. The point is this: Childbirth is *painful*. Very, very painful.

God was not kidding when he said, "With pain you will give birth to children."

Nothing in a man's natural lifespan even comes close to the searing agony that accompanies a baby tearing herself from her mother and squeezing out into the world. Sure, there are industrial accidents involving heavy machinery and testicles, but there is nothing that lies almost inevitably in our biological routine.

Unfortunately, we have fallen victim to pathetically unrealistic television portrayals of labor. These try to convince us that labor is little more effort than a rigorous afternoon aerobics session. The hapless woman pants a few times, blows a few breaths through clenched teeth and then, with a Herculean effort and a final gasp, the screaming baby is born. The woman has merely shed a light sweat.

This is bull. Total and utter bull.

If you think about it, childbirth is like trying to push a camel through the eye of a needle.

The camel is very big.

The needle is very small.

The needle will experience a lot of pain.

There is no such thing as painless childbirth. This concept only exists in the mind of men who are time-locked in the fifties. A few months ago a friend of mine lent me a cassette—one of those motivational things by some infomercial-making business guru. There is one phenomenal part of the tape where the guru says, in a thick southern drawl, "With thuh burth of mah furst chahld, my wahf and ah had uh paaynless layburr."

I played this to Meredith. She didn't think it was very funny.

I mean, not only did this fool believe that labor could be naturally painless, but he also had the audacity to assume that it was his labor as well. Although I'm not a medical giant, I am now a veteran of three births and therefore think it's fairly safe for me to claim that, generally speaking, childbirth is not really physically painful for the male. That is, unless you're a Cayapó Indian male. They have ropes attached to their testicles for their laboring partners to yank on during contractions, just so *they* know what it feels like.

This next story may help you arrive at some understanding of the pain of childbirth. Soon after I found out that Meredith and I were going to be parents, I naturally became quite inquisitive and anxious about the whole labor process. But aside from textbooks, I had no source of information. Then one day at a party we met an old friend who had just had a baby herself.

What a perfect opportunity! Unashamedly, and in retrospect idiotically, I opened our conversation by asking her if childbirth was painful.

The look on her face betrayed the fact that she clearly knew I was the stupidest man on earth. Fixing me in her steely stare, she said: "Imagine you are holding an umbrella."

Mmmm, OK so far, I thought.

"Now," she said, pausing for dramatic effect, "insert it into your penis."

At this, my legs involuntarily crossed and my eyes began to water. I tried to break eye contact, but she could see that her words were cutting me like a knife. She held me in her gaze and pushed on mercilessly.

"Now open the umbrella," she hissed.

With alarm bells clanging loudly in my head, I staggered to my feet in a feeble attempt to escape the anguish in my groin. But there was no escape. She grabbed my arm and snarled in my ear,

"Now pull it out. Yank it—hard."

She was reveling in the paralyzing effect of her words. And her words had had the desired effect.

"That's what childbirth is like," she snickered as I hobbled off.

Lights, Camera, Action!

A few years ago I spent some time teaching English in Japan. At one point I had some time off so I did what any self-respecting tourist would do: I packed my backpack and hit the road in search of adventure and major scenic attractions.

One day I ended up in the Todaiji Temple staring at the 1200-year-old, 450-ton *Daibutsu*, which is the largest bronze statue on Earth. I remember this not because of its breathtaking size, nor because of its artistic lines, nor for the overpowering sense of history that the place commanded. I remember this place clearly because of the busload of American tourists who arrived just as I got there. These people had obviously been briefed on "American Etiquette Overseas" and had all had lessons in *How To Be a Typical Texan Tourist in Foreign Climes*. They had twangy accents. They had gaudy clothes. They had big hats. They had condescending attitudes: "The giant Buddha in Dallas is twice as big as this, Cyndi." But most of all, they had cameras.

Lots of cameras.

Lots and *lots* of cameras.

Super 8. VHS. 35 mm. Polaroid. Disposable. Panoramic. You name it, they had it.

Now, most people like you or me would go to a tourist spot, take a look around for a while and then snap a few shots to remind us of the place in years to come. Not so with these guys. They were clicking, whirring and reloading before their golf shoes had even hit the gravel. Within seconds, they had deployed ranks of tripods and were grinning and posing for their automatic timers.

The ironic thing was that some of them were so busy taking photographs that they never even bothered to look at the statue itself. They didn't enjoy the experience of being there. They saw only through a viewfinder and appreciated only in terms of color, composition, light and focus.

I particularly remember one tobacco-chewing gentleman who obviously had a penchant for donuts. He walked up to his wife, who was looking around, and said, "Snap it now, Martha. We can look at it later."

I swear it's true.

The reason I've indulged in this somewhat tedious anecdote is as a segue into my next point: The birth of your first child is a momentous occasion and as such, you may feel the need to capture it for posterity. Fair enough. But how far are you going to go with this camera thing? How many photos are you going to take? How long are you going to videotape? And more important, *what* are you going to shoot?

There are three main rules that you should adhere to when shooting film during childbirth.

Rule One: Discuss It with Your Wife

This is perhaps the most important rule of all. During the labor your wife will be in no state to direct the photography. So discuss ahead of time what she wants or permits you to photograph. I have heard of some women who want no cameras of any kind within 50 feet of the delivery room. I have heard of others who want just a few tasteful snapshots taken after the baby is cleaned and wrapped up. I have heard of others who want every single gory detail captured at point-blank range on both video and still camera.

If the latter is the case with you, and you take thirty-six close-ups of "wife with legs in air and baby coming out," whatever you do, *don't* take the film to one of those photo-labs in a busy shopping center where the developed films scroll out of the machine in the storefront window. If you do, a small crowd will gather, usually made up of your wife's boss, an ex-girlfriend and the minister from your church.

Rule Two: Remember Your Job

Keep in mind that you are by your wife's side during the birth to provide support. Don't fool around with your camera when your wife needs words of assurance or simply your company and attention. You certainly don't want to antagonize her with unreasonable photographic requests.

Don't, for example, say things like:

- "Hey, that was great—can you make that face again?"
- "Can you lift your legs just a *little* higher?"
- "Don't push, don't push! I have to reload!"
- "Hey Doc, get outta the way, will ya?"

Which leads us to:

Rule Three: Don't Get in the Way

If you want to take a bunch of photos, using a flash may be a problem. The doctors, nurses and especially your wife and baby don't want to be blinded by constant explosions of light. It may be wise, therefore, to use a low-light film so your photography can be unobtrusive.

If you want to shoot video during the birth, that's your business, but stay out of the way. Medical personnel may not mind if you set a camera rolling in the corner, but you can expect opposition if you bring in a three-camera rig with light stands, mixing console, dolly grip and gaffer.

The need to capture it for posterity . . .

Zero Hour

The pager goes off. The phone rings.

OK, this is it. Zero hour.

Your wife's automatic system has decided that enough is enough and it's time to push the baby out into the real world. This may be signaled by a *show*, which is a euphemism for the expulsion of a big bloody messy glob of mucus that has been plugging up her plumbing for the past nine months. It may also be signaled when her "water breaks." This is when the uterine cocoon ruptures and all the amniotic fluid spills out like a scene from *The River* (A real thrill if you're at a nice restaurant!). Or it may be signaled by the commencement of strong and more regular *contractions*, which is another euphemism for the intense pain caused by your wife's uterine muscles getting together and deciding to push out the baby in strong bursts. This is the beginning of the first stage of labor.

For some reason, I always assumed that my wife's contractions would kick in at about 2 A.M., several days before the predicted date. I imagined scrambling for the car in pajamas and slippers and making a dash to the hospital in the freezing dead of night. Of course contractions can come at any time, and the onset of contractions does not usually mean that the baby is about to be born within minutes. Some people find that labor can be a very lengthy, and consequently exhausting and frustrating, process.

This frustration can be even worse if your wife has a false labor. The contractions kick in, everybody gets psyched up and you go to the hospital, but after a while the nurses send you home. Your wife's body was playing a practical joke on her! These premature contractions are called *Braxton-Hicks*. Mr. Hicks must have been a real jerk!

It is also frustrating when the baby is late. It is hard not to subconsciously psych yourself up for the due date, and you may be anxious if you only have a narrow window of absence from work. But then the big day passes. The next day passes, too. And the next. And the next after that. And then after that, the next day passes. Finally the day after arrives and then unceremoniously passes as well. The expectation and tension increases until you're a nervous wreck. You wind up like the Bill Murray character in *Groundhog Day*. Every day seems exactly like the last. And basically you just have to grin and bear it. *Que séra, séra* . . .

We were pretty lucky with the births of our kids. For our first child, Rachael, I woke up on a Friday morning ready to go to work after a good night's sleep and was confronted by my wife saying, "OK, I think this is it."

It was a beautiful summer's day. The sun was shining through the window and the birds were singing as we had breakfast. Rachael was born just after 11 A.M. She was two weeks late.

For our second child, we were just clearing the table after a pleasant dinner when once again Meredith said, "OK, I think this is it." Georgia was born close to midnight. She was one day late.

For the third birth, I was sure we could get it right on the day just to confuse our obstetrician. But then we traveled down the familiar road of one day, two days, three days late. Then on the fourth day, right in the middle of *The Simpsons*, Meredith said with great certainty, "This is it." Matilda was born a few hours later—twenty minutes short of being an April Fool. Whew.

The point is, "it" can come anywhere, anytime. It could be midnight or midday. You might be in bed or on the subway or at a dinner party or driving a plow. (As a matter of fact, it could happen right now.) But when the time comes, there's no point saying, "Can you hang on just a minute?" You must be ready. The bomb is about to go off.

There is one important thing to remember at this point. In the immortal words of Douglas Adams in *The Hitchhiker's Guide to the Galaxy*: DON'T PANIC. If it is not an emergency situation (such as the baby's head sticking out), remain calm and in control. Do not, for example, run around screaming, "What do we do?! What do we do?!" Do not run for the car half-naked from your interrupted shower with shampoo in your eyes.

This is where all your careful planning pays off. If you are having a home-birth, call the midwife and start running the bath. Boil some water and tear up a sheet into strips. I'm not sure why, but that's what they always did on *Little House on the Prairie*.

If you are going to the birth center or hospital, give them a call. They'll probably ask you a few questions about the space between the contractions and their duration and tell you when they think you should come in.

Most people make it to the hospital on time, but some don't. They get stuck in traffic, their car breaks down or the birth strikes sooner than anyone could have predicted. If it is an emergency situation, again, DON'T PANIC. Remember, childbirth is a *natural* thing. It has been going on ever since Eve said to Adam, "OK, I think this is it." Three hundred babies are born every minute in the world, most without the luxury of freeways and hospitals, so you're certainly not doing anything new.

Nevertheless, there is a certain protocol to observe if you're not going to make it to the hospital. If you're in the car, pull over somewhere safe. Don't stop in the middle of an intersection or outside an all-boys school during their lunch break. If you're in a taxi, make sure the driver turns the meter off. If you can, get someone to call an ambulance.

Then do your support stuff, just like normal. Don't freak out. Your wife will need you more than ever before and your panicking won't make things any easier for her. Help her to find her best birthing position, then get down near the baby-chute and catch it as it comes. Wrap up the baby in a T-shirt or towel to keep him warm. You don't have to pull on the umbilical cord or cut it. Birth is an automatic process; the placenta will come out by itself. Then go directly to the hospital. Do not collect two hundred dollars.

The next thing to do is place a classified ad in the paper, offering your car for sale at about 20 percent of its true value. It's the only way you'll sell it. Ever.

One final word of advice: If and when you do actually go to the hospital, *don't* wear a pair of good shoes. They'll only get ruined.

Stage 1: Before Birth

Birthing is something that still has a certain sense of mystique in our society. Some people liked it so much the first time around that they go to "rebirthing clinics" to try to experience the whole thing all over again. We even have a public holiday to commemorate the wonder of the birthing process. This is called Labor Day.

As you can see, my knowledge about birth is extensive but not very technical. So as you read this next section, let me remind you that I am not a medical doctor. In short, don't rely on a word I say. Also, in any discussion of childbirth it is necessary to talk in generalizations because every pregnancy and every childbirth is unique. For example, take the following cases from D. Wallechinsky's *The Book of Lists 2*:

- Georgias of Epirus was born in his mother's coffin during her funeral.

- In 1970, Grete Bardaum gave birth to twins—one black and one white.

- In 1955, the Schee twins were born forty-eight days apart.

- In 1875, a seventeen-year-old girl became pregnant after a bullet fired in the nearby Battle of Raymond lodged into her uterine wall. She didn't know that the bullet had already carried off part of a soldier's left testicle. Nine months later she gave birth to an eight-pound boy who had to be operated on to have the bullet removed. The soldier and the girl later married.

Believe it . . . or not.

Since trying to cover every possibility of birth would be impossible, here's a general overview.

OK. You've driven to the hospital and screeched to a grinding halt in the parking lot, waking an entire wing of patients who were just nodding off to sleep. Suddenly you realize you've left your wife at home.

Go back and get her.

Drive back to the maternity wing. Find someone wearing a uniform and give her all your personal details. Make sure she is not carrying a mop, because she might be the custodian. Eventually (when the custodian reports this information to the head nurse), you will be shown to a labor ward or delivery room where the hard part begins—the wait.

Your wife may have a quick labor: You arrive at the hospital. The baby is born. The End.

Or your wife may have a long labor: You arrive at the hospital. You hang around for ages getting tired, impatient and hungry. The baby is born. The End.

In reality, it is common for this stage of labor to be anywhere from two to ten hours long. During this time the contractions build in intensity. They are stronger, closer together in frequency and longer in duration. By the time of birth, the uterus has grown to be the biggest and strongest muscle in your wife's body, so you can imagine the strain and exertion this puts on her as the contractions increase.

Meanwhile, you are waiting for the cervix—the passageway out of the uterus—to get bigger, to *dilate* until it is big enough for the baby to pass through. Some people refer to this process as "waiting for the cervix to ripen," which always conjures up awful images of rotten fruit in my mind. But that's another story.

Normally the cervix is about two millimeters long, but it needs to stretch to about ten centimeters to allow for the baby's head. If my crude mathematics serve me correctly, this expansion is an increase of 5000 percent. To fully appreciate this muscular feat, contemplate the fact that the hole at the end of your penis is also probably about two millimeters. Pretty scary, huh?

From time to time a nurse will come along and give your wife an internal examination to inspect her dilation and check the progress of the baby. After the first cervix inspection, the nurse will probably say, "Two centimeters," which translates as, "You'd be lucky to give birth to a walnut right now."

Fifteen minutes later, when your wife has experienced so much pain that she is sure you could drive a monster truck through her cervix, the nurse will come back, inspect, and say, "Three centimeters." The nurse will then go and call your obstetrician and tell him how many more rounds of golf he could probably fit in before he needs to get to the hospital.

It is sometimes the practice at this stage for your wife to be given an intravenous drip. This may be glucose, which maintains fluid and blood sugar levels, or a synthetic hormone, which helps (cringe) ripen the cervix. When Georgia was born, I asked the nurse for a bourbon drip but she didn't think I was very funny. She must have had a long shift.

Your wife's abdomen will be palpated so the position of the baby can be felt. It is also sometimes the practice to give her an enema to clear out her lower bowel. This is for obvious reasons and I shouldn't really need to spell it out for you.

So labor can be long, painful, tiring and frustrating for mothers, many of whom by this stage are starting to have second thoughts about their babies and just want to go home and forget it ever happened. After you see your wife going through contractions, you will agree that there is no doubt the female of the species really drew the short straw as far as childbirth is concerned. However, you should also be prepared for the effects labor will have on you. Sure, you're not the one with the contractions, but you can't just stand back unaffected in the shadows either.

Childbirth for fathers is *draining*. It can be mentally taxing to focus on your wife for hour after hour on end. It is also physically demanding. You might have a sore back and be on your feet the whole time, and you might not have eaten or had anything to drink for ages. It may be particularly difficult if your wife has labored through the night and you've both been awake for more than twenty-four hours straight.

Because it's probably the first time you've witnessed childbirth, it can also be plain scary. You'll be in a strange and perhaps sterile place full of machines that go "beep" and "ping." Medical personnel will come and go and sometimes talk about things you might not understand. You might not be sure that everything is going as it should and on top of that, you may be anxious that the baby will be OK.

The experience can also be *harrowing*. The woman you love will be in agony. She will look at you with either pleading or accusative eyes and there'll be very little you can do about it. It won't be pleasant watching her suffer.

On the positive side, however, childbirth is a *thrilling* experience. It is awesome to see your child come into the world. It can also be emotional to finally meet the fruit of your loins and realize

"I'M A DAD!!!"

As your wife nears the second stage of labor—the actual birth—you'll notice her becoming vague. There will be a blank expression on her face and her comments will become more monosyllabic. Her breathing will change. All this is because a naturally produced opiate, endorphin, has kicked into her bloodstream. In short, she is stoned. She will internalize her thoughts, getting further away from the real world. Her body will be racked by pain as it prepares for the final moments.

Throughout this entire process, remember that *you are there to help*. Don't spend all your time with a camera locked to your face. You have work to do. Don't let your mind wander—focus. Encourage and support your wife. Hold her hand. Rub her back. Hum her a tune. Talk to her. Reassure her. Wipe her face with a towel. Stroke her hair. Help her move around. Help her maintain a comfortable position.

If she is in the bath, pour water over her back. Juggle a set of steak knives. In short, do whatever she tells you to do if it will make her feel better.

Of course, this is assuming that you can actually *understand* what she is saying in the first place. Women in labor have a special, secret language that is almost untranslatable to men. For example, she may point at the ceiling and say, "Grumph . . . hoooo . . . hoooo. Shup . . . den . . . plissss," which you will interpret as, "Nice shade of peach on the ceiling there, isn't it?"

Later you'll find out that she wanted a foot massage and a grilled cheese sandwich.

Your job then is to also *decipher* her noises and gestures. But it's not as easy as it sounds. When she was having Matilda, Meredith slowly twisted her arm up and pointed behind her back. She muttered, "Harumph . . . Sheejh . . . Carrrmooon. Hhooo . . . Hhrruuufffff."

I took this to mean, "Give me a really hard back rub, right . . . here." Which I did. Later I found out she actually meant, "Whatever you do, don't touch my back here."

Just do your best.

Another thing you can do to help is encourage her to use the breathing techniques and exercises you practiced in your childbirth-education classes. Breathe with her and coach her through the contractions. Remain calm and controlled. Be relaxing. Say positive things like

- "That's it. Good. B-r-e-a-t-h-e d-e-e-p. You're doing great."

- "Almost over now."

- "Relax, relax, relax."

- "Open, open, open, baby, baby, baby."

- "I can see the baby's head."

- "Oh Toto, I want to go back to Kansas."

Avoid saying negative things like

- "Wow, look at all that blood! Boy! I'm glad I'm not you right now! Hey! Is that supposed to happen? Don't make that face. You look silly. I don't think this baby's ever going to be born!"

- "Can you be a little quieter? You're embarrassing me."

- "Did you turn the stove off?"

- "STOP BEING SO TENSE!"

Once upon a time, women were supposed to be quiet and dainty while giving birth. But this is a reasonably unfair request, if you think about it. Try this exercise:

1. Put your hand on a solid surface.

2. Hit your hand extremely hard with a sledgehammer.

3. Stand still and make no noise.

I bet you ten bucks you can't do it. Of course you can't do it! If you've ever actually hit yourself like that, you know you scream, moan, swear, yell, pace back and forth, jump up and down, and so on.

"Noise and action" is a popular childbirth pastime. Encourage your wife to make whatever noises she feels like and to move however she wants to if it will help her cope. This could be rocking back and forth, slapping her hands on her legs, moaning, repeating words, making faces, steady strong breathing and panting. The main thing is, don't stand back and look at her like she is strange! Join in!

As the contractions get stronger and your wife's cervix opens wider, her pain level will increase. The urge to push will become irresistible. Things can get a little wild at this stage. Normally composed women may scream abuse and say things to their husbands they'll later say they didn't really mean, such as "I hate you for doing this to me," "I never want to see you again," "You're not really the father," and "Let's have another baby right away." It is common at this stage for women's heads to spin 360 degrees while vomiting green bile all over the delivery room.

Stage 2: Birth

This is the stage during which the baby is actually born. It can last from a few minutes to a few hours.

Now, let us consider for a moment how the baby feels about being born. For the past nine months, she has been happily floating in her own little world that she has come to call home. She spends her days sucking her thumb, dreaming and practicing for her black-belt exam. She probably really likes it in there and, if she had her way, would not come out until she was eighteen years old, thereby avoiding the terror of school and many awkward moments during adolescence.

Then, all of a sudden, things turn sour.

The nice warm fluid drains out and the baby is unwittingly pushed downward toward an impossibly small hole as if she has been caught in some sort of vaginal tractor beam. As you can imagine, she might not be happy about this turn of events.

For this reason the obstetrician may decide to keep an eye on the state of the baby on her journey. This is done with a *fetal heart monitor*. A small electrode or sensor will be placed on the baby's scalp and your wife's abdomen, and a machine making "ping, ping" noises will monitor the contractions and let everyone know whether the baby is "in distress." If your wife has had an epidural, she will almost definitely be wired for sound, because she won't be able to feel the contractions herself.

Meanwhile, the baby's head will be slowly negotiating the cervix and making its way through the pelvis. The crown of the head may now be visible. If there is a problem with the size of the passageway, an *episiotomy* may be performed: The doctor deliberately cuts your wife's vaginal opening to make it bigger and easier for the baby to pass through. The idea is that making a small, specific incision prevents large and uncontrolled tearing.

Yes, *tearing*. As in ripping. I am talking about torn skin and muscle. Just another reason why I am happy to be a guy.

At this stage, after much effort and labor from your wife, the head of the baby will pop out and spin around, followed by the rest of her body. She will shoot out into the world in a flurry of blood, mucus and gallons of unidentifiable Technicolor fluids.

Ta-daaaaaaaaaa! So, you're a dad! Take a few breaths. Take a couple of tasteful snapshots. Savor the moment. If you want to cry, do it. This is the new millennium. One day you'll look back and laugh.

Ta-daaaaaaaaaa!

Stage 3: After Birth

Right after he's been born, the baby's throat may need to be cleared of all the fluid and mucus and gunk that he's been soaking in over the past months. One of the nurses or the doctor inserts a tube into the baby's throat and sucks it all out—a job, I might add, I wouldn't do for a thousand bucks. The baby's reflexes will kick in and he will take his first breath. He will then be put right onto Mom's stomach for some warmth and snuggling.

At first, you may be surprised by how your baby looks. He might not be what you expected. This is because in commercials, TV and movies, all "newborn" babies are in fact photogenic eight-month-olds who have just had their hair shampooed. Most have graduated from acting school.

Real newborns aren't like this at all. They are wrinkly little things covered in mucky tomatoey gook. They are also coated in a thick creamy covering, called *vernix*, that looks like French onion dip. They are usually squashed and have weird-shaped heads, and they may have bruises or marks from the tight squeeze or from the forceps or vacuum extraction. Some are born with jaundice, which makes them all yellow, and some are born with a fine covering of body hair called *lanugo*, which makes them look like werewolves under a full moon.

Now you know why I think it's funny when people hold up a newborn and say, "Isn't he beautiful?"

In short, newborn babies are ugly and messy. All of my kids looked like Yoda when they were born. (But they're beautiful now. Really.)

Another shocking and rarely discussed feature of newborns is, well, how can I put this nicely? Um . . . you see . . . they have REALLY BIG GENITALS. Newborns are surprisingly well-endowed. Both boys and girls can have milk secretions. Girls are all swollen. And before you get too proud of the fact that your newborn son looks like some superhuman sex-god, his scrotum, which currently reaches to his knees, will get small again after a while.

If you look carefully you will also notice that your baby is still attached to your wife by a long thick strand of gray spiral pasta. This is the *umbilical cord*. But your baby can't stay dangling out of Mom forever. This would make even simple things like going to the movies a virtual impossibility. So the cord has to be cut. Some people ascribe great symbolism and significance to this event and often the father is asked to perform the complex operation, which involves squeezing a pair of scissors. If you do cut the cord, make sure of the spot, otherwise you might damage your son irreparably and—you guessed it—cause him much embarrassment in his high school locker room sixteen years from now.

Once the cord is cut, it is sealed off with a clothespin. At first I thought I had cut Rachael's in the wrong spot, because her new belly-button was four inches long! But it's supposed to be like that. In the next few weeks, the cord will dry out and drop off. If you're lucky, you will find the shriveled remnant in the cradle and can take it to work to show your friends.

Next, the afterbirth must be delivered. No, not in the same way that pizza or Chinese food is delivered. The afterbirth is all the stuff that comes out after the baby. It is like a giant peeled tomato, a red pillowcase that has been your baby's primary life-support cocoon for the past months. It is made up of the amniotic sac, the placenta and the cord itself. After the baby is born, the afterbirth will break away from the uterus and come out the same way. Sometimes an injection is used to encourage 't along. When it arrives it will be inspected to see whether it is hole, or whether in detaching itself it has torn, leaving nants inside your wife. If you're unlucky, the doctor will it in your face and show you interesting things about it. his stage, your wife might have to have some stitches if as occurred, or if she has had an episiotomy. And when ord stitches, I'm not talking about little teensy paper- finger stitches. I'm talking about *stitches* stitches. *Big* Meredith has a friend who had fifty-two of them. right. If you reread that last sentence, it will still say FIFTY-TWO. A buddy of mine who almost amputated his leg in a skiing accident didn't even have fifty-two stitches.

Anyway, enough of this eye-watering stuff. If you ask nicely, the hospital staff might let you take the afterbirth home with you. It sounds weird, but some people really do it. I know a couple who went to their friends' place one morning for coffee. It was a nice visit, with French vanilla coffee and croissants and pleasant company. Then the hosts, who had recently become parents, whipped out a shovel and a suspicious-looking plastic bag and invited everybody down to the backyard for an *afterbirth-planting ceremony*.

Pretty gross if you ask me. Then again, it's better than being a cat. They eat their afterbirth—but at least they have the decency not to invite their friends around to watch.

An afterbirth-planting ceremony

In the Silence

When the afterbirth has been delivered, most of the show is over. Equipment will be wheeled away. Some of the staff disappear. The mess is cleaned up. A strange quiet will fall over the room.

Your baby will be given an Apgar score, which rates her skin color, breathing, reflexes, heart-rate and muscle tone. She will be weighed, cleaned up and possibly even bathed. The diameter of your baby's head will also be measured. A hospital tag will be attached to her wrist detailing her name, weight and time of birth. This is to avoid confusion and prevent parents from fighting over the babies later on.

Your wife might have the opportunity to take a quick shower, but she'll probably need your help.

And that's about it.

The baby will be put in a nightie and wrapped up tightly in a blanket. Then the staff will probably leave the three of you alone to get to know each other.

After the noise, pain and turmoil of the birth, it's really nice just to enjoy your first moments alone together in the silence. After nine months of waiting, there is a certain sense of awe and wonder in seeing your baby for the first time. You will notice things, like her little fingers and toes, her eyes and ears, and the folds of her skin. This whole experience can cause an adrenaline rush that will leave you on full power for the next three sleepless days and nights.

And as the three of you sit there exhausted in the delivery room, you will start to think, "Whew, it's all over."

Don't kid yourself. Now the hard work really begins.

Bonding

You have probably heard of this thing called "bonding." My Webster's defines bonding as *the formation of a close personal relationship (as between parent and child) especially through frequent or constant association.* This word is thrown around quite a lot in birthing circles. Bonding is the process by which you feel joined to your baby; when you feel that "It" is part of your family; when you feel an emotional involvement, a link that unites you both.

I expected this bonding to occur the moment the baby popped out into the world. I would look at her and experience a warm glow of love and attachment.

I didn't.

I expected it to be magical, mystical and instantaneous.

It wasn't.

When my kids were born, it was pretty amazing and all that, but I didn't feel "bonded." I wanted to. And I was wondering where the violins and soft focus were.

To be honest, it took me a long time to bond with my children.

Looking back, I can remember several different points when I actually felt the bonding process occurring. These were times when the baby responded to me. The first time her eyes followed me. The first time she smiled or laughed at me. The first time she reached for me. The first time she fell asleep on me. The first time she vomited on me. The first time she said "Daddaddadda"—at least, that's what I think she said.

In retrospect, I realize my expectations were as limited as expecting to love my wife the first moment I saw her. Bonding is a relationship thing, and any psychology textbook will tell you that a rich relationship and feeling of attachment doesn't occur at the snap of your fingers. It takes time.

Like with most experiences in becoming a dad, everybody is different. I know some guys who really did bond instantly. They picked up their newborn (yuck!) and almost swooned. The coming days were spent totally obsessed with this new addition to their family. These are the guys who have the six rolls of photos developed one hour after the birth. Stay away from them.

I know others who, like me, were fairly nonchalant at first toward their newborns but warmed up after a few weeks.

Don't be stressed about bonding. It will happen in its own time. It takes me about eighteen months!

Celebrating

Well, congratulations. You can now officially call yourself "a dad." Welcome to the world of fatherhood. Such a monumental step as this is cause for a monumental celebration.

As a child of the TV generation, I was always entranced by the depiction of proud dads celebrating the birth of their first child with their friends. This largely involved drinking champagne, making a lot of noise and, most important, smoking cigars. And come rain, hail or shine, I knew that this was what I was going to do when my first child was born.

And so Rachael arrived. I was so charged up after the birth that I didn't sleep for a few days. Everything fell into a kind of timeless euphoric haze that had started off with a great celebration party. I invited everybody I knew to our apartment. Everyone congratulated me on the great job I had done. What an achievement! I could be proud of myself! That night, I drank a crate of champagne and smoked a box of cigars. This is kind of amusing in a weird sort of way, because the only thing that I detest more than champagne is smoke. But this was what had been programmed into my mind by years of sitcoms, so champagne and cigars it would be!

While I was celebrating and being thoroughly self-indulgent, my wife was lying exhausted in a hospital bed, trying to cope with a new baby. When I came to, not only did I feel physically exhausted and lousy, I also felt guilty that I had let her down like that. Perhaps I would have been better off saving my strength and spending a little more time at the hospital. Perhaps I should have postponed my celebration until both my wife and our baby could also attend. After all, they did all the hard work.

I had learned my lesson. When Georgia was born, the celebrations were a lot more controlled. I only smoked half a box of cigars and only stayed up for forty-eight hours. And when Matilda was born, I finally got it right. I celebrated with a small light beer and a pencil-thin filtered cigar. Then I went to bed early . . . and lay awake all night.

Take It Easy

It is easy to get excited about the birth of your first child. You feel like you have jet-lag and time loses its meaning. After all, it is a pretty big deal and usually all your friends make a huge fuss.

And after witnessing the miracle of birth, it's little wonder you get emotionally carried away with the whole thing.

However, you can start to lose your perspective and begin to think that the birth of your child is the single most momentous event of the twenty-first century. This is called *paternal tunnel vision* or, as the doctors call it, *PTV*.

The first signs of this syndrome are excessive photographing or videotaping. Being such an important event, you want to capture as much as possible on film. I wanted to record every single detail of our first child, so I shot a roll of twenty-four just of Rachael's feet. Fortunately, two of the shots were in focus.

The main problem, as any parent with two or more children will tell you, is that the first child ends up with fifteen photo albums and a box of three-hour videos documenting her first week of life. The second child ends up with one photo album and one video documenting the first year of her life. The third child ends up with one dog-eared photograph with her in the background and a five-minute guest spot on the end of one of the other children's videos. This documents her entire childhood.

Another symptom of PTV is an inability to talk about any subject other than your baby. You should take care to avoid lengthy monologues to neighbors, friends, relatives or colleagues regarding fatherhood. Remember that while your life has been turned upside down, their lives have gone on as normal. Most will want to know how the birth went and how mother and baby are doing, but they don't want sixty-minute reenactments.

If you go to the bar for a beer with your co-workers, you will find that they too probably won't want to discuss the ethics of intervention in birthing; they won't care about torn perineums; they won't want to debate the advantages of breastfeeding; and they won't be interested in updates on the progress of baby's feces consistency.

There is also common decency to consider. Some things are supposed to be private. For example, I'm not sure your wife would appreciate you giving graphic descriptions of her torn vagina or cracked nipples. I know my wife didn't.

I also made the mistake of subjecting our friends to video footage of "us having breakfast on the morning of the birth," "a quick tour of the maternity wing and miscellaneous interviews of interesting people I met there," "mother and baby minutes after birth," "floral arrangements in the labor room," "me free-associating in the parking lot after the birth" and so on. It was okay for the first two hours, but things turned sour after that.

Unfortunately, none of my friends come to visit anymore.

She's Got the Blues

I had heard about this thing called *the baby blues*, the period of moody sadness some women suffer following the birth of their babies. But I knew instinctively that it wouldn't happen to my wife. "The blues" were for other women, women who were emotionally weak or prone to depression in the first place. My wife, on the other hand, is just about the most level-headed, down-to-earth and in-control person you are likely to meet. So "the blues" didn't apply to her, right?

Wrong. During the last weeks of pregnancy and particularly during the labor itself, women overdose on their naturally produced opiate, endorphin. After the birth most women have enough hormones pumping through their veins to knock down an enraged bull elephant at twenty paces. But then the opiate dries up and they go cold turkey. Add to this the fact that childbirth is painful and physically demanding—women do not recover overnight, particularly if their labor was traumatic or if they have had stitches. The whole situation is then aggravated by the fact that new mothers are tired from balancing altered sleep patterns (or "lack of sleep" patterns) and a continuous stream of visitors. There is also the nervous anxiety and mental pressure of being responsible for a new and pretty demanding human being. The result is a potent emotional cocktail, also known as *the blues*.

Depending on what source you turn to, baby blues affect from 60 to 85 percent of women and can last up to a couple of weeks.

This is why when you visit a maternity ward, somewhere in the distance you can always hear the twang of a steel guitar, the wall of a harmonica and a chorus of mournful female voices singing:

> *I had a baby the other day*
> *And I can hardly walk*
> *My nipples are dry and cracked real bad*
> *And my husband and I don't talk*
> *I got the blues*
> *I said I got those moody bloo-oo-ues*
> *I got the baby-makin', breast-feedin', down 'n' out*
>   *maternity blues.*

All women will react differently, but the blues can be triggered by almost anything and usually manifest themselves in mood swings and spontaneous crying. You can't argue with it or talk your wife out of it. Your job is to help and support her in the most appropriate way possible. Be sensitive and understanding. Encourage her. Comfort her. Talk to her. Hug her. Be there for her and the baby as much as possible. She needs rest, so help out by taking the baby or screening the flow of visitors (see below).

Don't tell her what a great time you're having at home by yourself. Don't tell her about all the great parties you've been going to. Don't tell her she's being silly and that she should grow up and stop crying like a little girl.

Put your arms around her, damn it!

For some women, however, the blues don't go away. They just get worse. This is a serious condition known as *postnatal depression*. Sufferers can feel lost and confused, tired and miserable. The whole routine of domestic life with a baby can dull their senses. They may have trouble bonding with the baby. They may also feel emotionally on-edge and isolated from real life. Their world seems to be permanently off-balance.

This is a very real issue that you should not take lightly. Postnatal depression can last for months and sometimes even years. Be open to discussing this with your wife. Support her and spend time with her. Provide her with adult conversation. Tell her not to feel guilty or ashamed of her emotions. Help to organize the domestic routines and provide stability and order around the home. If appropriate, arrange for friends or relatives to visit her. Find out about local groups she can become involved in, such as mothers groups, playgroups, Bible studies and so on. Several support groups exist specifically for postnatal depression. If things are really serious, don't be afraid to seek professional counseling. Call your hospital or clinic or even your insurance provider for more information.

Whatever you do, don't ignore it or pretend it will go away. Your wife needs you, damn it!

Guests

It's good to have friends. Of course, your friends and relatives will want to share your newfound joy. Most will want to visit mother and child in the hospital and bring gifts and ogle over and maybe even cuddle the baby.

Visitors are also a good thing. They can break the monotony of the hospital routine for your wife and cheer her up. It's great to see familiar faces, and a few flowers around the room certainly brighten things up. But visitors can become a real pain, particularly if you have five hundred friends. The pain that they can become is mathematically correlated to the number of friends and relatives you have, the hours they choose to visit, the average length of time they stay, the volume of noise they produce and how hard it is to get rid of them.

The main problem is that visitors are exhausting. If you're really unlucky, your visitors will come in a constant stream, one after the other, like a prearranged tag-team. There will be an endless repetition of photos and questions and presents and chatter and laughter . . . all day long. Mother and baby will end up strung-out and irritated.

This is where you can help out. Most people are pretty reasonable and will probably call first to see when it's OK to visit. Most also know when it's time to leave. You may, on the other hand, find that distant acquaintances you haven't seen for ten years will arrive hours after the birth and want to stay a long, long time.

Be aware of your wife's needs. Maybe she and the baby don't want visitors right away. Maybe your wife is exhausted and needs a little time to recover. If this is the case, tell your friends to hold off for a few days and then maybe you can schedule them a little. Also, discourage them from visiting outside of the assigned hours. This will ensure that both your wife and the baby get some rest.

Also be alert to your wife's feelings. This may come as a surprise to you, but she may feel slightly uncomfortable about whipping out an engorged bosom for breastfeeding in front of all your softball teammates, particularly if baby is being uncooperative.

Don't be afraid to tell your visitors—no matter who they are—when it's time to leave. If they don't take the hint, most nurses carry around an electric cattle prod that usually works remarkably well.

Get Ready—They're Coming Home

Soon the time will come for your wife and baby to return home. If you're smart, there are a few things you can do that will help this grand homecoming run a little more smoothly. The general household routine will be pretty tumultuous for the next couple of months while you both get used to living with and caring for a little person in the house, so use the brief time you have alone to make some final preparations. This will get things off to a good start.

It's a great idea to have the house clean for their return. Some balloons and flowers probably wouldn't hurt, either. Trust me when I say that family life will not get off on the right foot if your wife comes home to unmade beds, a pile of laundry, ironing, dirty dishes, dusty shelves and an expectation that it's her job to straighten everything up.

An empty refrigerator will also not endear you to the heart of your wife, so make sure it is fully stocked. When my wife was still in the hospital with Georgia, I bought bulk supplies of ready-made stir-fries and marinades. I spent one morning in the kitchen cooking them all up and dishing them into disposable aluminium trays. I labeled them and filled the freezer to overflowing. Why not also fill up your refrigerator with pastas and sauces? Mixed with freshly cooked vegetables and rice, and interspersed with other meals and the occasional take-out or delivery, these supplies lasted us many weeks and helped especially on those days when things were a little hectic.

It is also important to get some sleep. If you are going to help out with the baby, you need to be rested and alert. All-night binges and TV marathons will just wear you down at a time when you need to be strong.

The Calm before the Storm

Until now, things have been kind of nice. You have probably been going to work and then popping into the hospital for the occasional visit. You've been able to hold your baby for a little while, spend some "quality time" with your wife, and then go back to the "real world." In fact, it's been almost like a vacation, living by yourself for the last couple of days. You could do whatever you wanted, watch your favorite TV programs and eat junk food.

This is simply the calm before the storm.

Your baby won't stay at the hospital forever. After four to six days, or even sooner, the doctor will say, "Adios! Time to get packin'!" When you walk out that hospital door, you're on your own. You pick up your wife, the baby, the bags, cards and flowers and drive home. The first thing you notice is that "the two of you" are now "the three of you." There is another human being in the back of the car.

This is where all your training and reading and discussion and contemplation gets put to the acid test. This is where theory clashes headlong with reality. You are about to encounter the storm after the calm.

It's time to enter survival mode.

CHAPTER 5

Surviving at Home

One day, when your baby is seventeen and asking you for driving lessons and contraceptives, you'll look back on these days as "the easy years."

Food for Thought

I have noticed something very interesting about weddings. People who are engaged seem to spend every waking moment planning their "big day." For months and months—years in some cases—their entire existence is directed at the thousands of small and intricate details that go into having the kind of fairy-tale wedding that Martha Stewart suggests they have.

And so comes the great event. After months of effort, everything goes smoothly. The wedding runs like clockwork and all is just perfect. In a flurry of rice and confetti, the bride and groom drive off into the sunset with a tremendous sigh of relief that it's all over.

Of course, it's not over at all—it's only just begun. My guess is that some couples spend so much time focusing on the wedding day itself that they forget to spare a thought for the more important part beyond: their lives together. And so for some, the early days of marriage come as kind of a shock.

The same applies to some people having a baby. So much time can be devoted to the labor itself—in books, conversations, birth classes and so on—that some parents-to-be may neglect to look beyond, to the more important part that is to follow: becoming parents and coping with a new addition to the home.

This is a fatal mistake. It is vital that you and your wife spend time thinking about and discussing life after labor.

The Times, They Are a' Changing

Do you remember your life before the baby came home? Life in your house with a newborn will not be like that. Babies are very demanding of time and the little time that they do leave you is necessary for sleep. As such, you will need to rethink many elements of your domestic life. To help you understand what I mean, here is a list of things that become difficult when you have a baby living in your house. Note that I said "difficult," not "impossible."

- listening to loud music
- going shopping
- washing the dishes
- washing the car
- washing clothes
- hanging out clothes
- ironing clothes
- mowing the lawn
- curling up with a good book
- watching television
- having a relaxing evening together at home
- having an in-depth adult conversation
- going out
- getting a good night's sleep
- sleeping in
- doing anything on the spur of the moment
- having sex on the spur of the moment
- having sex even if you plan it carefully
- cooking
- eating in peace
- cleaning the house
- practicing your musical instrument
- working at home (a fatal mistake)
- writing a book

The main consequence of this is that your home will look different than it looked before. You may have a spacious and airy home, a home built for entertaining, a home filled with interesting and beautiful things. You may have an obsession with tidiness and cleanliness.

All this will have to be overcome.

For the next few years, your home will be a wasteland. Your windows will be smeared with greasy fingerprints. Raisins and bananas will be squashed into the carpet. There will be a constant smell of urine and ammonia and every so often a hideous whiff of something ghastly that you just can't place or even find. Every nook and cranny will become home to a million tiny building blocks, bread crusts, stuffed animals, little cars, broken crayons and doll's clothing. All drawers and cupboards below the four-foot level will at one time or another have their contents strewn randomly throughout every room.

I wish I could say something like,

"No, wait! Babies do actually make your life easier! You'll hardly notice they're there."

But that would be a lie.

Babies are a lot of work. Being an active and involved dad, you need to share in that work. I don't know what your domestic situation is, whether your wife is going to be a full-time homemaker or whether she's going back to work after a while. It may even be that you are so liberated that you will be the one to stay home and take care of the baby. Or the economic reality of the day may mean that you both work full-time, in which case you both need to put a lot of thought into daycare and job division. Whatever your situation, you will need to discuss and plan your domestic duties and, once again, get your hands dirty.

Of course, the work you do may not necessarily involve the baby directly. Regardless of what your domestic habits or roles have been in the past, if you are an *I mow the lawn and wash the car and she does the shopping, washing, cleaning and cooking* kind of guy, then you'll need to do a little quick on-the-job training.

Whatever you do, never, ever, *ever* come home and say, "Why is the house such an incredible mess? What's for dinner? Haven't you ironed my work shirts yet?" A tired woman with sore breasts is not to be crossed—that is, unless you want a diaper bucket lobbed at your head.

Bosoms and Bottles

Topics people will always argue about:

- What killed off the dinosaurs?
- Jesus Christ: liar, lunatic or Lord?
- What really happened to Howard Hughes?
- Who was the superior Batman: Michael Keaton, Val Kilmer, George Clooney or Adam West?
- Should Texas become a republic?
- Is Elvis really working at a hamburger joint in Las Vegas?

And this golden gem:

- Should a mother bottlefeed or breastfeed?

The feeding of babies is a surprisingly touchy issue. Advocates of either method can become fiery about their beliefs. There are two enemy camps: The Bottle Alliance versus United Breastfeeders, and each side has its own support organizations, newsletters and surveillance satellites.

Given that most shelf-space in the bookstore parenting section is dedicated to feeding, it would be ludicrous of me to attempt to go into detail about feeding options. But just for the heck of it, here are the main arguments:

Breastfeeding

- is natural
- uses "live" milk, full of antibodies that strengthen the baby's immune system
- encourages closeness and bonding between mother and child
- can be awkward in public for some mothers
- can be frustrating and time-consuming
- requires commitment
- can't be done by you, the father

- can be affected by the mother's diet (onions, garlic and so on)
- can utilize bottle technology for baby-sitting purposes
- is cheap

Bottlefeeding

- is not done by any other mammal on the planet
- can be done by men
- is derived from cow's milk or soy or rice milk and supplemented with various vitamins and minerals
- keeps the mother's nipples in one piece
- means messing around with sterilizing the first three months
- can be more convenient for working couples
- is easier to prepare for baby-sitters
- costs money

You can tell that I have a personal bias toward breastfeeding. This is for two main reasons: First, pediatricians say, and I quote, "Breast is best." Second, my cousin is a lactation consultant and I'll never hear the end of it if I don't fly the breastfeeding flag, so to speak.

Either way, your role is important. Newborns feed about every four hours, twenty-four hours a day. This means getting up regularly throughout the night. If your wife breastfeeds, you can get the baby for her and put him back to bed. If your baby is being bottlefed, work out a schedule and split the workload.

You can also help by burping your baby. Because they guzzle and suck so greedily, babies often swallow air while feeding. This sits in their stomachs and causes them great discomfort, which leads to screaming, which in turn causes stress, tension and sleeplessness in their parents (see below).

To burp your baby, hold him upright with his head over your shoulder and gently pat his back while you sing a song. After a while, the baby will come forth with a deafening peal of thunder—the kind of burp you'd expect to hear from a beer-swilling Harley rider. It is also usually accompanied by a hefty, curdled, milky projectile spew, although this normally only happens when you've got a good shirt on or are giving butterfly kisses.

If your wife decides breastfeeding is the way to go, fantastic. If your wife is sick or under stress, or if the baby is unwilling to feed from her breast, don't worry. Babies are nourished by formulas everywhere in the world, every day of the year. So read some books, talk with your wife, discuss it with your doctor and the hospital lactation consultants to work out which option is best for your wife and your baby.

And two other things. I shouldn't need to say these, but I will . . . just in case.

- Don't ever use breast milk or formulas in tea or coffee. Taste it and you'll know why.

- Some women lactate with only the slightest prompting. Never, ever say to a breastfeeding mother stuff like, "Baby sucking . . . milk flowing . . . baby's little mouth going *schloop, schloop.*" Their blouse will end up so wet it will look like they just fell into a swimming pool.

The Ultimate Torture

I never knew that babies cry as much as they do. I think that is because as a child, the only baby I ever saw was Jesus in nativity drawings on Christmas cards. Have you ever seen a Christmas card where Jesus is crying? No! He is always asleep. What a deception! (Actually, I have friends who believe that this in itself is actually proof that Jesus was the Son of God. But I digress.)

We have a neighbor who has a faulty car alarm. I know it's faulty because it goes off at all hours of the day and night, for hours on end. *WWwwaaaaameeerrrm. WWwwaaaaaeeeeerri-m.* It is an excruciating, heavy metal wail that goes on and on and on until all the people on my street are driven to the point of insanity. When it starts, I feel like going over to his house and yelling at him and smashing his car with a hammer. Now *that* would be something to get alarmed over.

Now imagine having a car alarm that lives in your own house. It goes off regularly during the day and night. And imagine that you have to pick up the car alarm and cuddle it and kiss it. You sing to it and mumble soothing words and guess what? *It just gets louder!* That's what a baby in full cry is like. Yelling and hammers are definitely out of the question.

Babies cry. That's their job. They're particularly good at it. In fact, some babies love to cry. And when they cry, they are not doing it because they want to sound nice. A baby's cry is most often loud, incessant and irritating. That's what it's supposed to be like. It's an attention-getter. It says, "Hey you, come here! I want something!"

You see, when you or I want something, we go and get it. If we feel uncomfortable, we take care of it ourselves. If we're thirsty, we go to the refrigerator. If we're hungry, we order pizza. However, babies can't do this. Their single form of communication is crying. So they'll cry if they are lonely, thirsty or hungry, if they are cold or hot, if they are tired or wet, or if the TV is too loud. They'll cry because it was nicer in the womb, or because they don't like the way you decorated their nursery.

Basically, babies cry about just about anything. Of course the problem with this is that all beasts—from the Himalayan Rock Slug to the pinnacle of creation, *Homo sapiens*—have an instinctive, protective response to the crying of their offspring. But you must be careful. You don't want to smother the baby. You don't want to treat every whimper like a national emergency. If you spoil your baby, he or she will end up being one of those awful kids you see at hamburger places squealing, "I want fries! I want a party hat! I hate pickles!" And so on. But on the other hand, you don't want to be one of those parents featured on the seven o'clock news because they let their baby scream for two days in a row.

The fun that lies ahead for you is the guessing game that you will get to play trying to work out what is "wrong" with your child. You cannot win this game. You see, some babies cry just because they darn well feel like it. *And sometimes there is nothing you can do about it.*

And then of course there is the archnemesis of parents everywhere: COLIC.

Colic (translated from the German word *kärlech*, meaning "scream of death") is one of those things that occurs even though no one can explain why—like yawns, hiccups, sudden pen leaks and Steven Seagal movies.

Colic is a pattern of unstoppable screaming at the same time every day, usually in the early evening. These sessions can last up to a few hours each and may continue for a few months at a time.

When this behavior starts, it's best to consult your doctor just to confirm that the crying isn't caused by something more serious. Apart from that, you just have to do your best to cope with the noise. See if it's feeding time, check the baby's temperature, cuddle him, talk to him or change him. You can make babies more comfortable by massaging them, shoving a pacifier in their mouth or rocking their cradle. If that doesn't work, get a blanket and go sit in the garden, or take the baby for a walk in the stroller. The screaming never sounds as bad outside the claustrophobic confines of your home as it does inside. Why not go to a busy shopping center? It won't necessarily quiet the baby, but at least you can make all the other poor devils suffer as much as you.

If all else fails, you can always sing. When singing, avoid rousing renditions of AC/DC or Metallica. Make it gentle, soft and soothing. If you don't know any tunes, make one up. Your baby won't know the difference. In fact, you can sing any song you know, as long as you sing it slowly, softly and melodically. Sway back and forth in time to your song and tap a gentle 4/4 beat on the baby's bottom.

This whole crying game requires a lot of patience. A sense of humor doesn't hurt, either. The problem for us guys, as my mother constantly reminds me, is that

> *Patience is a virtue, bless it if you can*
> *Always in a woman, never in a man*

Yeah, great. Thanks, Mom. What can I say? Good luck. One day, when your baby is seventeen and asking you for driving lessons and contraceptives, you'll look back on these times as "the easy years."

Of course, most of us can cope with crying babies when it's a sunny day and the birds are singing and we feel alert and strong.

The real test comes at night when you want to sleep.

For many years, political dictators and dungeon masters have been developing and refining their methods of torture. They have used hot pokers, thumbscrews, the rack, "Brahms' Lullaby" and screenings of *Terms of Endearment* to make their victims beg for mercy. But there's one form of torture that is used more widely and more effectively than all the others:

Sleep deprivation.

Deprive a man of sleep and he will undergo a Jekyll-and-Hyde transformation of epic proportions. A normally mellow and easy-going Mr. Average can quickly turn into a tired and cranky animal—a short-tempered, bleary-eyed, babbling fool. All of a sudden, his whole life becomes a mess. Unshaven and unkempt, he'll be aggressive to co-workers and fall asleep on the job. He can no longer construct a fluent sentence. His eyelids feel like they are made of lead.

The problem is that babies don't live by the clock or the sun. They don't have the same culturally entrenched ideas about keeping "polite hours." The immediate consequence of this is that they wake up a lot during the night and need to be taken care of: fed, burped, changed and rocked to sleep. It's also likely that you'll hear a lot of screaming thrown in for good measure. And when a baby gets a good howl going in the wee hours of the morning, it's like a 747 thundering down your hallway.

Brahms was a sadist.

I'm not just talking about waking up once for a few minutes in the middle of the night. I know of a couple who called their son *The Screamer*. He only slept *four hours a day!*

Gasp! Shock! Snooze! I hear you cry. *Four hours,* did you say? That's inhuman! You're right. It *is* inhuman. But that's not the worst part. You see, he didn't sleep four hours at one time. That was merely his *cumulative total.* The four hours were made up of occasional twenty-minute snoozes! Meditate on this and you start to realize the impact a baby can have on your household.

Of course, I'm painting a somewhat pessimistic picture. Your baby could be a marathon sleeper. His cry might only be a barely audible whimper. You may have what is commonly referred to in fathering circles as "a really good baby." If you do, count yourself lucky.

My guess is that historically, Dad went to bed at the normal time and any nocturnal activity of the "waking-up-and-shuffling-around-with-the-baby-in-the-freezing-cold-dead-of-night" variety definitely fell under Mom's job description. But you need to remember that nowadays you are into shared parenting and active fathering. This is the time when you need to remember that if your wife is at home, she works all day, too, probably never gets a decent break from the baby and has to put up with that screaming *all the time*.

So, how can you help when the baby starts choir practice at 2 A.M.?

When Rachael was born, I thought I had a pretty foolproof escape clause from any nocturnal activity. My logic was that since I was lacking in the necessary equipment—that is, one pair of milk-swollen breasts—I was of no use whatsoever and could just roll over and go back to sleep. Of course, I watched my wife gradually turn into a zombie with dark eyes, a blank expression and monosyllabic conversation.

This "It's not my problem" approach is definitely a bad one. (In my defense, I did try to help. Whenever Meredith was up feeding, I would roll over and keep her side of the bed warm.)

When Georgia was born, I was guilt ridden and vowed to share 50-50 with my wife. Whenever she got up, I got up to make hot chocolate and keep her company. This had two immediate effects. First, my presence and talking prevented Georgia from nodding off, which kept us up much longer than necessary. Second, we *both* ended up as zombies with dark eyes, blank expressions and monosyllabic conversation. And it really is quite embarrassing to fall asleep at your desk in front of a class of high school students and then wake up, only to realize that you are dribbling and all the kids are staring at you.

So this "We'll share the torment together" approach is equally inadequate.

But what's the answer?

Without wanting to sound clichéd, the answer lies in a balance between the two approaches. It's no good letting one person do all the work, but it's no good for both of you to do all the work, either. As I said before, parenting is a team sport, so share the responsibilities. If your baby is being breastfed, play the delivery boy and get the baby from the crib and bring it to Mom in bed. You can take turns burping the baby and singing it back to sleep. This approach worked well when we had Matilda. Meredith still did all the feeding, but I tried to help with the burping, settling her down and pacifier patrol. When it's not your turn, the best thing you can do is sleep.

Discussion and job-sharing really are the keys to coping. When your wife is fed up, send her out to a movie or to a friend's place. And if you're fed up, be sensible enough to accept a break.

But of course, it's fine for me to come up with this great theory. The reality may be somewhat different. And it's only at this point that I must warn you about something.

Dealing with a baby, especially in the middle of the night, can be really frustrating. The crying is harder to cope with because all else is quiet, and this only accentuates the shrill pitch of the baby's cry. It's dark, and you feel like you're the only person on Earth who's awake. You feel even more lonely and isolated because often the only company you have is the people on TV and once you get past midnight, the quality of your television companion drops significantly, from mediocre to abysmal.

After a while it becomes easy to lose your temper. I had read about this in books, but because I am a mature and well-adjusted person, I knew that this would not be a problem for me. Right?

Wrong.

This fact dawned on me in the early hours one morning as I was playing a lengthy game called "Putting Georgia back to bed after a midnight snack." Every night Meredith and I played this game. My face would slide down the wallpaper as I huddled, half-naked and freezing, trying to rock her back to sleep (Georgia, that is, not my wife). After what felt like ages, she would doze off. I'd then spend twenty minutes sneaking down the hall like a kung-fu master walking on rice paper. I'd usually make it to within a few feet of the warmth of my bed before I hit that creaky floorboard. Then she would start up again.

She had just been fed, so she wasn't hungry.

She had just been changed, so she wasn't wet.

She was wrapped in a blanket, so she wasn't cold.

I held her warmly and sang softly and rocked gently. I mean, I was doing it by the book. But she was still screaming as if I were taunting her with red-hot irons. So I utilized the musical method that had worked well on other occasions. I patted the baby's bottom firmly and rhythmically.

On this occasion, it didn't work.

I started feeling angry. It was dark. I was tired. My best attempts at baby-soothing had been frustrated. Her scream was deafening. My feet were cold. My eyes were sore. So I patted her harder. It still didn't work.

Then all of a sudden, I had this uncomfortable feeling that my "pat" was becoming a "spank." I was losing control. So I went into the family room, turned on the TV and the heater and started over. It made me feel better and, more important, it helped me to cope a whole lot better.

You should be aware of this nocturnal frustration. It is real. There are ways of coping, however. Perhaps you could put on some nice music and make a cup of tea or decaf coffee. One couple I know would get up, put their baby in a sling and vacuum the house. The noise drowns out the screams, the house gets clean and the baby is eventually soothed by the rhythm. What more could you ask for?

If you start "losing it," put the baby in his crib where he can't hurt himself and go back to bed or hop in the shower. If things are really bad, don't be afraid or embarrassed to call a friend or relative to come and help you out. Even chatting with a phone counselor at 3 A.M. can lift your spirits (try Childhelp USA, 800-4-A-CHILD—a hotline available twenty-four hours a day, seven days a week).

Of course, it all depends on whether your baby is a dozer or a screamer and how well you and your wife handle sleep deprivation. But have the attitude of helping. Take turns dealing with the baby, and discuss what fits your situation best.

And good luck. You'll need it.

Do Not Feed the Animal

If you stick your finger in your baby's mouth, you will notice that it feels more like the mouth of a guppie than a tiger. There are no teeth. But it doesn't stay like that forever. At anywhere around the six-month mark, the first of twenty little white splinters will drive their way through your baby's gums. This is the first set of teeth, which your baby will have for about six years.

This has many immediate effects:

- Your baby will drool. There will be a continuous river of saliva running from his lower lip down to his navel, giving your baby a glistening appearance.

- Your baby may be very uncomfortable. He may be whiney and miserable and have trouble sleeping sometimes.

- If your wife breastfeeds, you will hear her scream intermittently as the baby's carnivorous instincts affect her nipples.

- The baby will produce diapers of such suffocating intensity and revolting consistency that you will wish you could die rather than change them.

- If your baby bites you, it will hurt rather than be cute.

Now this is all part of the natural order of things, because a newborn baby only drinks milk and therefore doesn't need teeth. But over the course of their first year, your baby will start his journey toward *real food*. This process is called *weaning*: His milk intake is lowered and solids are gradually phased in.

(I use the term "solid" very loosely here. To me, a *solid* is a filet mignon, or a Caesar salad with French fries on the side. To baby-food manufacturers, however, a solid is a banana that has spent an hour in a blender.)

You can start weaning your baby pretty much any time after three or four months, but don't expect it to happen overnight. It is a slow process that could start with a mouthful of slushy rice cereal at the beginning of each regular feeding. At the next feeding, your baby might eat a few more mouthfuls. After a few feedings, you can introduce a fruit purée either from a jar or, if you have the time, your blender. Pretty soon, some of the breast- or bottlefeedings will have disappeared and your baby will start putting away bowls of cereal or mushy fruit and vegetables or any combination of the above.

With this onset of teeth, your baby can start on foods of a more resilient consistency. You can throw your whole dinner into a blender and give him a semi-solid homemade meal. Later on you can introduce him to actual pieces of bread, cheese, (boned) fish and chicken, veggies, hamburger, fruit . . . in fact, pretty much anything off your dinner plate will do.

One of the problems, however, is that babies like to experiment with their food. This usually involves putting it into their mouth, chewing it, spitting it out, picking it up, rubbing it on their clothes, throwing some of it in your face, running it through their hair and then putting it back in their mouth again. Don't be too concerned if only a small amount of food actually gets into your baby's mouth. Recent studies have found that babies actually get the nutrition out of their food via the process of osmosis, whereby the vitamins and minerals soak directly through their skin.

The trouble is, this process tends to make a bit of a mess. For this reason, the only safe place to feed a baby is in one of those nuclear-shielded handling rooms where everything is done by robotic arms. But given that you probably don't have such a facility at your place, you could instead feed your baby over linoleum or in the center of a plastic tablecloth. Even then, you will still find morsels of food splattered on the ceiling on the other side of the room.

To protect the baby's clothing, many people use bibs. They are cheap, which means all your friends will buy you ten packages each as a present and you'll need a separate cupboard to store them in (the bibs, not your friends). But bibs are also funny things. Unfortunately, they don't work. Babies will get food on their sleeves and in their socks and no tiny piece of cloth with cute bunny prints is going to stop them. So not only will you need to wash their clothes (which you would have done anyway), you'll also need to wash hundreds of bibs as well, making your washing load increase by 200 percent.

The only outfit that will protect your baby's clothing is either a full-length wetsuit or a radiation suit.

Diapers

To many men, fatherhood is basically a scary prospect. They are nervous about all the awesome changes and responsibilities that accompany family life. There are also new financial pressures, a major change to the daily schedule, lack of sleep and more household chores. And if you are an obsessive worry-wart, questions like "Which high school will be best for my daughter?" "What happens if my son crashes the car?" and "What wedding reception venue will give me the best value for my money?" may soon begin to weigh heavily upon your mind.

But I have a theory.

To most men, one thing is scarier than all these other worries put together.

It is worse than any horror film.

It is the stuff that nightmares are made of.

It is . . . diapers.

Festering, steaming ones.

About twelve a day . . . if you're lucky.

Diapers really are incredible things. Like ants, babies can carry around in their diapers over one hundred times their own body weight. This is frightening, because then they need to be changed.

In the classic film *Three Men and a Baby*, when Tom Selleck is faced with the prospect of changing another "diaper," he offers his good friend Steve Guttenburg a huge amount of money to do it for him.

Of course, this sounds very funny. Ha ha. But you will soon realize that Selleck's bribery is completely understandable— some would even say a good value for the money. I have changed one or two memorable and breathtaking diapers that I would have gladly paid someone else a thousand dollars to do.

Toying with diapers is not something you will find as pleasant as toying with a nice red wine, for example. I found this out many years ago when I stayed with a friend who had a six-month-old baby. I was a "diaper virgin" and had never experienced a real, live 3-D diaper-changing with full smell-o-rama before. After witnessing the event, I never wanted to experience it again. I immediately went into "diaper shock," also known in psychological circles as "post-diaper traumatic syndrome." I lay prostrate on my friend's front steps, sweaty-faced and gasping for air.

He laughed at me and said, "It's OK, Pete. It's always bad with somebody else's kid. I couldn't change any other babies but my own. But your own kids—no problem."

I drew much reassurance from this, despite the fact that it turned out to be a complete lie. As far as I'm concerned, diapers are diapers, no matter who they come from.

Many years later, when my wife was pregnant, another friend told us that changing a newborn baby's diaper was like a "walk in a rose garden." This also turned out to be a lie. I've never seen a brown rose that makes you nauseated when you smell it.

And it's no use thinking that you can make it through the early years of your baby's life without changing one. You can't. If you want to experience fatherhood in all its glory, then you have to get your hands dirty (and trust me, when changing diapers, you *will* get your hands dirty). Being a dad is more than doing all the fun jobs like playing in the backyard and giving paternal lectures. Diaper changing, despite the opinion of many, is not an innately maternal pastime. So don't wuss out.

My first diapers were memorable.

I have always prided myself on my fortitude and steel stomach. After all, I do have a CPR-training certificate and have seen every Arnold Schwarzenegger film ever made. But my knees turned to jelly in the face of my first diapers. In fact, I dry-heaved. I didn't realize it at the time, but these were to be the first in a long line of reverse peristalsis experiences in the presence of Diapers from Hell. And now I look back on those first diapers and realize that in some ways, my friends were right. The diapers of a milk-fed newborn are chicken-feed compared to the diapers of a hefty toddler who eats red meat.

Then again, you get used to it. A veteran of three babies, I can now change the most nuclear diaper with my bare hands— in the dark even, although that's generally not a good idea.

When changing diapers, follow two general rules.

Rule One: The diaper must NOT come off under any circumstances. A loose diaper can drop off of its own accord. Older babies can also figure out how to take them off. Use electrical tape, an arc welder, superglue—whatever it takes to make the diapers secure. If you don't, your baby will use the chunky stuff as paint ... or worse. Trust me when I say that it's really hard to bond with a baby who has a brown ring around his mouth.

It's really hard to bond.

Rule Two: Hold your breath while changing. Fumes from diapers are poisonous. NASA scientists actually use diaper fumes to simulate the atmosphere of Mars in their astronaut-training program. If you happen to suck in a lungful without protective breathing apparatus, you can be rendered unconscious and keel over.

In your role as diaper changer, you have basically five choices:

Choice one: disposable diapers
Environmental researchers tell us that disposables have the same half-life as toxic waste. Which is not surprising, considering that diapers *contain* the chemical equivalent of toxic waste. They will still be intact and lethal at the local dump when your children are having children of their own. So if you're at all concerned about the environment, disposables are not for you.

Also, babies go through diapers about as quickly as you can put them on. At first you will use about twelve a day. At about $10 to $15 a pack, diapers will cost you a tidy sum, especially considering that babies are in diapers for about two years. And if your garbage is collected only once a week, you will soon find that the saunalike effect of the garbage can on the seventy or so little bundles will lead to a marital dispute over who gets to put the trash out. And the garbage collectors will probably hate you, too.

In addition, some disposables actually accentuate the smell when they are wet. Also, being plastic, they don't "breathe," so your baby's bottom will get steamed in ammonia, which can cause diaper rash.

And in case you think that buying disposable diapers is easy, think again. It is easier to buy a used car. There are more varieties of diapers than there are types of dog food—all with computer-designed, color-coded, sex-differentiated, scientifically proven features.

Of course, disposables are by definition *disposable*. Herein lies their main attraction. They are quick and convenient to use. When they're "soiled," you simply wrap them up and throw them away. This is of particular importance if you are out for the day and don't wish to carry around a plastic bag of fermenting sludge. So if you are not philosophically opposed to nonbiodegradable diapers and if you have a healthy bank account, disposables are for you.

Choice two: cloth diapers

Ah yes, just like mother used to use on you. Unlike disposables, when cloth diapers are "soiled," you have to "empty" them (this has to be experienced to be believed), soak them in a bucket of sterilizing fluid and wash them. It sounds complex and time-consuming, but once you have a regular system up and running, it's really pretty simple.

Initially, you need to buy a couple of buckets with lids and a stack of about forty diapers and a few pairs of plastic pants. After this, the only thing you need to invest is time.

However, there is one sinister disadvantage to using cloth diapers.

Pins.

They lurk underneath the cloth and wait for the soft flesh of your fingers to come within range. Then they suddenly burst through the thin fabric with a force of close to 4000 pounds per square inch and wedge their steely spears deep into your tender digits. This is incredibly painful, particularly if you score a direct hit under a fingernail.

Next time you see a man pinning a cloth diaper, watch his face carefully. It is a picture of excruciating expectation, of contorted anxiety. He knows what's coming. He just doesn't know *when*.

Fortunately, some bright light has invented a three-pronged clip that serves the same purpose as pins. This is widely available and is considerably easier, quicker and less painful to use. That is, unless you step on one with bare feet.

Choice three: the combo

No, not a new meal deal from your local fast food restaurant. Most of my friends use a combination of both disposable and cloth diapers. With this, you get the best of both worlds: cloth diapers during the day and around the house, disposable diapers for trips away from home.

Choice four: diaper service
Tom Selleck should have thought about this! Then he wouldn't have had to offer a thousand dollars for someone else to do his dirty work.

While you still have to deal with the stuff at the bottom end, with a diaper service you don't have to mess around with scraping off or washing the diapers themselves. You can have someone drop off a giant bag of crisp clean diapers at your front door once or twice a week. At the same time they'll take away a giant bag of wet, sludgy ones. Of course, this gets more fun as the week goes on and the bag fills—especially in summer. This is also a great way of getting back at neighbors you don't like who live downwind from you. Even better, it keeps door-to-door salesmen and various representatives of religious cults away.

If you have a friend or relative who wants to buy you a post-partum present but isn't sure what to get you, a couple of weeks' worth of diaper service will be a gift you'll really appreciate. Trust me.

And don't worry. You'll soon get over your reservations about the fact that the diaper you're putting on your beautiful baby has been pooped in by more than two hundred other babies in your city.

Choice five: no diaper at all
Unfortunately, babies do not have the manners that we adults have developed over the years. The most pressing consequence of this is that for the next couple of years, they'll "go" *where* they want, *when* they want, and they'll do it *often*. Somebody's got to clean it up because if you don't, your baby will eat it and your friends won't visit as often anymore.

Choice five is very stupid. Don't even consider it.

No matter what option you choose, however, invest in a diaper-changing outfit. A wetsuit, scuba tank, welding mask, blacksmith's gloves and a wooden spoon will do the trick.

Splish Splash

Babies have to be washed. If you don't wash them, they will start to smell and you won't like having them around.

While you may think it is the easiest option, hosing down your baby in the backyard is generally considered to be socially unacceptable, particularly in winter. One easy option is the frequently used sponge bath. This means the baby stays partially dressed and you just wash his face and bottom with a washcloth. If you use the same washcloth for both parts, it's generally a good idea to wash his face first.

Every so often, though, you do need to give him a bath. You can do this in a "safe" sink (a sink free of taps sticking out at skull-cracking angles), or in a baby bath like the ones I told you about in chapter 3, placed either on a counter or on the floor. If you're up for it, you can take your baby into the big tub with you.

You must be very careful with the water temperature. It is easy to scald a baby. But how do you get the temperature right? Some friends of mine actually use a thermometer.

Many people say that the best way to test a bath is to dip your elbow into the water. To be honest, I think this is a stupid idea. Since when has the human elbow been known worldwide for its sensitivity? My elbow is as tough as elephant's hide and has the sensitivity of a slab of concrete. You need to dip something really sensitive into the water. (No, not that!) I found the best way was to run the bath and stick my head right under the surface. Sure, it was messy, but I quickly started getting the temperature right!

Of course, you can also lower the heat on your water heater so that it's impossible to get the water too hot, but then you give up your own hot showers and baths.

Never leave the baby alone in the bath, not even for a second. Babies can drown in just an inch or two of water. You also need to be careful to support the baby's rolling head at all times. It is really important too that you set up the bath and dressing area with everything you need *before* you bring the baby into the picture. That way, you don't have to leave him alone on a changing table or whatever while you go hunting for this or that.

When dressing your baby after a bath, put the diaper on first, particularly if your baby is a boy. Boys have an instinctive defense system, linked to their penis, that transforms this organ into a high-pressure rotational urine squirter on demand. This squirter has its own sighting mechanism and is always aimed at your face. Don't say I didn't warn you.

Out and About

It's hard to be a social butterfly and a new parent at the same time. With the baby's patterns of feeding, sleeping and soiling diapers, going out isn't as easy as it used to be. A simple thing like visiting friends or shopping becomes a journey of monumental proportions. Outings like an afternoon at the park, a spur-of-the-moment movie or a weekend sail with your wife become virtually impossible.

Not that your life comes to a complete standstill. It's more like a radical screeching down through the gears. Your social calendar will need to adjust to your changed home environment. This doesn't mean that you have to make like Rapunzel and stay locked indoors until your baby leaves home at eighteen. Outings simply become a little more complicated and require a little more thought and planning than they used to.

Once upon a time, going out was a relatively simple thing. Typically you could make it out of the house in seconds. Grab your car keys and wallet, brush your hair—thirty seconds, tops. It doesn't work like this anymore. *Operation Desert Storm* was easier to coordinate and initiate than *Operation Getting Out the Front Door*. This requires organization on a grand scale.

The baby has to be washed, changed, dressed, bundled and held. This reduces the holder to one arm. The bag has to be packed with a blanket, extra diapers, plastic bags, bottles, pacifiers, creams, gels, stuffed animals with bells and so on. The car seat has to be refitted and the stroller folded into the back seat. The travel crib or playpen has to be folded and squashed into whatever available space you have left. (By the way, most colleges offer engineering degrees specializing in travel-crib construction.)

Once supply lines have been established, you have the plan of attack to consider. If you're going to your mother-in-law's for lunch, for example, make your estimated time of departure half an hour earlier than normal. That way you'll ensure that you only miss the first course. But just when you're ready to go, you can bet that your baby will decide it's time to feed, and you'll have to postpone your trip.

Lunch becomes an afternoon snack.

And if it's a really big night—somewhere your baby just can't go—you need to start planning weeks in advance. You need to call a baby-sitter and if your wife is breastfeeding, she needs to express and freeze an adequate supply of breast milk.

One final word of warning about going out and about.

You will quickly discover that many malls have been designed by sexist architects who position baby-changing rooms in the women's restrooms. So if you are trapped in a large suburban shopping center and your baby develops a severe case of "toxic diaper," you have only two choices:

Choice one
Assert your rights as a modern man and barge into the women's restroom. At best, you'll get the baby changed before anyone notices. At worst, you'll get beaten up by a pack of paranoid grandmothers and possibly get arrested.

Choice two
Squat on the floor, lay down a mat and change the diaper in the middle of a busy department store walkway. I know a guy who actually does this! Interestingly, it won't take long for your "diaper terrorism" to make an impact. Depending on how bad the diaper is, architects will probably be brought in within the week, and a month later, after substantial structural renovation, you will be able to use the store's new multi-million-dollar unisex diaper-changing room.

Let's Party

Babies are a lot of work. It's important, however, that you don't get so wrapped up in the maintenance duties and chores that you forget to actually have some fun with your baby. It's important that you spend time playing with your baby so that the two of you can get to know each other and build a relationship.

When you do play, give your baby your undivided attention. Some dads seem to think that "play" means either sitting them in front of the TV or shoving lots of expensive toys in their face. As far as I'm concerned, the best toy is you.

Play can start immediately. What you do depends on the age of your baby. Play at the baby's level, not yours. For example, babies are generally hopeless at contact sports. The best suggestions I can make are

- Be inventive.

- Laugh a lot.

- Don't do anything that scares them.

- Keep one hand over your testicles at all times.

Here's a list of suggestions for playtime:

Play newborn babies enjoy
- staring at the ceiling
- being jiggled
- looking at your face
- soothing singalongs
- watching you shake fluffy toys with bells

Play older babies enjoy
- chewing
- making faces
- making silly noises
- rolling around on the floor or bed
- cuddling
- dribbling on Dad
- urinating on Dad
- vomiting on Dad

(continued . . .)

- horsey rides on Dad
- clapping and singing songs
- peek-a-boo
- getting raspberries on the stomach
- being tickled
- squeaky toys and picture books
- going for trips in the stroller

Play babies don't *enjoy*

- playing with any toys suitable for babies
- watching soaps on TV
- squash
- gardening
- computer programming
- white-water rafting
- rides on rollercoasters
- mountain climbing
- board games
- reading adult fiction without pictures

Spend time with your baby from Day One. Cuddle him. Talk to him. Sing to him. But whatever you do, don't talk or sing to your baby in what you think is his own language. I don't understand why adults insist on doing this. Science has proven that given the right stimulus, three-month-old babies not only can speak, but also can conduct a decent conversation. Unfortunately, most don't because they can't figure out what all the adults are saying.

I mean, could you learn to talk if the only thing you ever heard was, "Bootchie-wootchie-coo-coo. Bubba wanna car-car? Daddy loves his baby bitsy poo poo. YeeeEEEsssss?" You'd grow up to be a total moron!

No wonder babies take years to develop.

Having something of a penchant for music myself, I've always found singing songs to be a most successful and enjoyable form of play. But be warned! Most childhood ditties were composed by mentally deranged lunatics. The words usually make no sense on the surface and subliminally turn your baby into a zombie. For example, what self-respecting father would sing this scary tune to a child?

Rock-a-bye, Baby
On the treetop
When the wind blows
The cradle will rock
When the bough breaks
The cradle will fall
And down will come Baby
Cradle and all.

One alternative is to make up your own songs. I always use established tunes but free-associate my own words. Remember, it doesn't really matter *what* you sing, it's *the way you sing it* that matters.

For example, to the tune of "Old McDonald Had a Farm":

The Dow-Jones just went up five points,
Ee-eye, Ee-eye, oh.
I'll buy more shares in IBM,
Ee-eye, Ee-eye, oh.
I'm reading a book,
There is snot up your nose,
My feet are sore
and I've got to wash clothes.
Hurry up and go to sleep,
Ee-eye, Ee-eye, oh.

Or this gem, to the tune of "Amazing Grace":

I'm wearing jeans and you are not,
My tax is due today,
The weather is nice,
I like ice cream,
And my favorite TV show is Gilligan's Island.

Well, at least I try.

Step Right Up!

When Rachael came home, I was ready to play the happy dad, just like the ones on the TV commercials. Walks in the park, wrestling on the carpet, throwing her in the air, lots of laughter and fun and tummy-tickling and making faces. This was all great in theory, but it did not take me long to discover that newborn babies tend to be pretty mellow.

Some would even say boring.

Newborn babies in fact only perform four basic functions, which they repeat with monotonous regularity: They sleep (somewhere around sixteen hours a day, unless you have a baby like *The Screamer*); they cry (a lot, when they're not asleep); they drink milk (they want to cry, but their mouth is full); they fill diapers (all the time).

At first I was slightly annoyed that my backyard campouts, fatherly lectures and fruit juggling would have to wait until Rachael was more developmentally mature. But in the depths of my despair, something wonderful happened.

I'm not usually doting or sentimental by nature. But one day, soon after the homecoming, Rachael wrapped her tiny hand around my index finger and squeezed it like she was milking a cow.

That single little action was a ray of light that made me realize that I was in on the growth of a little person. At that stage she really did nothing except the usual—poop, cry, drink and sleep—but I suddenly realized that in the coming months, I would see her grow, change and develop. I would see her come to recognize me. I would watch her first steps. I would hear her first words.

And this is exactly what has happened to me three times now.

Like I said, I'm not really doting or sentimental, but with babies, almost every day brings something new. I discovered that it really is thrilling to participate in the life and growth of your baby. But don't expect too much at once. Most new parents spend a lot of time staring at their babies, cameras poised, waiting for the next important developmental milestone to occur. And as soon as the baby even moves, they respond like the Salt Lake City Olympic Bid Committee hearing the 2002 decision.

"Did you hear that? Did you hear that? Beethoven's *Fifth*! Child prodigy!" they will scream at regular intervals while watching their one-year-old beat the keys of a piano with clenched fists.

Even I fell into this trap. One day, Rachael was lying on her stomach during her third month. Her leg went into a spasm and kicked out the way babies' legs do—and she nudged forward an inch.

The next day, I told some of my work colleagues that Rachael could crawl even though she was only two months old. They looked at me with the knowing smiles of parental experience. Their faces had "new father with ridiculously high expectations" written all over them.

Growing up is a slow and laborious process. Your baby won't do everything overnight. But then again, that's part of the fun. So what exactly can you expect, and when? Well, here's a rough guide of the developmental stages of babies. Remember though that I'm not a medical doctor or a child psychologist or anything like that. The following list is less the result of any serious empirical analysis and more the result of watching babies down at the local supermarket.

At zero months, your baby will probably

- cry, drink, vomit, poop, sleep (repeat)
- be a blob on the carpet
- get stuffed animals from your friends

At three months, your baby will probably

- smile
- smack the hell out of a rattle
- play with his hands
- start to lift his head
- perhaps start on "solids"
- be responsive to you

At six months, your baby will probably

- start getting teeth
- bite you with these teeth
- produce "teething diapers" (the worst you'll ever experience)
- use hands to pick up disgusting objects
- put disgusting objects into mouth
- gurgle and sing to himself
- sit up for a few seconds without bashing his head on the floor

At nine months, your baby will probably

- sit up
- stand up while holding onto things
- crawl
- never stop emitting sounds

At twelve months, your baby will probably

- recognize his name
- eat finger food
- take off his own diaper and eat anything found within
- walk with assistance
- bite you a lot
- throw tantrums in public places

At fifteen months, your baby will probably

- start on basic words (that is, if you count "Dog! Dog!" as speaking)
- stumble around dangerously at high speeds
- eat small servings of what you eat
- have favorite toys or books

- get into places where a baby shouldn't be
- know the head signals for *yes* and *no*
- own shoes that are more expensive than yours

At eighteen months, your baby will probably

- point at things he wants
- demand to have your attention all the time
- understand basic commands, like "No!" and "Fetch!"
- break something very valuable
- contract a mystery illness that will make you very worried
- take half an hour to dress
- flush valuable items down the toilet

At twenty-four months, your baby will probably

- use a "big" toilet, with some assistance
- use a spoon
- play by himself
- have a basic vocabulary and primitive sentence construction
- have a junk-food addiction

At thirty months, your baby will probably

- ask unanswerable questions, such as "Where is the world? Why is red? Why aren't I a tree?"
- ride a tricycle
- know the jingle from every irritating commercial on TV

At thirty-six months, your baby will probably

- read a couple of words
- stumble into your bedroom every night
- operate complicated home-entertainment-unit remote controls

- know what foods he dislikes
- strike up conversations with strangers at the supermarket with lines such as "You're fat!" "Where's your hair?" "Do you have a penis? My dad does."

At 108 months, your baby will probably

- start asking for a bigger allowance
- want a horse or drum set for his birthday
- want every souvenir at the state fair
- try out his first swear words

At 180 months, your baby will probably

- bring home a first love, whom you won't like at all
- get suspended from school
- spend hours in the bathroom
- triple your phone bill

At 216 months, your baby will probably

- go to an R-rated film
- come home at 2 A.M. and get grounded for ten years
- want a cell phone

At 252 months, your baby will probably

- be earning more than you
- have a baby

Yep, as they get older it just gets better. This way, you enjoy it more, like a fine wine.

By the way, kids never perform any of their new feats in front of strangers. They are like Mr. Ed, the talking horse. Mr. Ed would chat away to Wilbur all day, but the moment someone else entered the stable, he would be just an ordinary horse again.

Your baby might be able to clap hands or play peek-a-boo. He might be able to stand on his head or discuss environmental issues in a second language. He might be able to sing opera or perform complex mathematical functions while tap-dancing.

But the moment guests arrive at your place, he will go back to being a baby. You will ask him to do things and he will stare at you dumbly and your friends will think you're an idiot.

So when you have guests, never say, "Baby David . . . come here . . . yes, yes . . . come on, atta boy! Tell Aunt Sue the square root of nine."

The baby will look at you and invariably respond with, "DOG!" or, if you're really unlucky, "SNOT!"

And be assured that the moment Aunt Sue steps out the door, the baby will mumble, "Three."

Secure the House

Once things have settled down a little in your home and you and your wife are getting used to the idea of living with a baby, you'll need to make some more changes around the place.

As I mentioned earlier, newborns don't move around much by themselves. With the exception of changing tables, they basically lie wherever you leave them, like a turtle on its back. Therefore they don't really have much of an impact on the way your place is arranged. However, in the coming months your baby will learn to crawl. Some babies have a top speed that would impress the most athletic cheetah in hot pursuit of a wounded wildebeest. You put them down, blink, and all you can see is a vapor trail of diaper fumes as they tear off down the hall. (Your baby, that is, not the cheetah.)

The problem is that this newfound mobility gives your baby access to all sorts of wonderful dangers around the home. Babies are naturally inquisitive but have no concept of danger whatsoever. So it's really important to baby-proof your home.

Here are some ideas:

- Stairs, windows, balconies, swimming pools and fish ponds should be secured. Fences, railings and banisters should have vertical slats inserted between the bars to prevent small bodies from squeezing through or climbing over. You could even put gates at the head and foot of staircases to prevent any unsupervised acrobatics.

- Every ground-level outlet should be fitted with plastic plugs to prevent infant electricians from experimenting with death. Also make sure that adapters or surge protectors are secure and out of reach.

- All dangerous household products (fluids, cleaners, sprays, powders, knives, openers, Bee Gees records and so on) should be put in top drawers or locked cupboards. This is particularly the case in the kitchen, bathroom and laundry room. In North America, a child is poisoned every thirty seconds, and 50 percent of these poisonings occur at home, when they've guzzled something they shouldn't have. There are a range of easy-to-install devices in your local hardware store to prevent this from happening, ranging from plastic hooks to an electrified chain with a six-digit computerized combination lock. Such a device will keep your baby out for about two or three days.

  Also check that roach motels and mousetraps are inaccessible, and remember that kids can reach above their heads. I learned this the hard way, when Rachael cleaned her teeth one morning with a disposable razor I'd assumed was "out of reach."

- If there is water around, *do not take your eyes off your baby.* If the phone rings during bathtime, take the baby with you or, better yet, just don't answer it. Always keep the lids on diaper pails and put them in an inaccessible room. Our pails live in our bathroom, but we make a point of always keeping the door shut. When you've finished using the diaper pails, empty them and turn them upside-down.

- Secure free-standing shelves, drawers and cupboards. Babies are good at climbing, but their King Kong–like behavior may lead to disaster if their weight is enough to topple a piece of furniture.

- Make sure that there are no saucepan handles sticking out or electrical cords dangling down from anywhere. To a baby, a dangling cable is an inviting vine on which they will inevitably try to swing like Tarzan. The problem is that it is probably attached to an iron or toaster. You can imagine the rest.

- Guard all fires, including heaters and stoves. If you can, keep your baby dressed in natural fibers such as cotton or wool, which are more fire-resistant than manufactured materials. Also keep matches far away from babies. If they don't light them and cause irreparable damage, they might eat them or stick them up their nose.

- Don't leave plastic bags lying around, and don't let your baby put buttons, nuts, coins, the eyes of stuffed animals and so on into her mouth. She will choke. A good rule of thumb: If the object can fit through the center of a toilet paper roll, it's a choking hazard.

- Make sure that all things you value—especially electrical items—are suspended from the ceiling by cables or are only accessible by ladder. If you've ever seen the damage a bowl of spaghetti can do to a CD player, you'll know what I'm talking about.

Even after you've done all these things and a couple of others that you thought up along the way, there is one more thing that you must do. It sounds kind of weird, but it's the most effective way of finding out how safe your home actually is. Here's how it works:

- First, get down on your hands and knees and pretend that you are a curious baby.

- Second, crawl around from room to room, seeing how much damage you can do to the nice things within your reach. Also see if you can find some computer disks to chew or some fragile ornaments to smash.

- Third, crawl around from room to room, seeing how much damage you can do to *yourself*. Try to find great heights to leap off and nasty things to stick in your mouth. You will be surprised by what you discover!

There's one other thing that you must remember at all times. It doesn't really apply to baby-proofing your home—unless you live in a glass house, that is—but it's vitally important anyway: You must understand that a newborn's skin is about one thousand times more sensitive than your leathery hide. This is not helped by the depletion of the ozone layer. So never put your baby out for a suntan. (In fact, never put *anyone* out for a suntan.) This particularly applies to outdoor outings such as to the beach. Avoid exposure to the sun, especially in the middle of the day, and always make sure your baby is wearing at least 15 spf sunscreen, a hat and preferably something covering his shoulders as well. You could even get a little pair of wrap-around shades and make him look like the third Blues Brother. Also, put a shade or towel in your car window to stop the sun from frying him in his car seat. Make sure, though, that you put the towel on a side window, not the *front* window. This will improve your driving visibility.

The Truth about Cats and Dogs

Some friends of mine recently had a dilemma. They had two big dogs that they had raised from pups. These dogs had been the sole guardians and masters of their house for years and were regarded and treated almost like children.

But that had to change because one day, my friends had a baby. Some of the canine privileges would obviously have to go. So while mother and baby were resting in the hospital before the homecoming, the brilliant father thought up a grand scheme to desensitize the dogs to the baby.

I remember sitting in their living room days before the big return. This buddy of mine sat the dogs down in front of him and produced from a plastic bag a wad of used diapers that he had brought from the hospital. He rubbed the dogs' faces in them and said the baby's name over and over: "Anna, Anna, Anna . . ."

It seemed like a good idea at the time, but something didn't seem quite right. The dogs' eyes were glistening a little too brightly for my liking. All I could think of was an old black-and-white movie I had seen in which a British lord threw his bloodthirsty hounds a shirt belonging to an escaped convict. They sniffed and growled at it and then galloped off across the moors to hunt him down and rip him to pieces.

Maybe it wasn't such a good idea after all.

Some people are dog people. Some people are cat people. Some are hairy-nosed aardvark people. I don't have any pets . . . that is, if you don't count the cockroaches and ants that live in our kitchen. I'm not much of a pet person. I had a dog when I was a kid, but I had to clean up after him, which scarred me for life. I vowed I'd never have a pet when I got older. So I don't know much about them. But if you do have a pet, you need to think through the implications of bringing a new member of the family into your house.

Pets can *get jealous.*

The main problem is that pets can get jealous. Dogs can eat a baby before you can blink, particularly if they are called Killer and wear a studded collar. Cats have been known to attack newborns by sticking their tail into the baby's mouth until it gets a furball. (The baby, that is, not the cat.) I shouldn't even need to mention boa constrictors.

As far as I can figure, there are only a few pets you can keep when you have a new baby in your house. Birds are stuck in a cage, so they can't fly over and rip your baby's throat out with their steely talons. Guinea pigs are just plain stupid. If you've got mice, they're probably okay. They aren't too dangerous, but be warned—they can get stuck in your baby's throat.

Come to think of it, horses are probably okay, too, as long as you don't let them into the nursery.

Something Else to Think About

You and your wife used to be a couple. Now you're a family.

You used to be a pair. Now you're a trio.

You used to be tennis partners. Now you're almost a basketball team.

The point is this. Having a baby in the house changes your relationship with your wife. This is because you don't spend as much time together as you used to. You used to go out to dinner and go for walks and see movies and talk intimately and all those other things that couples supposedly do. You used to have lots of time to invest in the maintenance and development of your relationship.

But that was before the baby. Sure, there are many things you can still do, but it certainly won't be as easy anymore. The threat to your relationship is reflected in the words of some old famous poet I studied at school: "No time. No time. Too much to do." The baby needs to be fed. The shopping needs to be done. The baby needs to be changed. The diapers need to be put on the line. The baby needs to be sung to sleep. The house needs vacuuming. The baby needs a bath. The dinner has to be cooked.

The problem is that you and your wife can end up running around doing baby and house maintenance duties and then all of a sudden you wake up one morning and wonder who the strange person next to you in your bed is. The face seems oddly familiar . . . oh . . . that's right . . . you're married to her!

If you're not careful, your relationship with your wife can go out the window. I've even heard of parents who, after many years, when their kids leave home, sadly realize that they don't really know each other anymore. They were so busy being parents that they forgot to be husband and wife.

This is tragic.

The message is, *don't forget to be a good husband.*

Don't neglect your wife.

You must both make a deliberate attempt to spend some time alone together—even if it is only a few desperately grabbed moments. Have a cup of coffee together. Try to have a meal with just the two of you. Lie in bed for ten minutes before you get up. A little ways down the road you can extend this. You might be able to catch a movie or play a game of tennis.

Your relationship with your wife is really important. Don't forget it. And don't assume that Mother's Day is the only day of the year she gets treated to something special. Mother's Day is a disgusting concept dictated by retail stores wanting to make a quick buck.

The best way to show your appreciation is by your words and actions. Give your wife love offerings like a cooked dinner or a clean bathroom floor. Watch the baby while she goes out and does whatever it is she wants to do. Buy her roses, chocolates and a new car. Tell her you love her and that you want to do that thing with the cooking oil and the lampshade.

Even More on Sex

Many new fathers find that sex is relegated to that part of their brain clearly labeled "distant memory." According to some statistics, nearly all mothers and 50 percent of fathers are less interested in sex during the postbirth period.

The problem, though, is that nothing can shatter a husband's ego like a wife disinterested in sex. It's easy to feel a little resentful that things aren't how they used to be. You can resent the baby because if it weren't for his crying, crying, crying all the time, your sex life would be great, great, great. You can become jealous of all the attention your wife lavishes on your baby—attention she used to lavish on you.

You can also resent your wife for not being as interested in you as she used to be. But this lack of attention is perfectly understandable, given that moms are usually exhausted from working twenty-four hours a day. The last thing they feel like is another physically and emotionally demanding marathon in bed. They need sleep.

Be sensitive to this. Do not start reading *Playboy* in bed at night.

A friend once told me a horror story about "a friend of a friend" of theirs who had just had her first child. She was sharing her hospital room in the maternity ward with another woman. According to this friend of a friend, the husband of this other woman came into the room soon after her labor and "had his way" with her.

Stuff like this makes my skin crawl. Given that this happened to a woman known by a friend of a friend of a friend, I really hope that it is one of those urban myths, up there with the likes of the alligator in the toilet, the hitchhiking ghost, the murderer on the roof of the car and the department store sale where you can actually pick up a bargain.

If, on the other hand, there really are men like this in the world, it makes me embarrassed to be called a man. The guy obviously had a sloping forehead and scars on his knuckles from where they scraped along the ground. This type of behavior is Neanderthal and completely inexcusable.

Once you see what happens to your wife's body in childbirth, particularly if a Cesarean or episiotomy was involved, I'm sure you will begin to understand why your wife would rather be left alone than mauled by you. Her postnatal body-weight distribution and maternity bra probably don't help make her feel like Aphrodite anyway. Rumor also has it that cracked nipples are not conducive to sensual arousal. If you can't comprehend this, give your pectorals a fifteen-minute massage with a sheet of sandpaper and then see how revved up you feel.

When you start playing the role of the active dad and get into night feedings and diaper changing and baby bathing, you'll probably get an inkling of why she's not so interested in sex. But for the moment, let's go back to the anecdote about the umbrella and your penis. Meditate on this for a while. Imagine stretching your penis so far that you can scratch your nose with it. Imagine unmentionable acts with your scrotum and a garbage disposal. Imagine urinating a grapefruit. I'm sure you wouldn't feel like a heavy session of intense passion after that. And you wouldn't appreciate your wife giving you the "nudge nudge, wink wink" treatment, either.

In this regard, then, let your wife call the shots regarding your mutual re-entry (I'm sorry, I couldn't help it) into the world of lovemaking.

Of course, it's not just your wife's recovery from the physical trauma of labor and birth that inhibits your sex life. It's also the fact that you are both perpetually exhausted and are lucky if you have a moment to yourselves. It's also a little-known fact that newborn babies have a psychic link with their mothers, which means they can detect any sexual arousal or activity within a 100-foot radius. This will immediately trigger a screaming response just at "the right moment"—if you get my drift.

Some Advice

No one expects either you or your wife to be an instantaneous parenting expert. Even if you have read widely and spoken to parenting pioneers, there will still be times when you feel out of your league and unsure if things are going as they should.

Your baby may not sleep well. He might look pale, or he might cough all the time. He may cry constantly and without obvious reason. He might not take to the breast very well. Blotches or marks may appear on his skin.

Sometimes, you need practical advice or help. Sometimes, however, people want to give you advice even when you don't want it or need it. Suddenly everyone is an expert and knows exactly how to solve your paternal problems.

If anyone without kids of their own gives you advice, disregard it totally. They don't know what they're talking about. If they are persistent, ask them to change your baby's diaper. That'll shut 'em up.

If any strangers in the supermarket try to give you advice, pretend you don't speak English.

Family is a little different. After all, your parents brought you up and you turned out OK. But remember that it was your mom who used to put butter on your burns when you were a kid, and your dad who still calls your expensive home entertainment system a *hi-fi*.

My grandmother raised her children before the Second World War and always seems full of good ideas, but how much can you trust a woman who thinks pure lard on toast for breakfast is a pretty good idea?

Seriously, though, there are hundreds of organizations for parents throughout North America. Hop on the internet, look in the phone book or ask your healthcare practitioner.

Don't be afraid to get help!

One More Thing

Earlier in the book, I spoke of the lines from the Ron Howard film *Parenthood*: "You know, you need a license to buy a dog or drive a car. Hell, you need a license to catch a fish. But they'll let any . . . assh—e be a father."

And here is also where I will close this book.

It took me four years of college to become a qualified high school teacher. Four years of lectures, seminars and tutorials. Four years of burning the midnight oil, writing impossibly long essays and papers and drinking industrial-strength coffee. Four years researching and analyzing expert opinions in gigantic leather-bound volumes found in the darkest recesses of the labyrinthine library.

But it was all worth it. At the end of the four years I was ready to set the educational world on fire. I knew all there was to be known. I was an expert in school policy, child psychology, curriculum development, time management and literary analysis. I had done the work and was ready to assume my God-given role in life: Superteacher.

With a brand-new diploma under my arm, I sailed out of college into a job in a private school. At the end of a lengthy summer vacation, I turned up for my first day of work sporting a new haircut and a new suit. I held my head high, because I had graduated *summa cum laude* and I knew this would demand instant respect in the staffroom and guarantee me obedience and honor from the student body for the rest of my life. I was instantly recognizable as an expert. It was all downhill from here. Easy.

Then I met Graham.

Graham was my department head, a man who looked like he forgot to get out of his clothes before he threw them into the dryer. I'll never forget our first meeting. He sat me down in his small office and, with a dose of drama, said, "Welcome to the real world. You've spent four years with your head up in the clouds in some educational ivory tower. Now it's time to come down to Earth. Forget most of the stuff you learned at college. It's bull. Get into the classroom, keep 'em under control, teach 'em something and get out alive. That's it. Any questions?"

I was shocked to say the least. Hadn't this man seen my curriculum vitae? Didn't he know who I was? Didn't he know that I had read all the books and had sat at the feet of the great academic masters? I'd graduated *summa cum laude*, for heaven's sake! But before I could voice an objection, he was on his feet and out the door. With a glance over his shoulder, he added, "You're going to learn more this week about being a teacher than you did in four years of reading books. Have a nice day."

He was right. At the end of that first week, I realized that I really knew squat about teaching. I was a humbled amateur and each night as I crawled exhausted into bed I would think, *Why didn't anybody tell me about this? Why wasn't I warned?* I was an expert in theory, but expertise in practice would have to come in time.

A few years later, I became a father. I had read all the books and been to all the classes and knew all the theories and was ready to assume my other God-given role in life: Superfather. And exactly the same thing happened. I learned more in that first week after Rachael's birth than I did in nine months of thought and preparation.

You can read all the books and magazines on parenting in the local library. You can watch every movie on childbirth ever made. You can ask questions of medical staff until their ears fall off. You can study all the current theories and attend birth-education classes until you're a world-famous expert. In fact, it is your responsibility to do these things.

But it will still be "academic." It will still be head-knowledge.

And now that you've almost finished this tome, I'll let you in on a little secret. Are you ready? It's printed in bold letters so you can't miss it. OK, here it is:

Nothing can really prepare you for becoming a father.

I hope you're not disappointed, but I had to put this earth-shattering statement at the end of the last chapter, otherwise you might not have read the book.

Until you experience fatherhood in all its rewarding and painful glory, you can't really know what it's like in the 3-D, stereo-sound sense of the word. You have to *live it* to get the full sensation. Only when you feel the kick of your unborn child do you feel the thrill of expectation. Only when you see a woman give birth do you really understand how painful it is. Only when you hear crying at 3 A.M. do you know what it is to be tired and cranky. Only when you change a diaper for the first time do you know the true meaning of nausea. Only when your baby says, "I lub oo, dabbee," when you tuck her in at night do you feel that bursting pride of fatherhood. But that's OK.

The whole idea is that dadhood is a *learning process*. It's on-the-job training of the most important kind. And you better get used to it, because before you know it, your wife will be pregnant again (and again). Just when you think you're in the home stretch, you'll be back at Go without even collecting the two hundred dollars.

Just remember to get in there and get your hands dirty.

Well . . . what are you waiting for?

The Last Word

If I were to leave you with one message as you face the months ahead, no matter what stage you are at, it would be this:

Don't give up.

Sometimes things don't go the way you plan.

Being a dad is not always great and wonderful. It's not always holding hands and piggy-back rides and "I love you, Dad." There are busy times, rotten times, tired times, times when you are irritated and feel lousy.

The important thing is not that you become the perfect father, because there is no such thing. The important thing is that when things don't look so good—when things go wrong, when you make mistakes—you try again.

It took me a while to learn this. My dad tried to warn me, but I didn't listen.

He said that fatherhood was like riding a bicycle. I didn't understand at first. Riding a bicycle is about moving fast, wearing tight shorts and grazing your knees. Fatherhood, on the other hand, is about changing dirty diapers and not ever getting a good night's sleep.

Not all that similar if you ask me.

But there was a message in the heart of old Dad's metaphor. You don't learn to ride a bike by studying the principles of circular motion, gear ratios and muscle development. In reality you get on the bike, you pedal hard, you fall off and then you get on again and repeat the process until the "you fall off" part doesn't happen with such frightening regularity anymore.

Just like fatherhood.

You have to keep going. You have to keep trying. You have to keep getting back on the bike. You don't bail out.

So you're now the full-fledged father of a real, live baby. You have navigated the pregnancy, survived the labor and stumbled through life at home with a newborn person. Soon, you will get used to this new life and you will start to feel comfortable and in control again. You will find your feet and look back and wonder what all the fuss was about in the first place.

To an extent, this is an appropriate feeling to have. But don't be deceived. Don't start relaxing. Pretty soon, your baby is going to learn to walk and talk.

Soon your baby will turn into . . . a toddler.

That's when hell really breaks loose.

But I'll leave that for the sequel.

So to you, my paternal comrades, I offer my congratulations on being given the awesome responsibility and tremendous privilege of being a father. I hope you embrace it in all its richness and wonder. Savor the golden times, struggle through the frustrating times and work hard at it.

I hope in some small way this book has given you a glimpse of both the pain and the comedy of dadhood. I hope it has helped you prepare for your own journey as a dad.

I used to think that this journey down the parental road was a pretty straight one. You walked down it for a while until you arrived at your destination—parental perfection. I've since come to realize that this road is in fact a winding and complex maze. Sometimes I don't seem to be getting anywhere. And the further I travel through this maze, the more I realize that there is in fact no destination. There is no exit. I'll never get to a point where I stop being a parent. I'll be journeying until the day I die. Until then, I'll plow ahead, keeping one eye to the front and the other on the lookout for puddles.

Occasionally I look back on where I've come from and realize that I am content. And although I suspect parenting just gets harder from here on, I'm really, really looking forward to the years ahead.

I hope you are too.

Good luck on your journey . . . Dad.

Glossary

This is not an extensive glossary. It just contains a whole lot of words that I know.

aaarrgghh, no, it can't possibly be true, it must be a nightmare, I'm going to vomit . . . uurrgghblecchpphhhh. The words often spoken by dads changing their first teething diaper.

afterbirth. 1. The time immediately following the birth of the baby; 2. All the stuff that comes out of the mother after the baby is born.

afterpains. The pain you feel after the birth when the bills start arriving.

Alfa Romeo. The car your doctor drives.

amniocentesis. The extraction and testing of the amniotic fluid for abnormalities in the fetus.

amniotic fluid. Fluid inside the bag that the baby grows within for the first nine months of his life.

amniotic inversion. This is nothing, really. I just made it up.

amniotic sac. The bag the baby grows within for the first nine months of his life.

anesthetic. Thing that helps you cope with pain. Often used by mothers during labor (injections) and fathers getting used to a newborn (bourbon or beer).

Apgar test. 1. Test used to upgrade a level within the Swedish Civil Service; named after Thor Apgar, Swedish prime minister and mountain climber; 2. Used after birth to rate the newborn's heart rate, breathing, skin and muscle tone, reflexes and sense of humor.

Audi. The car your obstetrician's spouse drives.

baby. The technical name given to your child after she's finished being a fetus.

Beta hCG (human chorionic gonadotropin). A nasty hormone.

beta. Obsolete although technically superior video recorder.

bilirubin. 1. The pigment that builds up in the bloodstream, giving jaundiced babies their telltale color; 2. I know you're not going to believe this, but I actually went to grade school with a kid called Billy Ruben. I swear it's true. Kind of.

birth. When the baby comes out of the mother.

birth canal. 1. Salt-water inlet located approximately fifty miles south of the Suez Canal; 2. The passage that the baby has to navigate to get out of the mother.

blues. 1. Soulful music portraying a depressed character and morbid worldview; 2. Sadness felt during postnatal period, largely attributed to hormonal changes in the mother's body; 3. Hues between green and violet.

BMW. The car your obstetrician drives.

Bond. British super-spy rated with a 00 license to kill. First name: James.

bonding. What happens when you pick your baby up with hands covered in superglue.

bottle. Container used for formula transfer to baby.

bouncer. 1. Gorilla-like male who stands outside nightclubs and decides whether you're trendy enough to get in; 2. A device for baby bouncing.

Braxton-Hicks. Irritating and extremely inconvenient false labor contractions. (See also *Corporal Hicks.*)

breast. 1. The part my family always fights over when we have roast chicken for dinner; 2. One of the two outermost points on your wife's frontal area, usually impressively swollen to 747 size by the time of birth.

breastfeeding. 1. When victor of our family roast-chicken fights eats their meal; 2. When the baby drinks from its mother's breast.

breast pump. Gigantic device that looks like the bug-catcher you got for your seventh birthday. It makes *schloop, schlurp* noises and sucks breast milk out.

breech birth. When the baby is born rear-first.

Caesar, Julius. Roman statesman and general, 100–44 B.C.

Caesar Romero. Played *The Cisco Kid* and the original Joker in *Batman.*

Caesar salad. A tasty mix of romaine lettuce, croutons, bacon, anchovies, egg, parmesan cheese, oil and vinegar.

Cesarean section. 1. The quarter of Rome where Caesar's supporters lived; 2. The surgical removal of stubborn unborns.

cervix. The bottom of the uterus. Something akin to the plughole.

chromosomes. Microscopic, threadlike structures that contain thousands of genes. Each cell has twenty-three chromosomes. (See also X *chromosome* and Y *chromosome*.)

circumcision. Cutting off the flappy part on the end of the penis. Not to be confused with castration or circumlocution.

colic. A condition during which babies scream and scream and yell and wail and you go psycho-bananas trying to cope with it.

colostrum. A rich breast secretion, jam-packed full of proteins, antibodies and other nourishing stuff, which flows for a few days after a woman gives birth, before her milk kicks in.

conception. When the fertilized egg buries itself in the uterus.

condominium. 1. Fancy apartments; 2. The smallest size of a rubber contraceptive. The other sizes are condomoderate and condomaximum.

contraceptive. Well, it's too late for a definition now, isn't it?

Corporal Hicks. One of the heros of the movie *Aliens*. (See also *Braxton-Hicks*.)

crowning. 1. When a monarch receives her symbolic headpiece of power; 2. When the baby's head appears on the way out.

delivery. When somebody brings you something, such as a pizza. Or a baby.

depression. A state of sadness or moodiness encountered by parents. For mothers, it usually occurs after the birth. For fathers, it is when they realize that babies are really expensive, cause sleep deprivation and ruin their social and sex lives.

diaper. Poop catcher.

dilation. The process of being made wider. For example, the pupils of your eyes when you enter a dark room, or the cervix when it realizes that the baby is about to try to pass through it.

duff. 1.The decaying organic matter on the forest floor; 2. The brand of beer favored by Homer Simpson.

eight-thirty P.M. The universally acknowledged time for parents to leave parties.

embryo. Another name for your child; technically from implantation until about the twelfth week of pregnancy.

enema. Totally excellent activity for the whole family in which you get a little squirt of fluid up the old recto and everything hiding in your lower bowel comes out in a hurry. Women in labor sometimes receive this. However, in California you can get one done just for fun.

engaged. 1. When you promise to marry your girlfriend; 2. When the baby gets ready for birth during the last month of pregnancy by turning into the eject position.

engorgement. This is when the mother's breasts go overboard on the milk production and get bigger and bigger and sorer and sorer. If left untreated, they can explode and cause a lot of damage to entire city blocks.

epidural block. 1. The anesthetic procedure of numbing the entire lower half of a woman by injecting stuff into her lower spine; 2. A football strategy.

episiotomy. A surgical cut in the perineum to make it bigger so the baby can get out. This is done to prevent or impede tearing.

estrogen. A hormone produced in large quantities during pregnancy.

eyelet. The plastic covering on the end of a shoelace.

Fallopian tubes. The tunnels between the ovaries and the uterus where *fertilization* takes place.

fertilization. When the sperm and the ovum get together. This is the very first step in the production of human life.

flaccid. Soft and drooping.

fetal distress. When complications arise during birth causing a shortage of oxygen to the baby; for example, when the umbilical cord gets tangled or pinched.

fetal-distress flare. A bright red emergency light that shoots out of the vagina and into the delivery room to let everyone know that problems are developing.

fetus. The name of your baby after the period when it is an embryo; technically from after the twelfth week of pregnancy until birth.

fontanelle. 1. The soft spots on the fetus' or newborn's head where the skull has yet to join together; 2. A region of Italy known for its cheese, mushroom and pepper sauce. Next time you're in an Italian restaurant, ask for *Fontanelle Ravioli* or *Fettuccine Fontanelle*.

forceps. Gigantic baby-grabbing pliers.

foreskin. The flappy part on the end of your penis, but if you are of my generation, you probably don't have one, so don't bother looking. (See also *circumcision*.)

Gamma globulin. When the travelers in the classic series *Lost in Space* get thrown off-course because of the malevolent but ultimately likeable Dr. Zachary Smith, they miss Alpha Centauri and crash-land on Planet EV 36, also known as Planet Gamma Globulin, where they encounter a horrific giant Cyclops that throws rocks at their spacecraft.

gas. Babies have lots of this. It means they have air in their stomachs and it has to come out via the holes at both ends of their body.

genes. 1. Expensive denim pants with designer labels and French names; 2. Little, really, really microscopically tiny things that carry genetic information within cells.

getchadamhanzoff. Common maternal expression yelled at inconsiderate groping husbands.

glossary. Pathetic and see-through attempt to beef up a book by slapping another couple of irrelevant pages on the end.

gynecologist. A doctor of woman's things.

harp. The metal hoop that supports a lampshade.

hepaticocholecystostcholecystenterostomy. The surgical formation of a passage between the gall bladder and the hepatic duct.

hormones. Chemicals in the bloodstream that act as messengers to activate specific organs in the body to some type of response. During pregnancy, women have a lot of these floating around (chemicals, that is, not organs).

hospital. A place with doctors and nurses where you go when you're sick . . . but that's not important right now.

immunization. The process involving shots that protects your child from certain deadly diseases.

implantation. This is when the sperm-ovum blobby thing picks out a cozy spot in the uterine wall to call home.

incubator. A sealed crib used for monitoring newborns.

induction. 1.When presidents are officially put into office. This is usually accompanied by tears, moving words ripped off from JFK, appearances by Michael Jackson and saxophone playing; 2. The artificial triggering of labor.

intravenous drip. A slow feed-line of fluid from a bag into the vein by way of a catheter.

ixoye. I'm not sure what this means. I think it's Greek or something historical like that.

Jaguar. Your obstetrician's other car.

jaundice. A common newborn thing when the baby's liver doesn't do something or other and something else happens and then the baby turns yellow.

labor. The hard work experienced by a woman in getting the baby out of her.

lanugo. A covering of body hair at birth, usually accompanied by the comment, "Oh look, it's a carpet!"

let-down. 1. When a woman's milk drops into her breasts; 2. The feeling you get when you go to the movies and pay twelve bucks to see *Highlander 2*.

lopadotemachoselachogaleokranioleipsanodrimhypotrimmatosi lphioparaomelitokatakechymenokichlepikossyphophattoper isteralektryonoptekephalliokigklopeleiolagoiosiraiobaphetra ganopterygonn. The English translation of a Greek word meaning, "A goulash composed of all the leftovers from the meals of the last two weeks."

Mars. The place where your wife would rather be than on the delivery bed.

mastitis. Painful breast problem when breasts get lumpy and as sore as testicles that have just been stomped on by River Dancers.

meconium. The technical name given to a baby's first bowel movements. In some Third World nations it is used to pave roads. Don't let it come into contact with bare skin.

memory. The place in your brain under which you should file "sex."

Mercedes Benz. The car your obstetrician drives when she's sick of the Jaguar.

midhusband. There's no such thing, but this is a perfect example of how the degenderization of our language only works one way. (See also *midwife*.)

midwife. A nurse who specializes in childbirth.

milk. Nutritious stuff that comes out of cows and women.

morning sickness. When a woman feels so gross and nauseated during pregnancy that she wishes she were watching reruns of *The Love Boat*.

mucus. Nasal discharge.

navel. Lumpy thing on the lower stomach.

nipples. Two lumpy things on the end of the breasts.

obstetrician. A specialist doctor who delivers babies and drives an expensive car.

osseocarnisanguineoviscericartilagininervomedullary. A term detailing the structure of the human body.

ova. Plural of *ovum*.

ovary. Place where ova are produced.

ovulation. Time when the ovum comes out of the ovary.

ovum. Singular of *ova*—egg.

owchyaschlong. Where semen comes from.

oxytocin. A hormone that encourages uterine contraction and milk production.

pain. The feeling you get when you stop a high-velocity wet leather soccer ball with your groin. There is a lot of this involved in childbirth. (Pain, that is, not soccer balls.)

pediatrician. A children's doctor who drives an expensive car.

pelvic floor. The muscles in the base of the pelvis that hold everything together. They are attached to the pelvic walls, pelvic ceiling and pelvic viewing gallery.

pelvic thrust. Put your hands on your hips and hold your knees in tight. Yep, it almost drives you insa-yay-yay-yay-yay-yane!

pelvis. The bones of the hips, as shaken widely by Elvis Presley.

perineum. The area between anus and vagina.

placenta. The interface between mother and fetus that controls life-support and waste disposal.

Porsche. The car your pediatrician drives.

postnatal. Time after the birth.

postnatal depression. Depression during the time after the birth.

postpartum. An express delivery service offered by the Postal Service.

practertranssubstantiationalisticafly. The act of surpassing the act of transubstantiation.

pregnant. When a woman has a baby inside her.

premature. When a baby is born before it reaches adolescence.

progesterone. A hormone produced in large quantities during pregnancy.

prostaglandin. A hormone that encourages labor contractions. It is found in prostaglandin gel, suppositories and semen.

quadruplets. Four children born from the one pregnancy. This will guarantee you an appearance on a current affairs show.

quintuplets. Five children born from the one pregnancy. Guaranteed front cover and photo spread in at least two women's magazines.

Qaqa kwaze laziqukokeqika. Xhosian tongue-twister that translates as "The desert rat falls and bursts its larynx."

rash. 1. Skin irritation caused by a wet diaper; 2. Your behaviour the night your baby was conceived.

reverse peristalsis. What you do when you change a diaper that looks like a special effect from a horror movie.

rooting reflex. 1. When pigs poke around in the dirt looking for morsels; 2. When a baby pokes around on the breast looking for the nipple; 3. Oh, forget it! You're pathetic.

Saab. The car your anesthesiologist drives.

scrotum. Ugly wrinkly dangly male thing containing the all-important testicles.

semen. The goopy stuff, containing sperm, that comes out of your penis.

sex. Memories . . .

show. A sign of the onset of labor. It is when all this blood and mucus and stuff comes out of the woman's vagina. (Think about this the next time someone invites you out to "see a show.")

sit on a potato pan, Otis. A hilarious palindrome.

SK-70. The name of a rock band I played in as a teenager. We reached new heights in anonymity and the crowds flocked to our gigs in twos and threes.

sleep-in. I've forgotten what this is. Sorry.

sperm. The male reproductive tadpole. There are about 300 million sperm per human ejaculation, which though impressive is not as awesome as that of the pig, which produces about 45 billion a go. That's *billion*, not million. The hamster, on the other hand, only has a fairly uninspiring three thousand, which is why there are so few hamsters around.

stirrups. Once used widely by women to get their legs up during birth. Also used by ranchers to get their legs up on a horse.

stitches. What you get sewn up with; usually applicable to the perineum.

term. The period of the pregnancy. To *go full-term* is to carry the baby to the end of the pregnancy.

testicles. You should have two of these unless you played soccer when you were a kid, in which case one is probably wedged back up where it's not supposed to be. This is the storage tank for your sperm; also referred to as the family jewels.

tofu. The most disgusting foodstuff ever invented.

transition. The painful period between the first and second stages of labor.

trifecta. Something to do with horse racing and the number three.

trimester. A third of the full term of pregnancy; three months.

triplets. When you have three kids from the same pregnancy.

twins. When you have two kids from the same pregnancy.

ultrasound. The technological wonder that creates a picture of the fetus by using high frequency sound waves. It's like sonar but instead of looking for enemy submarines, you're looking for hands, feet and a head.

umbilical cord. The supply line between the mother and the fetus.

uterus. Thingy where the baby grows; another word for womb.

vacuum. Used sometimes to suck out wedged babies.

vagina. Where the penis goes in and the sperm comes out and then nine months later the baby arrives.

vernix. The creamy goop used by newborn babies and ocean swimmers to keep them warm.

virgin. Your pregnant wife isn't one.

virgule. The oblique stroke used between words or fractions.

Volvo. A car driven badly by people who live in the suburbs.

water. Euphemism for the fluid inside the amniotic sac. When the water "breaks," all the fluid spills out onto the floor or the expensive lounge or wherever the woman happens to be at the time.

wet nurse. You thought I was going to say "a nurse who has fallen in the water," didn't you? Well, you're wrong.

womb. 1. Another word for uterus; 2. What Barbara Walters calls the walled compartment within a building.

X chromosome. A genetic sex indicator. All ova are X. If an X sperm fertilizes the ovum, the baby will be a girl.

xylophone. A musical instrument often found in children's alphabet books because it is easier to illustrate than xenon, xenophobia or xerography.

Y chromosome. A genetic sex indicator. If a Y sperm fertilizes the ovum, the baby will be a boy.

You #!@%&!. Term of affection directed at husbands by wives in the throes of labor.

zebra. A striped horselike animal from the African plains.

dyslexia. Problem with reading ability, usually associated with letter confusion.

Appendix 1
Parent Education Films

Your local video store is a veritable goldmine of educational films that can teach you all you need to know about conception, pregnancy, labor and life at home with a new baby. Here are a few suggestions of some to see . . . and some not to.

Alien
Watch, and be grateful that human babies aren't born like this.

Aliens
Nothing to do with fatherhood but a great movie anyway.

Alien Seed
Women are impregnated by aliens. Yuck.

Babies
Young couples struggle through pregnancy, sperm testing, infertility, ultrasounds and so forth. All is wholesome at the end. Realistic labor sequence as mother gives birth to a clean eight-month-old!

Baby
With a name like this, you'd expect some decent parental education. But no! It's about a dinosaur.

Baby Boomer
No, not a film about a dynamite truck crashing into a maternity ward. Instead, Diane Keaton is a successful businesswoman *and* a competent full-time mother. Then I woke up.

Baby of the Bride
Saccharine drivel of the worst kind as hordes of soap stars tip-toe through the land of pregnancy. In true Hollywood fashion, they even made a sequel. (See *Mother of the Bride*.)

Baby Talk
Yuppie couple strive for pregnancy. Clichés everywhere. See the special effects wizardry as mother gives birth to a baby with a navel!

Betsy's Wedding
This is what lies ahead of you! (See *Father of the Bride*.)

Breeders
Close encounters of the pregnancy kind. Pass me that bucket.

Cactus Jack
Nothing to do with babies, but it's one of Arnold Schwarzenegger's first movies in which he plays a cowboy. Good for a laugh.

Dances With Wolves, the Director's Cut
A very long movie, good for those long nights with a screamer.

Dolls
I knew it! The dolls come to life, with horrific consequences!

Don't Tell Mom the Babysitter's Dead
Not to be watched before your first baby-sitting experience.

Embryo
Horror flick about an embryo that . . . oh, never mind.

E.T.
The star looks kind of like a newborn baby.

Everything You Wanted to Know about Sex, but Were Afraid to Ask
See Woody Allen play a sperm about to meet his fate.

From Here to Paternity
One of the great classics of parental education.

Father of the Bride
This is what lies ahead of you! (See *Betsy's Wedding*.)

For Keeps
Real footage of conception over the credits. Molly Ringwald and her husband try to balance diapers, postnatal depression, work and parenting while their lives fall apart. The birth sequence is quite realistic and even has a real newborn playing the part of the real newborn. Ignore the sequence where Mom holds the baby in her lap in the car.

Frozen Assets
Comedy about a sperm bank. Say no more.

Ginger Ale Afternoon
Tense fighting between jealous arrogant chauvinist pig husband and his pregnant wife. The star is the pregnant actress Dana Anderson who spends almost the entire film in a bikini. Has to be seen to be believed!

Ishtar
Put a screaming baby in front of this and she will go to sleep.

Look Who's Talking
Great special effect sequence over the credits of sperm hunting for the ovum followed by the development of the fetus.

Look Who's Talking 2
I haven't seen this one.

Look Who's Talking 3
I haven't seen this one, either.

Look Who's Talking 4
I don't think they've made it yet. I hope they don't. I won't see it.

Made in America
Worth seeing just for the great sperm donation sequence. After that, turn it off.

Maybe Baby
He's 57, she's 37 and pregnant. Clichés galore!

Modern Love
Burt Reynolds *and* Rue McClanahan are in this film. Need I say more?

Mother of the Bride
Rue is back! The people who made this must have been hard up for cash. Either that or they lost a bet. (See *Baby of the Bride*.)

Mr. Mom
Michael Keaton plays a full-time dad and finds that it is not as easy as it looks.

Parenthood
Steve Martin shows you what lies ahead for us dads. Great stuff.

Parents
Horror spoof about bad parental role models who always have lots of "leftovers" in the fridge.

Paternity
Burt Reynolds hunts for an incubator. (See *Modern Love*.)

Problem Child
The worst film I've ever seen.

Problem Child 2
Even worse than the first one.

Robin Williams Live
Includes some comical insights into labor and parenting.

Rosemary's Baby
Woman gives birth to the antichrist. Don't let your wife see it.

She's Having a Baby
One of the best fatherhood education films ever made. Naíve Father Type II (see page 9) faces the trials of sperm testing, birth classes and the hospital experience. Realistic labor sequence and excellent suggestions for baby names over the final credits.

Spawn
Woman gives birth to hideous alien. Don't let your wife see this one, either. (Also not to be confused with the demon-turned-superhero film of the late nineties.)

Terminator
A film about the conception of John Connor.

Terminator 2
See how much pregnancy changed Sarah Connor's life.

That's My Baby
He wants a baby, she wants a career. Avoid.

The Abyss
When you want a change of pace, this film has NO babies in it.

The Brady Bunch Christmas Special
Contains the most unrealistic labor sequence ever filmed.

The Color Purple
Contains a pretty realistic birth sequence.

The Exorcist
This is a good film to prepare you for labor.

The Hand That Rocks the Cradle
Another "not to be watched before your first baby-sitting experience" movie.

The Hunt for Red October
Wonderful underwater epic. The submarines make noises just like inside the womb.

Three Men and a Baby
The best fatherhood-education film ever made. Three successful corporate guys (Danson, Guttenburg and Selleck) are thrown headlong into fatherhood. Great insights into feeding, diapers, bathing, shopping and so on.

Trois Hommes et un Couffin
The original *Three Men and a Baby*, but in French.

Appendix 2

What My Friends Had to Say

Because the whole focus of this book is the "common" man's experience of fatherhood, I thought I would invite all my fathering comrades to have their say as well. I asked them to free-associate about pregnancy, birth, life and whatever else came to mind.

This will also ensure that they buy their own copy of the book, instead of borrowing mine.

So, here it is—the wisdom of those who have walked the road ahead of you. Read it with a grain of salt.

ADRIAN
Father of Lyndall, 6 weeks
From the age of fifteen, I planned out my life . . . what sort of job I would like, the type of girl I wanted to marry and the place where I wanted to live. I fulfilled my plans but then found myself uncomfortably out of control of my life. I feared not being able to plan anymore.

The first part of the pregnancy was really rough, with a threatened miscarriage. I was really anxious about being at the birth, but I was trusting in someone greater than me. I was praying everything would be OK.

When the day came, Annie's water broke at home so we scrambled to the hospital. It was really exciting. When we arrived, she was two centimeters dilated. I put on my swim trunks and got in the shower with her. Then things got wild. It all happened so fast, I was in shock. The pains came hard and sharp. I didn't know what was going on.

Thirty minutes later Lyndall was born. I was overwhelmed. Two hours later I was still gaa-gaa. I was totally occupied with my new family. That was when the doctor pointed out that I was still in my trunks and I should probably put some clothes on.

AL
Father of Amy, 9, Beth, 7, Gareth, 5, and Josephine, 2
My advice? Be around and make it fun to be a kid.

ANDREW
Father of Zoe, 8 weeks
I was really annoyed that everyone was so negative about how being a dad was going to really change things. I haven't found it to be like that at all. I expected my life to be over. Some things of course have changed, but it's nothing you can't adjust to.

We've just come back from four weeks hiking and camping, with Zoe bobbing around in a front sling. She survived four-wheel driving and a jog down a steep mountain trail to escape a storm. Our tent collapsed one night and she didn't even wake up. On one part of the trip, Gaia kayaked while I drove the car with the baby in it down a riverside road. When she needed a feeding, I'd just pull over and honk the horn.

I think it's all a matter of attitude. If you focus on the negative and talk yourself into a corner, you'll of course end up being defeatist and looking for problems in the whole thing.

In terms of the birth itself, that was pretty wild. I came home from work and Gaia had walked a few miles up to the hospital. I got up there about four in the afternoon and we went through 'til seven the next morning. We were even sleeping in three-minute bursts between contractions—we were so exhausted.

When Zoe was born, I was just blown away. It was the most awesome thing to see. I've done lots of stuff in my life across the globe, but the birth was the most amazing thing I've ever encountered.

(Oh yeah? Let's see if you're still as cocky in six months' time, Mr. Smarty Pants—P.D.)

BILL
Father of Talitha, 3 days
Everyone keeps telling me that "BC" stands for "Before Children." It makes me nervous and curious about the changes in our lifestyle. I am hoping and praying that I can meet the challenges and be a good father.

The birth was pretty moving. We went to the hospital and then got sent home again because nothing was happening. By the time we got home, the contractions had started again. We went back to the hospital. That was at 4 P.M. Talitha was born around four the next morning. I was surprised that I was invited to "catch" her on the way out. She was so slimy! I'm glad it wasn't me giving birth.

DANIEL
Father of Zachary, 4 months
Well, I'm not too sure. I think it's some sort of infection. Like a skin disease, with lots of scabs caused by parasites or something . . . What? Oh, *babies!!* I thought you said *scabies!!!*

DAVID
Father of Simon, 3, and Timothy, 15 months
As a father, you don't have to be one of The Magnificent Seven, but here's the good, the bad and the ugly of being a father.

The Good: that magic moment when the head first crowns, the first smiles, first steps, first words and cuddles.

The Bad: sleep deprivation, sleep deprivation and sleep deprivation.

The Ugly: ties stained with breast-milk vomit, first solids, leaking diapers.

ERIC
Father of twins Harrison and Jordan, 8 months
I don't think you can imagine how hard it'll be. I've got seven nieces and nephews, some of whom I helped raise. But holding down a job and living with them twenty-four hours a day under one roof . . . that's another story.

It's fifty times harder and a hundred times better than I ever imagined. My advice? Get all the help you can.

GABE
Father of Daniel, 10, and Joel, 7
My first thought when I got into the labor room was, "There's no way that baby is gonna fit through there!" I sure am glad I'm not a woman.

The labor was pretty exhausting. What I remember most is the hunger I felt. Deb went into labor at midnight and twenty hours later I still hadn't eaten. We got all psyched up for a natural childbirth and then they realized the baby was posterior and in distress, so Deb had to go off for a Cesarean. That was a little unexpected. And to be honest, I was afraid that something might go wrong.

When we brought the baby home, it didn't change our lives much. We still made it to restaurants and just put him under the table! The big change was that I used to be a surfer. Gone were the days of getting my board and heading out for an afternoon of waves. Taking a baby to the beach meant umbrellas and diaper bags, clothes . . . oh, you name it. The surfing had to go.

GRANT
Father of Alex, 3, and William, 3 days
Becoming a father is full of unexpected joys and spontaneous pleasures. Children make life simpler but richer. They bring less peace but greater fulfillment.

Accept all the advice you can handle, ask for help when you need it and don't overlook your wife.

JAMES
Father of Anna, 6 hours
The prenatal classes turned out to be a waste of time because we didn't do any of the stuff we'd practiced. Sarah didn't want to be walked or rocked or massaged.

It was frustrating when all the staff were saying, "Look— there's the head" and stuff like that. I couldn't see a thing because Sarah had me in a headlock. I felt like I was in a football scrimmage.

I was really surprised when Anna was born. She was covered in thick white goop, like glue. She looked like a long-distance swimmer getting out of the Channel.

Anyway, it was really exciting. Unbelievably emotional. I wouldn't have missed it for anything.

JAMIE
Superfather of twins Caleb and Daniel, 2, and twins Sam and Hannah, 8 months

When Annie started showing at five weeks, everyone started getting suspicious. She grew rapidly. When she had the ultrasound, it confirmed that we were having twins. We were really excited. My only fear was that there were more than two in there. I kept thinking, "There's one hiding, there's one hiding." But there wasn't.

The second time was different. I never, never thought for one moment that we would have twins again . . . I thought that it was statistically unlikely and I kept telling myself not to worry.

When I found out, I was in a state of shock. I was numb . . . like a zombie. Four kids in two-and-a-half years . . . I didn't know anybody who had lived through it. The next morning, though, I was fine.

It's such a fantastic moment when your child is born. You hold him up and look into his face for a moment and it's almost like you're holding a mirror. It's such a buzz when the nurses exclaim, "Doesn't he look like his dad!" To see yourself recreated like this is breathtaking, and it's something that makes being a dad so special.

For me, seeing myself in my kids and sharing so many experiences together, watching them grow and having the privilege of taking care of them, is what makes being a dad important.

Having four kids in the house . . . it's hard, but it's not overwhelming. Our babies have been really good, and it's pretty special holding a baby or two in each arm. It makes you feel . . . tall.

JEFFREY
Father of Nathaniel, 4, Tyler, 2, and The Bump, minus 7 months and counting; foster father of Dugald, 34, and Tyrone W. Dawg, 4
They say that nothing can prepare you for being a father. Well, babies don't come with a set of instructions like my software, but I actually think that everything in life prepares you for being a father.

Like, for example, the gridiron. You have your first child, and it's two on one. That's pretty easy. You have your second, and it's one on one. That's still manageable. After that, you get into zone defense plays. The kids know all the moves. Each parent handles one child each, but that still leaves one to wreak havoc. They work it all out beforehand.

Or science. Each kid is like a charged nuclear particle. Their behavior is dependent on how much space they have to move in, the ambient temperature, how fast they're traveling, how many collisions they have and how many other particles there are in the immediate vicinity. Then you introduce control rods—the parents. They absorb all the energy and prevent huge amounts of destruction.

Having a new baby in the house does change things. You miss the little spur-of-the-moment things, even like getting on your bikes and going for a ride. It's physically tiring, but not really exhausting. I mean, it's not too different from studying to get through college or staying out a lot. But it takes a truckload of mental energy. Babies demand your attention all the time. You can't just leave them to amuse themselves.

(My favorite age is four to seven months, which is when they're at what I call the *Self-Entertaining-Non-Mobile* stage. You can put a rattle in their hand and get to the fridge or bathroom for five minutes and you know they'll be where you left them when you get back.)

Being a dad is rewarding and humbling. It's helped me appreciate my own parents and put it all into perspective. You take your own parents for granted, but when you have kids, you realize how much time and effort it takes.

It's an incredible responsibility—molding a person. Scary, but exciting.

JIM
Father of Michelle, 3, and Madeleine, 7 months

Everyone has always heard stories about new fathers and how nothing can really prepare you for it. It makes you appreciate your own parents in a way you never thought you would. It makes you realize your own selfishness and it gives you a new sense of responsibility.

The birth itself is extremely stressful, mainly because you feel helpless. At the same time, the imminence of the birth itself is really exciting.

I remember a great relief when our baby was born. The pain for my wife was over and our baby had all the right bits and pieces. It is not an experience a woman should go through alone. My baby looked lovely . . . not like those ordinary ones that other people have. I mean that. If she were horrible, I'd admit it.

Nowadays, my life has totally changed. No longer do I have all the time to self-indulge the way I used to. There's no doubt I sometimes wish I could get more done, but the time with your kids is worth too much.

JOHN
Father of Angus, 19 months

A "hood" is a garment. Why this word is incorporated into the term "fatherhood" is inexplicable to me. There are no similarities between the state in which I find myself and any garment I have ever worn. Clothing is easily put on and easily removed at the whim of the wearer. Not so with fatherhood. It is not something you slip into casually. Once acquired, it is something so integral to your being that it can never be removed.

Whereas clothing is usually made to fit the wearer, you cannot alter the role of fatherhood to fit yourself. It comes as it comes and you have to adjust to it. It affects every aspect of your life: daily routines, sleeping habits, social life, finances—nothing escapes the influence of that bundle of joy.

It is something that can never be fully anticipated. All the information and advice in the world (no doubt all contained in Downey's weighty tome!) cannot prepare you for the extremes of emotion at the birth, the mind-numbing exhaustion as you set off for work after a week of sleepless nights spent having your ears assaulted by the screams of a baby for whom you don't know what to do, and the myriad other experiences that await you on the other side.

So what does fatherhood have going for it?

Nothing can prepare you for what is in store when that little face lights up with a smile. The pleasure of fatherhood is so deep and so lasting that it easily surpasses the short-lived pleasure experienced during the baby's creation.

JOHN
Father of David, 5 months

I always thought that when the time came, I would be Superdad and that it would all come naturally to me. It didn't take me long to realize that fathering takes a whole lot of work, frustration, self-sacrifice and humility. It's turned my life upside-down, but I wouldn't give it up for anything.

I've done lots of things in my life that have given me satisfaction and a buzz. Being a dad, however, has been better. It's given me a sense of completeness as a person.

MALCOLM
Father of Rebecca, 2, and Joshua, 7 months

Let me warn you. To go anywhere with kids involves a car-load of strollers, playpens, highchairs, changes of cool clothes, changes of warm clothes, sunhats, toys and books. You're going to need a bigger car.

Suddenly your house doesn't seem so big or so clean.

To go anywhere without your kids involves cajoling, persuading and begging friends, family or baby-sitters. You find yourself staying home a lot.

And I didn't used to consider getting up at 6:30 A.M. "sleeping in," either.

But nothing prepared me for my daughter's declaration of, "I love you, Daddy," or the beaming grin that erupts over the face of my son when I walk through the door at night.

MARK
Father of Laura, 3, and Katie, 21 months
(Mark is actually overseas at the moment, but I know he wouldn't want to be left out so I wrote something for him in his own biting and largely sarcastic tone of voice—P.D.)
Fatherhood . . . ah, who wouldn't want to be a father? It's wrecked my life but who's counting? It's great. Wonderful stuff. No, really. I have the best kids in the world. I enjoy being their dad. I love the smell of diapers in the morning.

MARK
Father of Adam, 9, and Matthew, 4
Was it really this hard for my dad?

MATTHEW
Father of Jordan, 1 week
Look, I'm not particularly fazed about it all. It's been done a million times before. And if everybody else on the planet can do it, we can too.

I don't want our lives to be dictated by the baby. If we go out to dinner, we'll put the baby in his car seat and take him with us. Maybe I'm naïve. I don't know. I mean, I know we'll spend more time at home, but I don't want to get locked away like in a fortress or something.

We've been stashing money so Tracey can take time off work, and then I'll take my leave and we'll swap the care-taking.

That'll give me about three months solid at home. What a great opportunity!

OWEN
Father of Sophie, 2, and Rosanna, 2 months
The worst thing I could imagine about having a baby was not getting enough sleep. So to prepare ourselves for the worst, we fully expected to have what is referred to in baby-rearing circles as "a screamer." I'm not sure if it's possible to store up sleep for a later date, but I calculated that by the time Sophie arrived we could have gone without sleeping in for about six months.

Strangely, our new arrival had no trouble sleeping through the night—sometimes for more than twelve hours straight. We kept tip-toeing into her room to hold a mirror up to her nose to see if she was still breathing. I think we learned that trick off *Murder, She Wrote*.

The moral of the story is sleep in a lot before the baby comes and *don't* expect a sleeping angel.

When Rosie came along, I suspected it might not be too much more work. It's more like tag-team parenting now. One stops, the other one starts. The babies seem to know. In a way it's twice the work, but it's certainly twice the fun.

PHIL
Father of Samuel, 5 Laura, 3, and Cameron, 6 weeks
The births have been the most amazing experiences. Just being there has been incredible. We went to a birth center, where the father plays an important role. I was helping with hot packs, massages, showers, gentle rocking . . . you know, just being there.

When each of my kids was born, I bawled my eyes out. It's just so miraculous and exciting. You finally see and hold your new baby.

I think it's gotten easier the more kids we've had. The first was kind of a shock to our domestic sphere but then all the baby stuff—crying, diapers, interrupted sleep—became the norm. The third one's really easy.

I love being a family man and watching my kids grow up.

RAY
Father of Lachlan, 2

Parenthood messes up your life —*Ray*

   No it doesn't —*Ray's wife*

   Actually, it's parents who mess up your life —*Ray's son*

   I could have done without the competition —*Ray's cat*

   My life is now complete —*Ray's mother-in-law*

   It's the only worthwhile thing he's ever done in his life
      —*Ray's mother*

   No comment —*Ray's father*

   He should spend more time on his golf swing
      —*Ray's father-in-law*

Seriously, before my wife and I stopped using contraception, we asked a few friends what it was like to be parents. The thing they emphasized was that unless you really, really, really, really, really, really want children, you shouldn't have them. This was an understatement.

So if you're about to be a father, there's a hell of a lot of stuff I could tell you to make it easier. But I'm not going to. You can find out yourself. But I'll tell you this: Every fear you have is worse than you expect, and every hope is better.

SANDY
Father of The Unborn, minus 6 months and counting

Pascale brought home a home pregnancy kit just to stir me up. She'd just come off the pill so it was kind of a joke.

The smile was wiped off our faces when the little strip turned purple. We just sat there and stared at it, waiting for it to fade. It didn't.

The next morning she got up and checked it. Still purple. In fact it's been several weeks now, and the damn thing's still purple. We check it every morning. Every morning it's still purple.

It's slowly starting to dawn on us what this little purple strip means. It's hard to come to terms with. It just "happened." The funny thing is, I don't feel like I'm a "parent." I'm just a normal guy.

SIMON
Just married
Look, Pete, I know I'm not a dad yet but I'm trying really hard, honest! Give us a few years and we'll be right into this parenting thing. Can't I be in your book, please? You put Mal and Sandy in.

SIMON
Father of Christina, 6 months
One of the best things about being a dad is crashing in the living room on a Sunday afternoon with my daughter and watching football together. She is such an enthusiastic spectator; eyes wide, arms flapping and legs kicking. She doesn't care who wins, as long as they wear a red uniform. Just by being there, my daughter turns an ordinary event into a special one.

What does concern me, however, is how she is in 'the habit of calling out "Daddaddadda" to every player on the field.

WAYNE
Father of Brittainy, 18 months
Look, Pete, I was going to try to have it ready by tonight but I'm too damned busy being a father. Hey . . . why don't you just print that?

Resources

You can contact my virtual self at: ozdad@ozemail.com.au. I'll try to reply. No promises, though, because I'm not really sure what buttons to press and I keep erasing things. Also check out my website: www.ozemail.com.au/~ozdad.

Child Care Aware
800-424-2246

Couple to Couple League
P.O. Box 11184
Cincinnati, OH 45211
513-471-2000

Doulas of North America (DONA)
1100 23rd Avenue E.
Seattle, WA 98112
206-324-5440

Family Resource Coalition
200 S. Michigan Ave.
16th Floor
Chicago, IL 60604
312-341-0900

Family Service Canada
600-220 Laurier Ave.
West Ottawa, ON K1P 5Z9
613-230-9960

Fatherhood Project
c/o Families and Work Institute
330 7th Ave., 14th Floor
New York, NY 10001
212-465-2044

International Cesarean
Awareness Network
1304 Kingsdale Ave.
Redondo Beach, CA 90278
310-542-6400

International Childbirth Education
Association, Inc.
P.O. Box 20048
Minneapolis, MN 55420
Tel: 612-854-8660
Fax: 612-854-8772
Website: www.icea.org/

La Leche League International
1400 N. Meacham Rd.
Schaumberg, IL 60173
Tel: 800-LA-LECHE or 847-519-7730
Fax: 847-519-0035
Website: www.lalecheleague.org

Ligue La Leche
CP874 St. Laurent
Quebec H4L 4W3
514-327-6714

New Mothers Resource Group
c/o Anne Fownes
Box 1271
Liverpool, Nova Scotia B0T 1K0
902-354-2479

Pacific Postpartum Support Society
#104-1416 Commercial Dr.
Vancouver, BC V5L 3X9
604-255-7999

Postpartum Education for Parents
(PEP)
P.O. Box 6154
Santa Barbara, CA 93160

Index

Navigating through a Strange Land

A Book for Brain Tumor Patients and Their Families

Second Edition

Edited by Tricia Ann Roloff

Fairview Press, Minneapolis

Published by Fairview Press, a division of Fairview Health Services,
2450 Riverside Avenue, Minneapolis, Minnesota 55454.

Library of Congress Cataloging-in-Publication Data
Navigating through a strange land : a book for brain tumor patients and their
families / edited by Tricia Ann Roloff.--2nd ed.
    p. cm.
  Includes bibliographical references and index.
  ISBN 1-57749-108-4 (pbk. : alk. paper)
    1. Brain--Tumors--Popular works. 2. Brain--Tumors--Patients--
Biography. I. Roloff, Tricia Ann, 1958-

  RC280.B7 N38 2001
  362.1'9699481--dc   2001040728

First edition published by Indigo Press, copyright © 1995 Tricia Ann Roloff.

Acknowledgment for previously published work on page 153.

First printing of second edition: November 2001
Printed in Canada
04 03 02 01   6 5 4 3 2 1

Cover design by Laurie Ingram Duren
Interior by Corey Sevett

Medical Disclaimer
This publication is designed to provide accurate and authoritative information
in regard to the subject matter covered. It is sold with the understanding that
the publisher is not engaged in the provision or practice of medical, nursing, or
professional healthcare advice or services in any jurisdiction. If medical advice
or other professional assistance is required, the services of a qualified and competent professional should be sought. Fairview Press is not responsible or liable,
directly or indirectly, for any form of damages whatsoever resulting from the use
(or misuse) of information contained in or implied by these documents.

For a free current catalog of Fairview Press titles, call toll-free 1-800-544-8207.
Or visit our Web site at www.fairviewpress.org.

NAVIGATING THROUGH A STRANGE LAND

This book is dedicated to the authors who made it happen. They gave their time and dedication without compensation to help others, and that is the most noble of all gifts.

Creative people do not try to run from their feelings of non-being, but by encountering and wrestling it, force it to produce being. They knock on silence for an answer, they pursue meaninglessness until they can force it to mean.

— Rollo May, from *The Courage to Create*

Table of Contents

Foreword

At some time in our lives, most of us face a medical challenge either personally or while supporting a loved one. We manage these challenges the best way that we can. We try to understand and make sense of what is happening. We try to work with our healthcare providers for the best possible results. During this time, the most helpful support often comes from a personal story or experience shared by someone who has lived through a similar challenge. The opportunity to learn from other people is invaluable.

Ms. Roloff has gathered a range of individual experiences with brain tumors – from people who face this diagnosis, family members who have provided support, and professional caregivers who work with brain tumor patients. These personal stories are not intended to show a "right" or "wrong" way to manage living with a brain tumor. In fact, it is reassuring that no two stories are exactly the same. The stories convey individual experience and the shared universal concerns – personal fears, small victories, and the disappointments and uncertainties of living with a brain tumor.

The stories include both benign and malignant diagnoses, first-person accounts of treatment and recovery, reflections on experimentation with alternative therapies, and what steps people took to participate in their own healthcare decisions. Also included are the perspectives of family members on the death of parents and children, and the advice and observations of healthcare professionals.

In addition, Ms. Roloff provides practical information to assist in the understanding of brain tumors. She asks people to be more assertive about their wants and needs in the delivery of their healthcare. She describes coping techniques, advice for financial and legal planning, and a generous resources section (organizations, books, pamphlets, support groups, and professional contacts).

With the wisdom, dignity, and knowledge of shared experiences, this book can help empower anyone facing the challenge of a brain tumor.

STACY COSGROVE, MLIS
Institute for Health and Healing Library of the
California Pacific Medical Center of San Francisco

Preface to the First Edition

Months after having surgery in 1984, I came upon a small eight-page booklet (no longer in print) that described in a few paragraphs pituitary tumors and common problems associated with them. I found that booklet very comforting; I clung to it, in fact, for several months, until I could come to grips with my own struggle with a pituitary tumor.

I believe that people do rebound from most difficult situations, given time. However, this time period varies for person to person. And it seems there are natural recurrences of what I call "reflective grief" throughout a person's lifetime.

From 1987 to 1989, I worked as editor for the National Brain Tumor Foundation and helped publish their newsletter. This book is somewhat an extension of what we did there: highlighting people's experiences. At the same time I was hired by the University of California, San Francisco, and worked for seven years in an administrative position in a research lab.

I worked on many scientific manuscripts. Research is a slow process, and it takes many, many years to understand the results and develop treatments for illnesses. Because research is so slow in getting answers, it's even more important that there be emotional support for people.

I have always believed that truth can only be expressed as a result of personal experience. Therefore, I made it my goal to put together a reference book that reflected the experiences surrounding a brain tumor diagnosis. I believe I have accomplished what I set out to do: I have given you stories of triumph, stories of death, stories of pain, and stories of gratitude. There were no great heroics, only day-to-day realities.

Preface to the Second Edition

Welcome to the second edition of *Navigating through a Strange Land*. With the help of Fairview Press, this popular book will continue to be available. As many of you know, I was able to keep the first edition in print for over six years under my own label, Indigo Press. It's been a lot of work but incredibly rewarding. I am indebted to the many nurses and doctors all over the country who have supported this book from the very beginning and who have helped keep it alive.

We have not changed the format of the book. We have kept the original stories, added some new stories, and updated the resources. I have appreciated all the comments I have received over the years from patients, family members, and professionals. They have affirmed my belief in the purpose of this book: to help people process a very uncertain and frightening time in their lives. Many have said that the original stories were instrumental in their understanding of brain tumors.

Several people who wrote for the first edition have died. I have kept these stories as reminders of their courage. Those who have passed away include Chris de Jong, who was studying at the University of Oklahoma, and Kristin Randolph, who was an inspiration to many people with her incredibly positive attitude about life. Also, Harry Smith's wife passed away several years ago. Harry cared for her for over twenty years while she lived in a nursing home. That is love, and Harry's story has moved me to tears every time I've read it.

Harry's essay reminds me of a comment made by Rabbi Harold Kushner, author of *When Bad Things Happen to Good People*. At a neurological surgeons meeting in Baltimore, he said, "Maybe it is not in the asking of 'Why me?' but in noticing the incredible compassion that others can show in times of need. That is the blessing."

Again, I thank all those who have helped me and this book in the past six years. I've enjoyed talking and working with each and every one of you. I hope you enjoy this expanded edition.

TRICIA ROLOFF

Acknowledgments

There are many people whom I wish to thank. First and foremost, I thank Sharon Lamb, RN, for her unswerving support of all my efforts over the years. Her work and genuine concern are an inspiration to all who know her. Thanks to Dr. Maribell Leavitt, whom I met at the beginning of this project, for his positive influence; and to Dr. Charles Wilson for his initial interest in this publication, which gave me the confidence to pursue it.

Many thanks to Kris Simonsen, who was the initial inspiration for this book. It was her idea to publish a book to help other pituitary patients, since we both had experienced this illness and there was no literature dealing with it. Over time, the book expanded to include all types of brain tumor experiences.

Thanks to the staff at the University of California, San Francisco, for their encouragement and advice. Special thanks to my former colleagues Charlene Bayles, Debra Jan Bibel, and Jane Leong.

Many thanks to my sister Sue and my friend Lisa Peterson, who told me I had to finish this project when I felt like quitting.

Thanks to Jeff Fink, for his love, and for critiquing and editing various sections of the book.

Heartfelt thanks to Dr. Robert West of International Scholars Publications for his invaluable publishing assistance.

I acknowledge with great appreciation all the people at Dickson Street Book Exchange for their humorous conversations and much needed business services, and the gang at the Fayetteville Public Library, in particular Susie and Ann.

I would like to thank the principals and workers from all the brain tumor foundations across the country, in particular Janice, Rob, Naomi, Larry, Roberta, Sheryl, Gillian, Rebecca, and Samantha. We have traveled this path together for a long time, and I cherish our friendship.

Special thanks to Gute.

And, thank you, of course, to my parents, whose love sustains me.

Introduction

SOMETHING IS JUST NOT RIGHT

For a time, you will be traveling through a land that is foreign to you. Many have been there before you, although their landscape will look a little different from yours. May this book help familiarize you with the terrain.

Dealing with the diagnosis of a brain tumor is tough. It is not like a broken arm, or another part of the body that one can look at and say, "Okay, just five weeks and we'll be back to new, maybe even a little stronger." It is more like a heart attack, where a person feels that a part of his or her very being has been disturbed – the part that pumps life, that hurts when things feel bad, that breaks when a love affair ends.

With an illness in the brain, we fear our very mind will start slipping away. Depending on where the tumor is located, areas that control motor function, memory, orientation, balance, coordination, speech, sight, and chemistry can easily be affected, either temporarily or permanently. This makes the diagnosis particularly scary: it is sound intellectual function that allows us to do our jobs, raise our families, and create our own special lives.

NOT ONE DISEASE, BUT MANY

There are over 120 types of brain tumors. This presents researchers and physicians with a difficult task in finding the cause(s) and in determining the treatment(s).

According to the Brain Tumor Registry of the United States report 1992–1997, every year approximately 185,000 people in the United States and 10,000 people in Canada will be diagnosed with a primary (originating in the brain) or metastatic (traveling to the brain from another part of the body) brain tumor. Metastatic tumors are the most common, occurring in 20 to 40 percent of all cancer cases.

Brain tumors are the leading cause of cancer death in children under age twenty, and the third leading cause of cancer death in young adults ages twenty to thirty-nine. Diagnoses of brain tumors in people sixty-five years and older has also risen dramatically.

Some tumors are termed "noncancerous" or "benign," for example, meningiomas and pituitary tumors. These are generally slow growing and are often noticed only when they affect a part of the brain that controls eyesight, coordination, hormones, or other functions. "Slow growing" and "benign" are considered by some to be misnomers, since all tumors within the brain are potentially life-threatening if left untreated.

Some tumors start growing in adulthood; others, like craniopharyngioma, medulablastoma, and brain stem gliomas, often start in childhood.

MOVE OVER, I'M A BRAIN TUMOR!

Brain tumors are generally described as "cancer," which means that the cells keep dividing and multiplying instead of stopping at a certain point. The cranium, or brain box, is designed to hold only the brain, and there is very little space for expansion. Therefore, a tumor pushes against and into vital structures within the different lobes, or sections, of the brain.

Different parts of the brain affect different functions of the body. The frontal lobe, for example, affects memory. The hypothalamus controls mood. Because the brain controls thoughts and behavior, a tumor can cause disruption in either of these areas. That is why, when a patient gets angry, depressed, or violent, it may be due to physical placement of the tumor.

Brain tumors are unique. Although classified as "cancer," they are really a neurological problem; they affect the body neurologically or, in the case of pituitary tumors, hormonally. Based on the location of the tumor, we can predict what functions it may affect.

What causes cancer? Is it genetic or environmental in origin? Philosophically, is cancer a manifestation of an ill society? Metaphysically, is it our deepest, personal conflicts expressed in a physical form? There is no evidence indicating any particular cause for brain tumors. For now, "Why do I have a brain tumor?" is not medically answerable.

No Rhyme or Reason

Some brain tumors are removed surgically or controlled by medication. Others go into remission for long periods of time after treatment and then return for no apparent reason. Some people live for many years with no lingering problems, while others need to adjust their routines to accommodate new conditions. Some people die, even when things seem to be going well. There seems to be no reliable way to predict the course of a brain tumor or its outcome. In a way, this unpredictability is good news; it allows each person a chance at survival, even if statistics say otherwise.

Current treatments for brain tumors depend on the type of tumor and the degree of operability. Treatments include surgery, chemotherapy (drug therapy), radiation, or a combination. If the "tentacles" of a tumor have spread into vital structures, removal of the entire tumor may not be possible, as this would pose a risk of impairing essential body functions. In that case, radiation or chemotherapy is recommended. Even if the entire tumor is excised, a few cells may remain. These may metastasize, or move to surrounding healthy tissue. Therefore, a combination of treatments is recommended.

The newest treatment is the Gamma Knife, a technique that uses magnetic resonance (MR) and computer tomography (CT) guidance to map the exact location of the tumor and shrink the tumor with radiation. This technique is less invasive than surgery and has proved successful in certain cases. It is used mainly on small tumors. Because it destroys normal tissue, it cannot be used on larger areas in the brain.

Dealing with Professionals

Unless it is an emergency, it is important to get several medical opinions after the initial diagnosis, and to investigate all treatment options. This is your right. Your first loyalty is to yourself, not to one particular physician or institution. When selecting a physician, consider level of experience and area of specialization. Most neurosurgeons specialize in a certain tumor type or area in the brain. Get referrals: ask respected physicians whom they would seek if they had a brain tumor.

While many doctors may be in private practice, some also work in large university settings where they can do research. Large hospitals are more bureaucratic and may be less personal than other medical centers; many people understandably feel lost in such a setting. Therefore, when dealing with a large hospital, it is important to select someone who will coordinate events during the hospital stay. A nurse or social worker can help you out-line and understand the course of treatment, care, and rehabilitation. This arrangement would allow you to make essential decisions while leaving the coordination to someone else, thereby alleviating unnecessary anxiety.

This is also a good time to organize your finances. A health insurance agent and the hospital financial planning office can help you determine your financial obligations for treatment. A comprehensive financial or estate plan is also important. An estate plan consists mainly of a will or a living trust and the following documents: healthcare power of attorney, financial power of attor-ney, nomination of conservator, letter of instruction, pour-over will with a living trust, and property agreement.

Although initially uncomfortable, taking care of these matters usually makes people feel more at peace; it is one less thing to worry about. One estate attor-ney speculated that the reason people do not plan is because they are afraid to face all their unrealized dreams. He commented, "What people don't real-ize is that we all only have time for so many things in life, so all our dreams get trickled down through a funnel into which only a few things can pass. And that's okay."

WHO CAN HELP?

> NEUROSCIENCE CLINIC STAFF AND NURSES

There are several people who can help during the hospital stay and afterward. A patient and compassionate physician can address concerns about the illness and the emotional turmoil experienced during treatment. Not all physicians, however, can devote themselves to the emotional needs of patients, and sometimes this has to be accepted. But that does not mean that there is no one to help you. A caring nurse can be one of your greatest assets while going through the medical system. Nurses have a lot of knowledge and experience. They will often take the time to talk with patients and guide them if the physician is unavailable. Many patients feel that a particular nurse or staff member is their sole anchor in the stormy seas of diagnosis and treatment.

For example, Peter Farbach of Washington, D.C., was treated for a brain tumor. It was his first experience in any hospital. He writes: "When I was struggling to save my identity and self-esteem in the spiritual darkness of that alien medical world, [my nurse practitioner] brought me a window of light and hope, by treating me one-on-one as a person, rather than just another chart-with-symptoms patient in a dressed-in-white bureaucracy. Though not a surgical nurse herself, she stayed in the operating room during all four of my craniotomies. I cherish and respect her selfless way in helping me and other people with brain tumors."

> SOCIAL WORKERS

Social workers are another valuable resource. Most hospitals have clinical social workers on staff. Many train as general social workers. Depending on the size and staffing of the hospital, there may be some who specialize in neuro-oncology. Clinical social workers can be a tremendous resource, as they are exposed daily to the needs of patients. They understand disability issues, vocational and rehabilitation training, and the network of social services provided by cities and counties. They should be consulted if available.

> CHAPLAINS

Hospitals also have chaplains. They can help patients and their caregivers deal with the emotions and strains that illness generates. A chaplain may be able to refer you to books, pamphlets, and other supportive resources. For example, *Living through Personal Crisis*, by Ann Kaiser Sterns, a hospital chaplain, is one of the best books on loss and recovery.

> THERAPISTS

After the initial treatment, psychologists and other therapists can have enormous value. In particular, a neuropsychologist and a family counselor can be extremely helpful during recovery.

A neuropsychologist defines neurological functioning, deficits, and strengths. Tests are given to determine whether or not symptoms, such as memory problems, are caused by the brain tumor. This evaluation identifies those skills that have been preserved, those that have not, and those that can be redeveloped in rehabilitation. Besides assessing various skills to determine the course of rehabilitation, a neuropsychologist can provide the written documentation required for a disability claim.

Marriage and family counselors (MFCC) are trained therapists who focus on interpersonal relationships. These therapists understand how individuals in the family interact and relate to one another. Families are bound as unified systems. Just as the moon affects the tide, what affects one family member will affect the entire family, changing the way members interact. Families are usually unprepared to handle the psychological aspects of a loved one's illness, and many hurt feelings can arise out of misunderstandings that may occur. In such a situation, it is imperative that the family seeks outside help.

How can I develop good coping strategies? How can I help my family understand me? Why do I feel depressed? Is there something I can do about it? A good therapist helps people to work through these issues, individually or with the family.

Don't Be Afraid to Be Choosy

There are many types of therapists: psychotherapists, psychoanalysts, counselors, art therapists, and so on. Titles from prestigious institutions are not necessary here; what is necessary is someone who makes you feel important and supported so that you can work on the issues that brought you to therapy. A "standard routine" approach to all problems can be damaging. Likewise, a cold and judgmental attitude is unhelpful. A brain tumor is not just any problem, and patients deserve someone who is truly there for them. Ask for referrals from friends. A good therapist can be a lifesaver, and a life changer. Also, therapy does not have to be a lifelong process. Short-term therapy, directed at a specific concern, is often all that is needed.

Your Friends and Fellow Brain Tumor Patients

Last, but most important, friends and others who have been down the road before you can be your greatest source of strength. Many people who go to a support group find that they instantly bond with others who are in the same situation: the usual barriers to communication are absent, and an open and honest dialogue is immediately established. Frustrations and triumphs are central to support group discussions. Many friendships begin at these meetings because people can be themselves, share ideas, and find humor in their predicament.

Some people are more reserved than others and prefer to handle the situation on their own, while others try a support group but do not find any benefit in it. Like everything else, these meetings are not for everyone; however, there are two instances where support groups can really help.

The first is during the acute stage of the illness, right after diagnosis or treatment. A group run by a professional can help to answer many medical questions. It can also give you an opportunity to meet people who have made it through. After the initial trauma period, other methods may work better for you, including individual therapy, in which you can get help without sacrificing privacy, or a phone conversation with a patient-volunteer.

The second situation in which a support group can help is if you have no primary support person – a spouse, partner, relative, or friend – close by. Doing everything on your own will be overwhelming and stressful. If you have a good relationship with someone who is emotionally available and can help with your day-to-day needs, this will take a great burden off of you. Remember, however, that being a caretaker is difficult if it extends for a long period of time. It is important to evaluate how much you can realistically expect of any one person, regardless of love. Over the long haul, family and friends will help hold you together, but be aware that professionals can help you, too.

In preparing this book, I wanted to offer hope to those who have been diagnosed with this disease, as there is still a belief that anyone diagnosed with a brain tumor is going to die. This is simply not true. I know this through my own experience, and through my work with the National Brain Tumor Foundation. In fact, every person I talked with during the writing of this book has known someone with a brain tumor. It is much more common than we think. As with every disease, some people will die. But there are many people who survive and live productive lives in spite of their brain tumor experience.

At the same time, even those who survive will experience some problems. Along with the difficult search for the "best treatment," there are psychological and physical changes that can occur because of the tumor. These are mainly related to changes in mental function or the emotional dilemmas faced by patients and their families. Mental changes are a little easier to determine, given the testing strategies that are available. Emotional dilemmas, ranging from denial of the disease to difficulty coping, are harder to identify. The personal stories that make up this book represent a realistic range of experiences and issues faced by brain tumor patients. You will see how very differently each person is affected.

Navigating through a Strange Land is meant to address the psychological issues that accompany a brain tumor diagnosis; however, you will have many questions and needs that are beyond the scope of this book. Accessing the appropriate information is the first step in dealing with the many issues you will face. There are numerous foundations and associations in the United States and Canada that can provide information on support groups, treatments, physician referrals, and more. Many of these associations are included on pages 137 through 148 in the resources section.

The intent of this book is to cover common areas of concern, to share examples of how others have dealt with their diagnosis and recovery, and to acknowledge the struggle you are going through. The following stories are divided into three sections: Part 1 is patient stories, Part 2 is family stories, and Part 3 is professional caregivers' perspectives.

Essays by Patients

BY KRISTIN RANDOLPH

Surround Yourself with Those You Love

Kristin Randolph was born in Chicago, Illinois. Before her illness, she worked as a full-time mental health counselor and part-time therapeutic masseuse. She enjoyed swimming, hiking, dancing, shopping, going out for lunch, reading, and hanging out with her family and friends. In 1993, Kris had surgery for a glioblastoma grade IV. She died several years after this story was written.

In late 1991, I began to have some problems: frequent headaches that no pain reliever could alleviate, strange bodily experiences that felt like energy rushing through my body and out from the top of my head. By February of 1992, the headaches were so severe that I would feel nauseated, and at times I was unable to remain upright. I was unable to focus visually and would see blotches instead.

The first time I went to my regular physician, I was told that I was having "tension headaches." My doctor prescribed exercise but agreed to do some tests to see if there was any medical cause. I called in March and was told that all of my tests were normal and that I was fine. At the beginning of April, I saw another physician, who referred me to a psychiatrist and prescribed pain medication. My boyfriend had become increasingly worried, and when I became disoriented, he convinced me to go to the hospital. After having a CAT scan, I was admitted on May 9 with a "large mass" in my brain. Within thirty-six hours, I had gone into a coma and needed emergency surgery.

The diagnosis was glioblastoma multiforme, grade IV. The tumor was the size of a lemon, located in my right frontal lobe crossing the midline. After surgery, which was a subtotal resection, I was referred to a medical center and agreed to take part in a clinical study. The treatment was aggressive: I had radiation twice daily for four-and-a-half weeks.

I do not remember the week preceding surgery or the few days following it. What I first remember is my boyfriend sitting next to me, holding an ice pack to my head for eight hours at a stretch. My mom and step-dad had come from Des Moines, and my sister had arrived from San Diego. I was disoriented; I could not tell where my family had come from. They stayed in my apartment during the two weeks of my hospitalization. They would visit me for eight hours every day. My mom brought me fruit salads because I refused to eat the tofu enchilada that arrived twice every day. My friends came after work and during work, even after my transfer to another hospital forty-five minutes away.

My family provided a positive and supportive atmosphere for me to recover in. When the social worker from the hospital told my family and best friend that I would never be the same and that I would be unable to drive or live alone, they did not relay the news to me. Fortunately for me, I think, for I kept getting better. My mother stayed with me in my studio apartment for four months following surgery, leaving her own life in Des Moines. She was my prime support, social worker, and good buddy. We had fun together, and I couldn't have done it without her.

I spent my days reading the books that my sister, friends, and friends of my family had brought for me. I worked hard to stay positive. I would visualize the tumor being swept away or eaten by animals. Therefore, I fully expected the tumor to be completely gone by the end of treatment. In August, I was shocked when I learned from my oncologist that this tumor usually recurs and that people die from it. I changed oncologists.

After the initial shock, activity kept me from thinking about the prognosis. My major fear was that others would not be able to go on without me.

Immediately following the treatment, my MRI results surprised all my doctors: the tumor had shrunk considerably. It looked even better a couple of months later. I had scans every two months for the first year. After that, an MRI was scheduled every three months. So far, there has been no growth and I am in remission. As a requirement of the clinical study protocol, the researchers at the medical center will monitor my progress for ten years.

Certain factors have played an important role in my recovery: my positive attitude and that of those around me, laughter, lots of love from so many people, prayers from people all around the world, and good medical treatment. Even on the bad days, like the one when I lost hair after radiation, Mom and I maintained a sense of humor. I am so thankful to have had the whole summer with my mother.

I had read about people who declared that they were thankful for their diseases. I had dismissed them as crazy. Eight months later, I am one of them! My life has changed dramatically, but I love every day of my life, even the hard ones. I appreciate the richness of my emotions. I feel more passionate about things, about making each day precious. I believe that this zest to embrace life has brought me closer to my family and friends. I have met other long-term survivors, and found our meetings inspirational.

For those facing a similar diagnosis, I would say to surround yourself with those you love. Get involved in support groups. Read books by positive thinkers, like Bernie Siegel. Practice visualization techniques; drawing the picture first can be helpful. Go easy on yourself; expect it to take some time for the effects to lessen. Explore alternative treatments as an adjunct to Western medicine. Keep asking your doctors when you know something is happening to you; they are not inside of your body. Talk about your fears; other people have them too. Do not let anyone tell you how long you have to live. They can only recite statistics.

BY GREGORY RAVER-LAMPMAN

Excerpts from Magic and Loss

Gregory Raver-Lampman is an award-winning journalist who wrote for newspapers and magazines for several years. He has traveled extensively both in the United States and abroad. When faced with the potentially fatal diagnosis of a low-grade astrocytoma, he began to write a series of letters to his three-year-old daughter, Emmy, which are excerpted below. He now lives in Norfolk, Virginia, with his family, and is working on a new novel, White Tribes.

Dear Emmy,

About two weeks ago I suffered a seizure and headed to DePaul Hospital nearby, where doctors discovered I had a brain tumor.

A neurosurgeon checked me into DePaul and removed the tumor. He believes it's benign. But he, and others, made it clear the tumor will most likely grow back. Maybe in six months, maybe in one year, maybe in ten — but at *some* point it will probably kill me. . . .

At times, fear and sorrow overwhelm me. Other times, confidence overwhelms me. I picture you and me twenty years from now huddling together, reading from these letters and laughing. Still, I write these letters with the understanding that that may never happen. These letters I write to you, Emmy, so you'll never forget your daddy and his undying love.

. . .

In the last few days you've found it punishing to be with me, hour after hour, as I lie in pain on the couch, so Mommy made arrangements for you to spend the day with friends. When you left this morning, I felt a pang of regret as I watched you drive away, looking out the window of someone else's car, waving goodbye.

In the last few days, I haven't been an especially good father, or husband, or patient. I read and re-read the medical articles I've gathered hoping to find some *answer*, some secret cure that doctors overlooked. Most were discouraging. Even worse, they contradicted each other. One study hailed a new kind of chemotherapy. Another study shot holes in the findings. . . . Some patients had inoperable tumors deep in the brain. Some, like me, had tumors that seemed entirely removed. . . . Some patients were old. Some were my age. . . .

Disease, in some ways, is universal. In other ways, it's extraordinarily personal. Disease has a way of becoming entangled with *life*. With plans and aspirations, attitude and will. . . .

Mommy and I really haven't talked much. Not *really*. We've talked about radiation and research. We've both read Medical Miracle books. Yet the research and these books seemed to distract us from our real fears, from our real sorrow, even from our real love and hopes.

This morning, as I sat on the couch, the books and articles that had me transfixed suddenly seemed irrelevant, useless, distracting. What does it matter what statistics say? What comfort can I take in them? Soon I'll become Patient X on somebody's chart. Where on the chart? I don't know.

Mommy came to the couch and sat next to me. She took my hands. We looked into each other's eyes. For several long moments, Mommy didn't speak. I knew we hadn't talked because we were scared to hear what was on the other's mind.

As Mommy sat looking at me, I saw the eyes I remember from so many years ago, in California, Greece, and Mexico, beautiful light-brown eyes flecked with yellow. Mommy's eyes glistened.

"I love you *so* much," Mommy told me.

"I love you, too," I said. Tears welled up in her eyes.

I tried to pretend I didn't know what she was thinking. "What's wrong?" I asked.

Mommy tried to keep from breaking down. "I don't want to be left *alone*," Mommy told me. "Please don't leave me alone."

It was like a knife to my heart. Mommy leaned over. I wrapped my arms around her. I ached to tell Mommy she never *would* be alone. But I knew I couldn't promise that. I couldn't promise anything.

· · ·

In our years together, your mommy and I have traveled over a good part of the world. . . . For me, these trips weren't part of a story I was writing. They were *adventure*. They were *life*.

That's what makes me feel so bad right now. This brain tumor is a big deal. But you have to know – this isn't me. This is something that *happened* to me, something threatening to destroy the person I was before.

I have a friend who lost the use of his legs and right arm when he was about thirty-five years old. Today, he gets around in a wheelchair. He once told me the toughest adjustment was growing accustomed to the fact that people never see him as he sees himself. They don't see the life that he lived for so many years, in which he was strong and healthy and athletic. They only see a man in a wheelchair.

He told me that when he dreams he walks and runs. Then, he wakes up in bed with his paralyzed legs, wishing that, for just one moment, he could *be* that man in the dreams, and wishing that somebody else could at least *picture* him running.

Today I wonder – will you be able to see through my illness, through all this trauma, through death even, to see the person who still lives in *my* dreams?

· · ·

Lately, I've felt a lot of anger. . . . In the books and articles my friends gave me, anger is often lauded, encouraged. Patients direct anger at doctors and hospitals and medical personnel. Theirs is an anger born of the sense that, with the right medical care, the right doctors, the right nurses, the right medical gadgets, we can escape suffering, can escape this defining characteristic of the human condition, our mortality.

It's easy to blame doctors. They are trained in the science of fixing the body. As such, they sometimes view the body as a machine. . . . The truth is, my doctor, my hospital, all those nurses and technicians – whatever their shortcomings, real or imagined – saved my life. Without them, I wouldn't be alive.

No, my anger digs deeper. It is born of fear. Fear of dying. Fear of suffering. Fear of separation. Fear of abandoning loved ones. Fear of being forgotten. Fear of having squandered this, my only life.

I'm not sure why this confrontation with mortality has shaken me so badly. I've always known death lay in store for all of us. When I lived in South America, that seemed especially obvious. . . . Death was undeniable, woven into the fabric of life.

When I got back to the States, I noticed how death seemed sequestered, disguised, tucked away. Cemeteries here look like parks. Funeral homes seem stately mansions. Public mourning is frowned upon. . . .

Mortality, thrust upon us, forces us to question everything we value, expensive suits, good jobs, nice cars, power, prestige, fame – writing. I remember one of my uncles who swore he didn't want to live if he were so ill that he couldn't snow ski. Yet, when he came down with liver cancer, he clung to life for all he was worth.

For me, that's been part of the trauma. In my life, what endures? What matters? What still seems important? . . . It frightens me that I may come out of treatment unable to write or think. I sometimes wonder whether my surgery has already caused damage when they scooped out some of my brain during surgery. But today, that issue doesn't seem as monumental as I might have expected.

All that seems to matter, to really matter at a gut level, is compassion, brotherhood, friendship, parenthood, love, these nebulous emotions we forget so often, but which grow so important toward journey's end.

BY LAURA SANTI

A Happy Ending after a Long and Confusing Journey

At age twenty-five, Laura Santi was diagnosed with ganglioneuroma, a rare tumor that contains cells from the neurons and tissue in between the nerve cells and blood vessels. It is a slow-growing tumor, usually treated with surgery, and occurs in the brain or spinal cord. Laura has had no recurrence of the tumor since surgery. She enjoys skiing, biking, walking, and reading.

It was the summer of 1985 and a very exciting time in my life. I had just graduated from high school and was looking forward to starting college. After going to Hawaii to celebrate my graduation, I went to Lake Tahoe for the Fourth of July. I don't know if the fireworks had any effect on me, but that was when I had my first seizure. I happened to be sharing a room with my mom, who woke up during the episode. Since I had never had a seizure before, my mom panicked and thought the worst. She called 911, and an ambulance arrived. I woke up with paramedics in my room and was totally confused. At first I would not agree to go to the hospital, but my family insisted. The doctor who treated me said that I had had a grand mal seizure.

When I came home, I went to see my regular physician. She referred me to a neurologist, who suggested I have a CAT scan and an EEG. All of my tests came back normal. After all the 'fun' tests, the neurologist concluded that I had epilepsy. He prescribed Dilantin. I filled the prescription but decided against taking the medication. I was not convinced that I had epilepsy and did not want to take pills that I felt I did not need. To this day I have not experienced another grand mal seizure.

11

Three years later, over the course of a few months, I started to have psycho-motor seizures. I would feel nervous, turn red in the face, get a metallic taste in my mouth, and feel queasy. The symptoms were so mild that only I noticed. At that time, I was unfamiliar with the term *psycho-motor seizures,* and called the seizures *spells* instead. I went back to the neurologist, who still felt I had epilepsy. However, I was still not convinced and felt that the spells were stress related. I was preparing to graduate from junior college and in the middle of changing jobs.

Two years later, the seizures recurred. Again I was going through a stressful time in my life. I was getting ready to graduate from college and begin my career. These seizures were more severe than the ones I had had before. They began to happen more frequently, from once to twice a week to every day, sometimes more than once a day. Stress and worry seemed to trigger these seizures. They lasted from a few seconds to a minute. Half of the time no one would know I was having a spell.

I became concerned. These spells were not going away as they had in the past. Reluctantly, I went back to the neurologist. I described the spells, and he called them psycho-motor seizures. That was the first time I had heard the term. I was scheduled for an MRI. The result showed a glioma. My neurologist used the words *glioma, temporal lobe,* and *cyst.* I was so confused. I just wanted to know what *cyst, glioma,* and *tumor* were. According to the neurosurgeon, my tumor was slow-growing, so he suggested that we monitor it. My endocrinologist explained that it was a ganglioneuroma in the right side of the temporal lobe, and he urged me to get a second opinion.

The second doctor confirmed the diagnosis and said I should have had the tumor removed a long time ago. I just sat in my chair and felt sick. I was speechless. I could not even comprehend the idea of brain surgery. I was dead-set against it. I made up my mind to not have the surgery.

A few days later, I decided to get a third opinion. Before going to the appointment, I went to a health library and spent hours reading about brain surgery, alternative medicine, and the definitions of all the medical terms being thrown at me. I contacted agencies such as the Brain Tumor Foundation to get more information. I became obsessed in learning all I could.

The third neurosurgeon agreed with the second. On February 18, 1992, I had my surgery. Before the actual surgery, I prepared myself mentally, physically, and spiritually. I had a positive attitude and knew I would be fine. I visualized coming out of the operating room, the doctor telling me that the tumor had been removed completely and that I would not have any more seizures. I would be normal again. I also attended brain tumor support group meetings. It was such a help meeting others who had gone through surgery and lived. It was also reassuring to know I was not the only one in the world with a tumor. I asked the nurses and members as many questions as I could.

The surgery was a success. I had very few permanent side effects. However, I developed aseptic meningitis from the surgery. I woke up with the worst headache. I was prepared for some pain, but this was beyond words. There was no magic pill to cure the meningitis. I just had to wait for the blood in my spinal fluid to work its way out. So for two months I had daily headaches and back pain.

One of my biggest fears was waking up after surgery and looking like a beast. Luckily, I did not have to lose all my hair, only the locks where the tumor was located.

After surgery, I had trouble with short-term memory as well as with using the right words in the present moment. At first I was frustrated, but in time my memory improved. In fact, people around me could see a difference. I had "circuit overload"; there was just too much going on around me at once. I learned to work with it. I still experience circuit overload as well as not being able to recall the right word for what I want to say.

Follow-up care consisted of MRI scans every six months, then, eventually, once a year. After surgery I was taking Dilantin. Since I did not have a seizure after surgery, my neurologist and neurosurgeon decided I could get off of the medication completely.

At first, the idea of brain surgery was out of the question for me. Then I did my research. I felt that this was *my* head and *my* body. I recommend anyone in the same situation to become involved in their treatment. The diagnosis can be overwhelming, and unless you take control, you will feel powerless. Support groups can be extremely supportive. I attended a meeting two weeks before surgery and three weeks afterward. I felt inspired by the members who had had surgery, and later I was an inspiration to new people at the meeting. I was able to give others hope. Also, the guides and pamphlets supplied by the group were helpful resources.

It took seven years to diagnose my condition. After going through such an ordeal, I realized that not only did I have the tumor, but everyone I knew had the tumor as well. It affected everyone around me. The love and support from my family and friends had to be the best medicine during my recovery.

Asking questions was an important tool in getting through the surgery. Every morning I would have a notebook ready with a list of things I wanted to go over with my doctor. I also had the phone numbers of people in my support group, as well as those of volunteers from the National Brain Tumor Foundation.

When you live through a crisis like this, other problems seem so trivial. I appreciated life so much more after surgery, and I was able to reevaluate my direction in life. It was a very difficult time. I felt as though I had been satisfied with my life before surgery but was totally dissatisfied with everything after. I felt I had been given a second chance and didn't want to waste a moment of my life. In time, I came to grips with these feelings and made positive changes. As a result, I learned a lot about myself.

When you are pushed against a wall, you definitely become a stronger person with a deeper connection to the universe. If anything, you have more appreciation for the simple things in life, like waking up in the morning and being able to open your eyes, see the sky, get out of bed, and put your feet on the ground.

BY LINDA KENDALL

Why Me? Why Not Me?

Linda Kendall underwent surgery to remove a tumor from the back of her neck. Paralyzed and unable to speak, she was told that she would never regain her independence. She defied the odds. Today, Linda lives in Los Angeles and works for the National Brain Tumor Foundation's outreach program as a community liaison, providing information and support to brain tumor patients and their families in the underserved minority communities. This essay is adapted from a piece she wrote for Search *in 2000.*

It started with a headache that would not go away. Then, my foot started to feel numb. I didn't think the two were related and neither did my primary care physician. She said it was probably stress related. "The headaches may be stress related, but the numbness in my foot?" I questioned.

A few months later, while I was watering the yard, my legs turned rubbery and couldn't support my weight. I fell. My physician sent me to a neurologist for a CAT scan. I was not prepared for the results.

The scan showed something, but an MRI was needed for clarity. The MRI confirmed that I had a brain tumor. The tumor, I was told, was the size of a pea, and operable. "It must be removed," my doctor crisply informed me.

I sat for a moment thinking that he was surely talking about someone else. I think I was in a state of shock. When that wore off, I was in a state of fear. I was thirty-two years old and up against the most difficult situation in my life. I left my neurologist's office shaking. I told my doctor that I wanted a second opinion. I got one, and the diagnosis was the same.

After having a private pity party, to which I was entitled, I had to deliver the devastating news. My parents, siblings, relatives, and friends never hesitated to assist me with anything that I needed. Their love made all the difference. My close companion never wavered, either – he did all that he could to help me with this most difficult journey. I felt blessed to have loving and supportive people around me. I did not feel alone in dealing with this life-altering condition.

I was scheduled to have a nonmalignant hemangioblastoma removed on March 26, 1986. The tumor was lodged in my neck, at the tip of my spine. My preexisting high blood pressure was monitored and I was put on insulin. I had never been diagnosed with diabetes. I did not anticipate any problems. The surgeon told me that there was a 50 percent chance of things going smoothly. I guess I didn't hear that the other 50 percent meant that things might go awry. I have a deep faith in God, and I had faith that everything would be fine.

My tumor was not the size of a pea, but a large grape. I went into surgery fully mobile, and woke up paralyzed from the neck down. I couldn't talk or move. I couldn't believe this was happening to me. I was alive but unable to function. I was on a respirator for several weeks. It paralyzed my left vocal chord. I developed blood clots in my legs and a high fever. One minute I was a young woman in the prime of life, the next minute I couldn't move or even tell anyone how I felt.

I can now recall the emotions and heartache that accompany a brain tumor diagnosis. It was like being dropped from an airplane without a parachute. I was frightened and scared. "Why me?" That was the question I asked myself repeatedly. I went from being an independent woman to one who was completely dependent on others. I was lucky that I had parents and siblings who took care of me around the clock. However, it was up to me to change my situation. I counted on my faith and personal strength to defy the horrible prognosis.

Physical changes can be shocking. It was bad enough that I couldn't move. Despite the fact that I didn't have chemotherapy or radiation, I lost my long, beautiful hair to antibiotics and anesthesia medication. Still, the loss of hair was a minor stroke of bad luck when compared to my rehabilitation evaluation.

I was transferred to a rehabilitation hospital where I was poked, stretched, and prodded by a gaggle of well-meaning specialists, including a speech therapist, an occupational therapist, physical therapists, and orthopedic surgeons. I was told that I would never walk without metal braces. The doctors told me, "Your incontinence will probably not improve; and your voice will never waiver above a whisper."

I was stunned. I couldn't thoroughly digest the news. Shortly after this evaluation, I became more introspective. I asked myself the same question: Why me? Over time, I began to ask, "Why not me?" The ability to move on with my life came once I accepted my condition. I had to dig deep inside myself to come up with a solution to the dreadful diagnosis. I wanted to get back on my feet. I chose hope and faith over doctors who said that it couldn't be done. I could not picture myself inactive or incontinent. Instead, I pictured myself walking, working, and being independent. It wasn't always easy. I had lousy days and good days, but I decided to take each day as it would come.

After four months in the hospital for rehabilitation, I was sent home with a wheelchair, metal braces, prescriptions, and medical equipment.

Often, I quoted Loretta Claiborne: "Forget about the disability and think about the abilities." I did just that. I gradually moved from the wheelchair to a walker, then to a cane, and eventually began walking on my own. I worked on my voice. While it didn't return to its original full capacity, it is decibels above what it was after surgery.

It took four long years to finally stand on my own feet. Thirteen years later, I can walk and talk and live a fairly independent life. I work from home as an independent medical transcriber, and I drive around the city.

While my doctors were happy with my outcome, they were stunned to see me walk into their offices. I think my determination to move past the medical prognosis allowed me to see that fighting a brain tumor has much to do with one's inner courage and determination. My faith, hope, and tenacity turned a demoralizing medical opinion into a positive, practical triumph.

Life isn't a bed of roses. The right side of my body feels different from the left. There is a constant numbness and tingling sensation. Fatigue can still be a problem. But I am a survivor. I see the word and savor it! I'm a long-term survivor!

BY MITCH MILLNER

Mitch's Journey

Mitch Millner is a former credit representative for a medical supplies company. Now retired, he reads books on finance and collects antique toys.

My journey began fifteen years ago, or at least this was the point in time when I first noticed subtle changes in my behavior. My grandfather had died, and, as the executor of his estate, I was under pressure to handle this responsibility as well as my own work schedule. I started to experience brief interruptions to my thoughts; they were like episodes of déjà vu. They would sidetrack me from my daily routine. I attributed these strange episodes to stress. I never mentioned a word about this to anyone.

Two years later, my behavior changed severely. My family and friends began to notice strange facial movements. They thought I was having trouble swallowing. My mouth would open and close and my eyes would get bloodshot. Then, as quickly as the symptoms appeared, they would disappear without a trace. My colleagues noticed that I would start to speak but would forget to finish the sentence. This pause in my cognitive thinking would last for a period of maybe fifteen to twenty seconds.

A year later, my symptoms became even worse. In September 1995, my family insisted that I seek medical attention. A battery of MRI and CT scans revealed a brain tumor. My seizures were caused by a bleeding angioma, which was growing and causing small strokes. I met my neurosurgeons in October. They advised me to have surgery immediately. The last test before surgery was an arteriogram; it allowed the surgeon to look at the tumor directly, but I had to stay awake for this uncomfortable test. After about an hour of drenching my brain with dye, the doctor informed me that he had found a large aneurysm located on a main artery near the brain tumor. Another arteriogram was conducted to rule out more aneurysms. While the brain tumor was life-threatening, the aneurysm, due to its size and location, could rupture at any time. The doctors stabilized the aneurysm with a small titanium clip that secured the weakened wall of the artery.

Looking back to that cold January day just before the surgery, I took a good look at myself and thought about my accomplishments and failures in life, and squarely faced my prognosis. The surgery was risky; however, I knew I would find the strength and courage to handle the remaining leg of this journey.

The surgery lasted almost six hours. The first thing I recall after surgery was my surgeon telling me, "You did beautifully." I told my mother, who was nearby, that I was not the same person. She kissed me and said she understood. I had a feeling of great relief and joy to be alive, but I was also understandably frightened.

I was anxious to get on with my life. I had to adapt to a variety of side effects from the surgery. I looked in the mirror after going home and saw a pale, bald, very thin man that I did not recognize. I wanted to reacquaint myself with this person. I had my family take a picture of me so I could see where I had been and where I would go.

The next few weeks were painful and difficult. I had to learn how to walk again, which proved more difficult than I had thought. There were times when I fell over the coffee table or fell getting out of bed. Though frustrated at my slow progress, I knew that I had to be patient and persist in my recovery. The muscles in my jaw had been cut during surgery; eating was painful, and I lived on liquids and very soft foods. I exercised to rebuild my strength. I could not feel any sensation on the entire right side of my head. I would bite the right side of my tongue and not be aware of it until I tasted blood.

I found that getting a sense of humor really helped through recuperation. I came to terms with my surgery. I was anxious to discuss my progress and feelings with my family, who had been so supportive and loving throughout my recovery.

I regained some of the weight that I had lost. My hair grew back, and I started to venture beyond the house. I was definitely making progress in my motor skills. Though double vision remained a problem, the swelling in my right eye gradually decreased. I found a new friend in myself. I could walk and I felt alive.

My colleagues were very supportive and understanding. I only needed those two things. I was not looking for pity or sympathy. I knew from the very beginning of this journey that my strength and determination would see me through. I certainly had my share of depression along the way, but I knew that each day was an improvement and I would be a functioning, active person once again.

It has now been six months since the surgery, and recent tests confirmed that I am healing well. There have been some neurological deficits, but I have come a long way. There have been bumps and detours on my journey, and a profound change in my attitude. I am more reflective, and I appreciate the world around me more than I had. I am ready to begin a new chapter in my life.

BY MARIE BECKERMAN
Healing Is a Lifelong Process

Marie Beckerman was born in Salt Lake City, Utah, and raised in Southern California. She has lived in San Francisco for the past thirty-one years with her husband and son, and enjoys quilting and reading mysteries in her spare time. Marie was diagnosed with a meningioma on her fifth cranial nerve. She subsequently had two operations and radiation therapy. The tumor has disappeared, and though she experienced some minor side effects, these, too, have subsided.

The odyssey began a lifetime ago, or so it seems to me now. Most of it is a blur, but it is easiest for me to remember the sequence of events as they relate to milestones in the life of our son, Aaron.

In February of 1988, when Aaron was in kindergarten, I visited my doctor for episodes of severe vertigo that I had been experiencing for a year. The first two attacks had been so debilitating that I was bedridden for a week each time, unable to even lift my head from the pillow. The third attack left me with ringing in the ears, loss of hearing in one ear, and loss of balance for months. Quite by accident, my physician discovered a small meningioma attached to the fifth cranial nerve on the right side of my face.

After seeing several neurosurgeons, it was determined that the meningioma had nothing to do with the vertigo. I was completely asymptomatic. The meningioma was monitored regularly, and I began a series of tests for the vertigo.

In May of 1989, Aaron was completing the first grade. I began to have tingling sensations on the right side of my face, just under the eye. They were intermittent and painless. By the time Aaron began the second grade in September, the meningioma had shown some signs of growth. I had surgery a week after school began. The neurosurgeon was able to remove most, but not all, of the tumor. Recovery went well, and I was back to work in two months.

In May of 1990, the pain began. It was, at first, very quick – around my teeth on the right side. The next occurrence was about two months later. This time the pain lasted a minute or two. Gradually, these attacks became closer together, lasting longer each time, until November, when the pain became continuous. It was a searing, electric shock that sometimes caused the right side of my face to vibrate from the intensity. It would wake me from a deep sleep. Talking and eating became extremely difficult. I was no longer able to read to Aaron, so he read to me.

My neurosurgeon felt that radiation therapy was in order for the meningioma. After getting a second opinion, I began my treatment in mid-November, 1990, five days a week for six weeks.

During this time, I experienced a great deal of fatigue and nausea. It reminded me of the first trimester of pregnancy. The radiation also affected my sense of taste; everything I ate tasted like soap. I began to have trouble keeping food down, my weight began to drop, and my head and face felt hot and dry to the touch. One day, as I left radiation therapy, it began to rain lightly. I have a vivid memory of how cool and refreshing the raindrops felt as they touched my face.

Midway through the treatments, the pain from the swelling of the tumor became excruciating. The Dexamethasone helped immensely with the pain and loss of appetite. I was soon eating and regaining the lost pounds. I suddenly had an enormous amount of energy and began cleaning and cooking a lot. Through all of this, I slept only about three hours a night.

I completed the treatments just after New Year's in 1991. There was some hair loss above both ears and just above the forehead. This was a temporary condition, and my hair regrew within the month. The facial pain, however, continued to plague me. I began taking Tegretol in February 1991. The effect would wear off quickly, so I began to take larger doses. By the following year, it was clearly not working for me any longer. The side effects became unbearable. I began to have double "rolling" vision. It was like watching a television set whose vertical hold control no longer worked, causing the picture to keep moving upward.

I went back for surgery. This time my doctor was performing a rhizotomy to sever the fifth cranial nerve, but cutting only the part that corresponded to the area of pain in my face. I was looking forward to this operation, thinking that I would finally be free of pain. But, to my disappointment, when I regained consciousness in the recovery room, the pain was still there. I also had some rather strange symptoms.

In the hospital, I developed an itch on the right side of my forehead. Whenever I would scratch it, I would feel the scratching on the top of my head. I also had a numbing sensation on my right eyelid, the right side of my nose, and the right side of my upper lip.

My doctor reported that the tumor was completely gone. Only scar tissue remained. The radiation had done its job. I was greatly relieved.

Nearly a year after the rhizotomy, the level of pain was quite low, and I stopped taking pain medication. I had a strange, slightly salty, slightly sour taste in my mouth. Intermittently, I had a sensation on the right side of my forehead that felt like an insect crawling down my forehead from the hairline to the eyebrow and then back up again. I experienced about two weeks of intense twitching and spasms under my right eye, followed by about six pain-free weeks. Eventually, the side effects subsided.

Several years later, at the end of 1997, my mother passed away. Two months after that, I was diagnosed with breast cancer. I had a mastectomy, followed by radiation therapy. This time, though, the hospital gave me guided imagery sessions along with the radiation. The guided imagery left me feeling soothed and relaxed. That may have been why I was better able to handle the radiation this time around.

I recovered nicely from both the surgery and the radiation. Sadly, my brother was diagnosed with stomach cancer soon after. He passed away in January of 1999.

It is now June 2001. I continue to have an MRI for the brain tumor every two years, along with a visit to the neurosurgeon. I am happy to report that there has been no new activity. And, I am now pain free. It took about a year for the pain to disappear after the second brain surgery.

As for my son, Aaron, he is almost nineteen. Happily immersed in college life, he has just completed his freshman year. I am pleased to say that he is becoming a very nice young man.

When I look back, it is hard to believe that I actually went through all of this and survived. But now, I am feeling great. I could not ask for anything more. In spite of everything, I count myself as one of the lucky ones.

BY MELISSA S. HARTMAN

The Last Lesson

Melissa S. Hartman is a designer and writer from Jordan, Minnesota. She is a recent graduate of University of Wisconsin-Stout and holds a BFA degree in graphic design/journalism. Melissa has made a full recovery and is currently working at an advertising agency in St. Paul, Minnesota.

I always had a plan. In college, I learned to be responsible, to organize, and to set formal goals for my future. After years of finding solutions to academic problems, I was under the assumption that every question had an answer. By graduation, I was ready to enter a new chapter in my life.

I don't believe I'll ever forget the first week. Four days after graduation, on a rainy day, I was diagnosed with a brain tumor. Miles away from home, I left the hospital devastated and alone. Somehow, for reasons I will never know, I managed to complete my finals in the center of all the commotion. Many of my friends were also graduating, celebrating, and soon moving on to new chapters in their lives. Unsure of what the future would hold, I shed as many tears as I possibly could the first night. Although close friends helped ease the pain, there were times when I could not hide from my fear of death, among other things.

At this point, I felt very vulnerable and fragile. I could not talk about the situation, or carry on any conversation, for that matter, without breaking down in tears. I chose to tell only a few close friends from college. I wasn't necessarily afraid of what everyone might think. I simply felt like I was now on the other end of the spectrum – I felt very different from everyone else – and I didn't want to be remembered that way.

People around me dealt with my news in different ways: some acted suddenly distant, for lack of words; some dramatized the whole thing; and, some acted perfectly normal, which felt most comfortable to me.

My journey began as I packed up my college belongings and headed home to my family, ready to face the situation. I was unaware at the time that future days, weeks, and months would be filled with overwhelming support from family and friends. I also had a special ally who gave me extra security: my best friend from high school had gone through cancer our senior year. Watching her experience and overcome all her obstacles years ago gave me the fuel I needed to battle my own obstacles. She listened to every tiny detail, and she knew exactly how I felt. I found an enormous amount of comfort and strength in this.

As the day of my surgery drew closer, I was on a roller coaster of mixed emotions. By this time I was experiencing intense pain. Part of me wanted to just get it over with and start the healing process. The other side of me was falling apart. The wall of strength that I had built was crumbling before me, and there was nothing I could do. I was so angry that I had to go through this when everyone else was going on with normal lives. All I could do was ask, why? But this time I had no answers.

It's true what they say: you have your good days and your bad days. But somewhere in between grows new strength, strength you never thought you'd have.

I started to look at things very differently. My outlook on life was changing, almost like I had been asleep for a few years and finally woke up to see the beauty around me. The smallest things started to catch my eye. I noticed how colorful and serene a sunset could be when you took the time to look at it. Blades of grass cascading along hills highlighted new, brighter shades of green. A small child's laughter became an instant remedy for a bad day.

I'm convinced that someone must have been watching over me. As it turned out, I woke up from surgery ecstatically happy to be alive and well. Words could never describe that moment.

The healing process was longer and more difficult than I had anticipated. I hadn't thought a whole lot about being completely immobile and dependent on others the first few days out of surgery. I also never considered the struggle to walk again or do simple tasks during the first few weeks. As anxious as I was to leave the hospital and go home, I grew nervous as soon as I stepped into the blinding daylight. I immediately felt different from everyone else. A day later at home, I examined my bald head for the first time. Ironically, a month before I knew of this whole situation, I had cut my hair short and donated it to the American Cancer Society.

That was the last painful memory that I have. After that, I convinced myself that I would fully recover over time. I wasn't scared anymore. I had this great second chance at life, and I wanted to take full advantage of it. I can't say that I never catch myself frantically stressing out about minor things anymore. I still feel the need to excessively plan almost every detail of my life. But I know now that life can throw a good curveball when you least expect it. I feel that everything happens for a reason, yet not every question is going to have the perfect answer. And that's okay. It leaves room for the wrong answer. It leaves room for the unimaginable. It leaves room for dreams.

BY ANDREA BLINN

A Different Path

Andrea Blinn was diagnosed with a brain tumor on September 17, 1998. She had brain surgery one week later, and the tumor, which was later declared to be a glioblastoma multiforme, was removed. Following surgery, Andrea participated in both conventional and alternative treatments. Her tumor has not recurred, and she attributes her health to both of these medical approaches. Andrea is now thirty-eight years old and lives in Pittsburgh, Pennsylvania. An independent consultant, she loves to travel, write, and relax by the ocean.

Ironically, even after two cancer diagnoses, I still consider myself a lucky person. I'll never be thankful for my cancers; however, when I was diagnosed with thyroid cancer five years ago and suddenly found the willpower to quit smoking, I learned that there is a gift in everything.

When I was diagnosed with brain cancer two years ago, at age thirty-five, I remember lying on the couch in a daze, wondering what cancer would bring to my life this time. As expected, brain cancer has brought many horrible, difficult losses. But fighting it has led me down a new path, and into a new world.

Symptoms of my glioblastoma started in February 1998. I was falling asleep when suddenly, ugly elflike figures invaded my vision. I was dreaming, but I was awake. A terrible fear gripped me. I sat up in bed, panicked, nauseated, heart racing. Within seconds, sudden nausea turned into dry heaves. After a few minutes the images disappeared, the nausea diminished, my heartbeat slowed to its usual pace, and I was breathing normally. When I asked my doctor what had happened, he told me it was probably due to stress.

In order to reduce the stress in my busy work life – I was executive director of a controversial, high-profile civil rights agency – I started to get frequent massages and work out regularly at the gym. But the visions, as I came to call them, recurred often. They were always the same. Although frightened, I never told anyone about them.

When the visions became unbearable, I complained to my doctor again, only to receive the same response. Daily meditations and an extra mile on my already two-mile daily run did not help. The visions came at the oddest times, even while I slept.

In desperation, I went to a spa for a week. I met a psychoanalyst there and told her my problem. She listened carefully. Although she was puzzled, she thought it sounded like a neurological problem. I was so happy to have someone tell me that I was not crazy! Much later, I learned that these episodes were actually seizures.

I shared the psychoanalyst's opinion with my parents. My mother asked me to go and see Lewis Mehl-Madrona, MD, a doctor who practices both conventional and Native American medicine. He told me I was having symptoms of either a brain seizure or a brain tumor. An MRI confirmed a mass in my brain. Dr. Mehl-Madrona told me to prepare for immediate brain surgery.

Exactly one week later, on September 24, 1998, I had the tumor removed. About five hours later, I woke up in the recovery room in terrible pain. I cried, begged, pleaded and screamed for pain relievers, but my doctor refused, saying that pain relievers could mask critical neurological symptoms.

I was in the hospital for ten days, nauseated and in pain. My family and friends saved me with their love and patience. I went to stay with my parents so I could receive constant care. Over the next four months, my father did endless research on brain tumors and their treatment. My parents and I interviewed many doctors before deciding to get radiation treatments and BCNU chemotherapy. My life became an endless stream of doctor's appointments. I ended up in the emergency room a number of times due to shingles, petechiae, pneumonia, seizures, and a host of other annoying problems related to chemotherapy.

Weak, sick, and exhausted from treatments, I slept the days away. I lost a quarter of my hair, as well as a good twenty pounds. Four months later, balder and skinnier, I moved back into my own apartment.

During radiation and chemotherapy, I saw Dr. Mehl-Madrona every week. I was incredibly weak and exhausted. On his recommendation, I began attending a weekly two-hour meditation session. Several patients would gather in the family room at the Center for Complementary Medicine for guided imagery with Dr. Mehl-Madrona. He would bring each of us into a world within ourselves that we'd never visited before. In a soft, gentle, and beautiful voice, he would ask us to focus on our breathing. Then he would lead us over the windy, rocky, and mountainous terrain of our psyches, and through the beautiful oceans of our minds and souls.

I benefited from each and every session. During the first session, the doctor asked each of us to go within ourselves to visit our illnesses. Suddenly, there I was, face to face with my cancer, a heavy gray goop dripping inside the darkest caverns of my brain. I was scared and sad at first. But by the time we finished the exercise, I walked out of my brain with fists clenched, ready to fight to reclaim my body.

I had recently returned to work but was still very weak. I realized that I had to create an environment of wellness in order to recover. Meditation helped in my physical, emotional, and psychological recovery. It slowly changed me and gave me strength to fight brain cancer.

I had heard Dr. Mehl-Madrona talk about attending Native American spiritual ceremonies and healing circles. I decided to participate in a ceremony at a sweat lodge. During the ceremony, we sat in a circle and prayed by singing and humming along to Lakota songs. We also prayed individually. This was the first time in my life that I had consciously constructed a prayer.

When it was my turn to pray, I gave thanks for my family, my friends, and my doctors for saving my life. I gave thanks for my strength and prayed for health. About two hours later, I emerged from the smoky lodge feeling refreshed, hopeful, ten pounds lighter, purer, and healthier. I had never felt this way after attending traditional support group meetings.

The community that Dr. Mehl-Madrona built through meditation sessions and sweat lodge ceremonies is still a part of my life, and a source of encouragement and support. I believe I've developed the attitude that my brain cancer is behind me. Of course, I have daily reminders: I must take a nap during the day, I have a terrible memory, I haven't worked out for over two months, and I may not be able to conceive a child.

Instead of dwelling upon what I've lost, I try to channel my energy into improving all that is in my control. I left my job, which was stressful and drained my energy. Now I am working as an independent consultant, which means I can set my own hours, work at my own pace, and take vacations whenever I want to. I practice yoga and am considering the beauties of adoption. I've also taken up crossword puzzles to help my memory.

I'll never be one of those people who feel thankful for their cancer. My losses have been too great. Too staggering. Too horrible. However, I've learned some important things. I've learned to surround myself with positive people. I have kept an open mind and experimented with alternative therapies; I believe that I have benefited immeasurably from both conventional and alternative treatments. I've changed my attitude toward life. I'm still alive. I'm still planning a future.

BY NORMAN KORNSAND

I Can Do Everything
I Dreamed I Could

Norman Kornsand wrote this story for Search *in 1988. He lives in Walnut Creek, California, with his wife and children. After being diagnosed with a grade-III astrocytoma in 1982, he was told that he had a 20 percent chance of living another two years. He has had five surgeries (two seed implants, and two to remove necrosis, but has had no recurrence of the tumor), radiation, and chemotherapy. Despite his prognosis, he is alive and well. He is the author of "Handicap Provisions: A Review and Assessment," for* Building Standards. *It traces the history of the Americans with Disabilities Act and the unified building codes for the disabled. Norman was in the building profession before his surgery.*

Giving up my career was the most difficult decision of my life. I had decided that I was no longer capable of continuing my job. The cancer and associated treatment had left my mind and body weak. They had won the battle, but I was determined to win the war.

I had so many questions. How would I be able to support my wife, two small children, and myself? I was pulling in a damn good income. Luckily, my employer had a good disability insurance plan. That and social security got us by. My wife's part-time job provided a little more income. What I did not foresee was how the system could trap us. If my wife made more than $510 a month, we received less social security benefits. I found that any income that I would get would be deducted from the insurance benefit, social security, or from both. Here I was, thirty-nine years old and essentially retired.

I had to figure out what I would do with all my time. I no longer had the opportunity to work sixty hours a week. I had to reorganize my life. I knew that it would kill me to become a couch potato, wasting my mind (or what was left of it) and my body watching what Newton Minow graciously called the "vast wasteland." What did I want to do? I could now do all those things I had dreamed about but never had time for.

Prioritizing was my first step. There were the kids. I spent more time with them. I helped them with their studies and homework. We did things together, as long as our activities did not require my left side too much and I did not have to run or walk too far. I really became a chauffeur, tutor, and referee. I helped out my wife by doing light housework and ran errands. Until now, I had not realized that they had lives that did not always include me. They wanted me to be there to help when I could, but to give them the room that they needed, especially the kids.

I was still left with the basic question: what should I do with all this free time? I had bought a computer the year before, but had not had much time to work on it. I had always wanted to reorganize our personal financial records. What better way was there than computerized records? However, I was a real novice when it came to computers. It had been almost twenty years since my college courses, and that's generations in terms of computers. I decided that the best way to learn was to actually do the work: I wrote my own programs. Although it was frustrating work, I finally got them to work. It had been fun. Now, I only had to maintain the programs.

I had free time again and did not know what to do next. I had heard that there is a great story in everyone and had always wanted to write a book. I had also heard that you must write about something that you know. I had written a number of articles for technical periodicals. I decided to write the first of what I hoped would become a number of books, using a character much like myself.

It has been a year since I started. My book is now in a semi-final draft, and I am well into my second effort, a mystery. I do not know if my book is publishable material, but that is almost irrelevant; I did it, and I am pleased with my accomplishment. I am not under any pressure to meet deadlines. I don't write if I don't feel like it. When I do feel motivated, I can sit at the computer all day long. I don't recall ever having this freedom before. It is the single most recognizable benefit of my disability; I have the freedom to set my own schedule with very few restrictions.

Ever since my diagnosis in 1982, I have accepted that life is a series of adjustments. Sometimes, these adjustments are forced upon us, such as adjusting to the effects of a chronic disease. Rarely do we get a chance to make adjustments that we want to make. When I realized that I could no longer pursue my career, I took a few steps back to reassess my life. I made the choices that were right for me.

Although we have to accept things as they are, we must cherish life; it is the most wonderful gift that we will ever get. It is up to each and every person to decide how to use that gift.

BY MARTHA AARONS

Moving On: A Musician's Journey

Martha Aarons is a flutist with the Cleveland Orchestra and a native of Los Angeles, California. She attributes her recovery to good general health, a positive attitude, sense of humor, good medical care, and marvelous support from family, friends, and colleagues.

I always thought this sort of thing happened to other people, people who were less fortunate genetically or in worse general health. I always dreaded breast cancer after seeing close friends and family struggle with it. When I got the worst headache of my life, it never occurred to me that I had a brain tumor.

I have had migraines since my twenties, but they are hormonally triggered and therefore predictable. I was in Boston, participating in a special benefit concert, when this headache crept in. At first, I just assumed that it was another migraine, but not only did aspirin fail to wipe it out, Imitrex, my usual foolproof remedy, could not lessen it. I ignored it, but by the next day I had chills and figured I had a virus or infection. By the time I flew home to Cleveland, I felt as sick as a dog. I had a headache, nausea, fever, and my neck was stiff. My internist diagnosed a urinary tract infection. As the week progressed, the headache worsened. I was sent to an infectious diseases specialist. I had a number of lab tests done that came back negative. Eventually, a CAT scan was performed and I was informed that I had a mass growing on my brain. An MRI confirmed the diagnosis of an olfactory groove meningioma, the size of a jumbo egg.

Despite the grave news, I was calm. I was actually numb. I did not shed a tear, which was quite out of character for me. My memory of those weeks is hazy; much later, I asked my boyfriend to reconstruct the events for me. By this time, my internist had arrived at the Cleveland Clinic, located the neurosurgeon he assured me was one of the world's best, and scheduled my surgery. I had complete faith in my internist and did not seek a second opinion.

I came in for preoperative tests and interviews the following day. MRI scans and computers would be navigational devices during my stereotactic surgery. My surgeon shaved a very narrow swath of hair, just large enough for an incision.

The surgery went very well but took seven-and-one-half hours. I woke up in the ICU tethered to numerous tubes and devices. The pain was easily manageable with medication. Although most of my memories of the ICU are hazy, certain episodes are vivid. I remember my head being unwrapped to remove a drain. I had many ultrasounds, and a machine massaged my legs to keep blood clots from forming. I looked repeatedly at a clock on the wall at half-hour intervals but the hands did not seem to move at all. I thought I was losing my mind. Weeks later I discovered that it was broken!

I had hardly eaten for over a week. Once I was out of the ICU and on steroids, I was ravenous. Within a day or two I was allowed to get up by myself. I was passing all the neurological tests from the first moments after surgery. I had lost my sense of smell on one side before the surgery. Now I could not smell anything; the other olfactory nerve had been damaged during the procedure. I was discharged from the hospital three days after surgery.

I missed a tour of my orchestra to Japan and China. My boyfriend stayed home to take care of me. All the stress and emotions that I had suppressed before the surgery overwhelmed me. I had nightmares and panic attacks, and I cried a lot. But my emotions subsided once I dealt with the reality of my illness. Part of my therapy was researching my condition and the surgery. I read the surgical report, asked questions, and discussed my experience in great detail with anyone who would listen. I had ample support from my family, friends, and colleagues. I was actively involved in my recovery and in monitoring my progress. I was gradually weaned off of my antiseizure medication, as it made me feel drunk, dizzy, and jittery all at the same time.

During the six weeks of recovery, one of my goals was to participate in the Aspen Music Festival. I play there every year from mid-June to mid-July. It is the highlight of my year: I enjoy the musical experience, and, being an avid hiker, I adore the mountains. I was recovering well. Except for the inevitable black eye from the craniotomy, there was little evidence of what I had gone through. My thick, curly hair covered the incision, and I was getting out and around by myself.

I got to Aspen and had the time of my life. I felt wonderful, especially by the end of my sojourn there. I was more appreciative of the small joys that life offers daily.

Today, I am less reluctant to indulge myself and more determined not to let stress interfere with my well-being. Although the intensity of these feelings diminished somewhat with time, they made a lasting impact on me.

I do not expect any complications, although I will be monitored periodically. The numbness on the top of my head has almost completely disappeared. I have been experiencing phantom smells for a couple of months. Perhaps the damaged nerves are healing. Even though my surgeon and oncologist tell me that the loss of smell is probably permanent, I still hold out some hope that I will be able to smell again. No matter how small your loss, you still mourn it, all the while knowing how much worse it could have been.

BY CHRIS DE JONG

It's a Cruel, Crazy, Beautiful World

Chris de Jong was diagnosed with a glioblastoma multiforme, the most aggressive and common form of primary brain tumor. He underwent surgery, then radiation and chemotherapy. When his tumor recurred six months later, he had a second surgery and Gamma Knife treatment. He died shortly after writing this essay. Chris, originally from South Africa, attended the University of Oklahoma.

My mother was born and raised in Oklahoma. Her mother was born in Pontotoc County, Indian Territory. My South African father came to the University of Oklahoma on a swimming scholarship. My parents met in the geology school and were married in Norman, Oklahoma. They moved to South Africa, where I was born, and lived there until 1990. With dual citizenship, I cherish being an American.

Two weeks prior to my diagnosis of a deadly cancer requiring brain surgery, I was in top physical form. In the middle of April 1993, I began to have severe headaches. Nonprescription pain relievers were not very effective. I grew tired quickly. I had been exposed to mononucleosis two or three weeks earlier, so I was not overly concerned about these symptoms. At the same time, I was experiencing déjà vu: I would suddenly remember events from five, six, or even ten years before. My mind would retrieve accurate memories at unrelated times.

On Wednesday, April 28th, 1993, my behavior changed drastically. I attended class as usual but could not recall being there. My short-term memory failed temporarily. I know that I was on campus because I have lecture notes from that day.

I went to the university health center with a terrible headache and was prescribed Norgesic, a powerful headache medicine. Later, I could not recall going to the health center; the only evidence of my visit was the medicine in my book bag and medical records documenting my complaint.

I took my headache tablets and apparently went about normal campus activities. I have very few recollections of that day. I felt as if I had woken up after being drunk and could only recall bits of information about the previous night. Apparently, I stayed on campus all day long, but I don't know what I did there.

What is certain is that I became incoherent and was almost incapacitated by headaches by the end of the day. At 7:00 P.M. I returned to the health center. By this time I was in excruciating pain and was very confused. My friend, Jim, took me to Norman Regional Hospital where I had a CAT scan and an MRI. The scans revealed a mass, either a lesion or an abscess, about the size of a lemon, in the right temporal lobe of the brain.

The mass had resulted in enormous swelling. I was told that I would definitely need surgery, but that the swelling had to subside first. The mass and the swelling had led to headaches and confusion. I could withstand the pain, but it was terribly frightening to feel my mind slipping. I was given antiseizure medication, pain relievers, and a massive dose of steroids to reduce the swelling.

Before the surgery on May 3, 1993, my neurosurgeon warned me of the risk of losing some cognitive ability, since the tumor was located near areas of the brain that are responsible for memory, emotion, and motor functions on the left side of the body. The night before the surgery was particularly bad, since the doctors could not administer painkillers for fear of masking more severe symptoms. During a five-hour craniotomy, my neurosurgeon removed approximately 95 percent of the golf-ball-size tumor, as well as a section of the right temporal lobe. The operation was a success and my condition improved immediately. I was conscious and coherent immediately after coming out of anesthesia. There was no long-term damage to my memory, emotions, or motor functioning. But it did take a while for my short-term memory to return to normal.

I have fleeting recollections of events surrounding my surgery. I do remember some things quite clearly, though. I remember actually fighting, using all my inner-strength against a deadly foe. I know that if I had given up that fight for a second, I would have died that night. I have never been afraid of death. I still had a lot to accomplish and was having too much fun living. It is still against my personal philosophy to give up on anything if there is even the faintest glimmer of hope.

The lab report indicated that the tumor was a glioblastoma multiforme grade IV, an extremely aggressive kind of malignant tumor that usually kills within six months or a year of diagnosis. I could now face my fear, since it was no longer an unknown enemy. It was a relief to know that my confusion and pain had been physiological and not psychological. As for the high mortality rate associated with the diagnosis of glioblastoma, I felt inclined to agree with Disraeli: "There are three kinds of lies: lies, damned lies, and statistics."

I have been a recovering alcoholic for more than three years. Knowing that I could successfully halt the progress of that insidious, terminal disease certainly helped me in dealing with this one. Throughout my entire ordeal, the staff and faculty at the university could not have been more accommodating. I will always be grateful for their kindness.

Although my physicians were extremely capable, there are some vast gaps in our understanding of cancer. For example, none of the doctors could say how long the tumor had been there, where it had originated from and why, or what might happen next.

My family was wonderful. My parents and three of my five siblings were with me in the hospital and during recovery. I am closer than ever to my family and friends.

Humor has sustained me throughout this ordeal, and I hope that I never lose the ability to laugh at myself. Many people were shocked at my apparent lightheartedness. I would simply tell them, "This is my cancer, and I'm going to laugh about it. Go get your own disease!"

The postoperative brain scans were inconclusive. I thought that if there was any residual tumor, it had shriveled up and disappeared. Positive thinking, a healthy attitude, and humor have been indicated in cases of spontaneous remissions. Why should I let things weigh heavily on me? I would much rather deal with cancer than shrivel up and die long before my heart stops beating!

Despite the success of the surgery, I needed further treatment for any microscopic cancer cells lingering in my brain. I had chemotherapy and radiation treatments. Apart from feeling a little tired, I lost hair in the areas that were irradiated. I saw the hair loss more as an indication of the effective radiation than as a side effect. I had great trouble staying awake in the afternoons and in the evenings for several months. Sometimes I would fall asleep at my desk while studying. I managed to keep up academically, and all indications are that my intellectual functioning is unhindered.

My friends in South Africa were obviously concerned for me and raised enough money to fly me home for five weeks in July. There I dropped the dosages of the steroid and antiseizure medication that I had been taking for seven months, since I had never had a seizure. My mental activity remained as sharp as it was before surgery. I gradually recovered my strength and returned to Oklahoma in August for the fall semester.

Most contemporary literature recognizes that the psyche has enormous power over physiology. Reading Dr. David Spiegel's *Living beyond Limits* helped me to understand the connection between my mind and body. Spiegel referred to the work of Dr. Bernie Siegel, who suggested that positive thinking and a will to live are almost as effective in battling life threatening diseases as medical science. While this is a crucially important idea, it can lead patients to blame themselves for the disease. Spiegel's research also showed that those who participate in a support group have longer periods of remission than those who do not participate in a group.

I found myself drawn to both theories, but I realized that, for me, it made more sense to stick with medical science and treat the disease. I have neither denied the existence of the cancer nor tried to wish it away. I think that I will be able to deal with it effectively again if it does recur.

I will be attending the National Brain Tumor Foundation's conference for patients, families, and professionals in San Francisco. I feel compelled to learn as much as I can about my condition, but also to encourage others to be strong in their recovery.

Why me? Why not me? I have reaped so many positive rewards from adversity. I have become a better person: more humane, caring, kind, and sensitive. While Johnny Clegg thought of the world as "cruel, crazy, [and] beautiful," a Xhosa proverb describes its true nature. *Ubuntu ungamntu ngabanye abantu.* In other words, each individual's humanity is ideally expressed through relationships with other people and in the acknowledgment of their common humanity.

While trying to remain positive, I probably get depressed about trivial things. But I have learned that there are no guarantees in life. Derek Walcott wrote, "Survival is the triumph of stubbornness." I may have this disease, but the disease does not have me!

On February 17, I had another brain scan. It was inconclusive. It was the best news that I could have hoped for. It is seldom that we are called on to live. We only live a little at a time. But that little makes a great difference in the grand scheme of things.

BY RUTH JACOBS, PhD

Overcoming Ageism and Illness

Dr. Ruth Jacobs is a gerontologist, sociologist, poet, and author of nine books, including Be an Outrageous Older Woman. *A college professor, she is also a researcher at the Wellesley College Center for Research on Women. She writes a monthly column for the award-winning* Senior Times *and serves on the editorial board of the* Journal of Women and Aging.

In 1996, on my seventy-second birthday, I got terrible news. A doctor telephoned to tell me that my MRI had revealed a brain tumor. I had consulted this neurologist because I was having trouble keeping my balance and kept bumping into people. A few weeks later, I had a craniotomy to remove a benign meningioma.

I was greatly worried about my mental functioning being affected because I am a college professor, writer, and lecturer. My intellectual acuity is very important. Fortunately, my memory and speech were not affected, as I could recite poems that I had memorized previously. I had many complications, though, including blood clots and pneumonia, which required four hospitalizations and intravenous heparin for four months to prevent more blood clots. Visiting nurses came into my home to check on my progress. I was impatient to return to work; I had already begun accepting dates for guest lectures. One of the nurses told me quite emphatically that it was pure fantasy to believe that I could be well enough to speak in public again. I was not surprised: many people think that sickly old people will remain invalids forever. The nurse's disbelief bothered me, but I was determined to prove her wrong.

The day my intravenous therapy was disconnected, I drove to an indoor swimming pool and got into the water to swim. I was badly out of form; I had been inactive for four months. I had developed osteoporosis from the heparin. As a result, I had two stress fractures in my lower back, which made movement painful. But I was determined to move and get reconditioned. Swimming seemed my best hope, and I moved in the water as best as I could.

Each day I swam longer. It was agonizing to walk from my car to the pool. I was in so much pain that I could not walk the last few steps to the dressing room. So, I wore my bathing suit under my clothes and changed poolside. If I dropped anything, I had to ask someone to pick it up. The fractures in my back made it impossible to bend. I had to go without socks as I could not bend; my feet were often cold.

As I grew stronger, I began to take very short walks, gradually increasing the distances. With the help of a physical therapist, I began a series of exercises to strengthen my bones and muscles.

Defying the medical professionals' expectations, I was able to make my speaking dates, including an interview on the *Today Show* in New York. I had to use a wheelchair in the airport, though. I made this trip to New York ten months after the brain surgery. Now I am out teaching, speaking, and traveling, and I can walk unaided.

I can attest to the fact that it is possible to recover from a diagnosis that may, at first, seem like a death sentence. I encourage older people with brain tumors or other illnesses not only to pray for recovery, but also to get physically reconditioned. This is possible with professional advice and a lot of care not to exceed one's limitations. Above all, do not give up on yourself or listen to those who have no faith in you or your recovery.

BY TRICIA ROLOFF

What It Means to Be Human

Tricia Roloff was diagnosed in 1984 with a prolactinoma, a hormone-secreting pituitary tumor. She is former editor and program associate of the National Brain Tumor Foundation. For the past fifteen years, she has been active in the publishing field as reporter, editor, and director of her own publishing company, Indigo Press. She holds bachelor of science degrees in fine and applied arts from the University of Oregon. Born and raised in Minnesota, she now resides in Fayetteville, Arkansas.

In October of 1981, after graduating from the University of Oregon, I set out to visit a friend in London, England. Having also obtained a six-month work visa through a university student exchange program, I was prepared to stay for at least this amount of time. Before leaving, a physician advised me to go on birth control pills since I was on an irregular, two-month cycle. I was against this but took the pills anyway. I stopped menstruating entirely. I was told by friends that it was probably just the stress of traveling and being in a new and very different environment.

By February of 1982, I had left England and was living in Madrid, Spain. I still hadn't menstruated, even though it had now been six months. It was around this time that I started to notice changes in my personality. All my emotions seemed exaggerated. Anger became rage, sadness easily turned to depression. I felt very anxious most of the time, even though there was nothing to feel anxious about.

My thoughts seemed crowded, rushed, and unorganized. One day I remember writing over and over, "Why am I so emotional about everything? Why is my mind racing so much? Why do I feel anxious all the time?" This just wasn't like me. Unfortunately, I lost that journal. Whoever picked it up must have thought I was really cracking up. I was so disgusted at the way I felt. It was maddening to deal with something I couldn't place or name.

But I was not willing to give up my travels, so I imagined that my body was not connected to me and hoped these feelings would go away with time. I suppressed the unpleasant and focused on things that made me happy. I lived in a large flat with several artists and spent my days sketching in the streets. I loved the richness of the sights, sounds, colors, and moods of the city. February always floods me with memories of blue skies, hot days, and the beautiful parks that I frequented.

A year later, I moved to San Francisco after working in Germany and San Diego. I was still having the same problems, but they were getting increasingly worse. I had many days when I could only drag myself home after work, sit in the bathtub, and then go to bed. I seemed to have a dull headache that never went away, and my body was always tense. I felt bloated and uncomfortable. Even a jog around the block would not ease my stress.

I alternated between feeling very energetic and ambitious, to feeling lethargic and without purpose. My body and my mind were exhausted from fighting whatever it was. I started to feel paralyzed by all the stresses and strains of living.

One very hot day, I lay on the roof of my apartment building, unable to move, until my face was burnt crisp from the sun. I didn't want to get up. I felt life being sucked from my bones.

Looking back, I realize that I simply couldn't admit to myself that something was wrong. I wanted to be happy. Instead, I was depressed.

During this time period, I occasionally covered media events as a freelance reporter. I was covering a television conference in Los Angeles when

I met a dentist. He told me that I looked as if I was about to crack from tension. He told me quite emphatically, "There's something wrong with you." I remember feeling embarrassed and wondering if I really looked that bad. I finally faced up to it and sought medical help.

I went to a gynecologist in San Diego where my parents live. I had not menstruated in two years and was producing milk. Tests showed that I had a high prolactin level, 200 instead of 5. "Ah," he sighed. "This often indicates a pituitary tumor. I suggest that when you return home you visit the hospital and have a CAT scan done." A week later I did, and my doctors discovered the tumor. I looked at the scan, a little perplexed at the pea-sized shadow, and thought to myself, "You! You are what's causing me all this grief!" I wanted to cry and laugh at the same time.

The pituitary gland is the master gland of the body because it issues many hormones and controls the functions of other glands in the body. It regulates the reproductive system, produces the growth hormone, and controls other major functions, including metabolism. If the pituitary is removed entirely or partially, medication is necessary to replace the natural hormones of the pituitary gland. A tumor of the pituitary causes the most problems for children because of the disruption of natural growth patterns.

The tumor in my pituitary gland was signaling to my body that I was pregnant. I was producing estrogen but not progesterone, and my breasts were full of milk, ready for a newborn. I felt as if I had premenstrual syndrome consecutively for two years, which resulted in the extreme mood swings. Water retention led to bloating, and the headaches were due to pressure on the optic nerves from the tumor.

At that point I just wanted to be rid of the tumor! All the anger and frustration that I had felt over the past two years welled up inside me. I was fed up. My doctors gave me several options, including drugs that would inhibit the growth of the tumor but wouldn't dissolve it. I would have had to take it for the rest of my life. I knew immediately that I would chance the surgery, because I was only twenty-five years old at the time.

Pituitary tumors are better news for neurosurgeons because often they can be completely cured in the first surgery. This was true in my case. I was in the hospital for a week, then at home for another week. I returned to work in the third week. Exactly a month after my surgery, I had my first period in almost three years. My senses of smell and taste improved noticeably. I recall that things started to seem clearer thereafter.

For a month or so after the surgery, I was ecstatic at my newfound freedom. And then, for some reason, I crashed into a depression. I still don't know if this was a physical reaction, emotional, or a combination of the two.

In search of normalcy after dealing with hospitals, bureaucracies, and life in the city, I moved back to my hometown. Tears welled in my eyes as the plane descended over the lakes and farmland that I had missed so much. "I'm home," I remember thinking. "It's over. It's really over."

I lived with my girlfriend in the country and worked downtown with a wonderful group of people. Every day I took an old, rickety bus for an hour-long trip through small towns along the lake. We would pass through the woods. I recall the changing of the seasons, how the green of the trees exploded into a kaleidoscope of color before turning white with snow. Just beyond the woods, we would find ourselves downtown. Sometimes old friends would happen onto the bus, and we'd talk all the way to work together. I was in heaven.

When you are recovering from a brain tumor, many people will say, directly or indirectly, "Oh, snap out of it! Get back to your old self." But that's unrealistic. We don't go back to the way we were. These things change us.

For example, I am much more emotional than I used to be, and I think that is good. I am also much more protective of myself. I am cautious about events that make me too anxious; anxiety only reminds me of how I felt all those years ago.

I was in great turmoil at times while working on this book. Whenever I started to write my own account, I'd get really depressed without knowing why. At one point, I quit the entire project even though it was almost done. It frightened me to think about that time in my life. I had never let myself feel fear at the time, but writing was bringing me in touch with it more and more.

Feeling a need to do something physical in order to focus my energy, I began to draw again. I found the creative process uplifting. After some conversations with friends, I decided to finish the book despite trepidation about putting my personal thoughts on paper for all to read.

It has been sixteen years and there has been no recurrence of the tumor, which is typical if the entire tumor is removed. When I hear the word "recover," it seems that people mean they want to recoup their losses, or themselves. But to me it means to integrate and evolve, to redefine what was and replace it with something new. Life is not linear; it's more like a topographical map, where new ideas and perspectives overlay the terrain.

There is always hope of a good outcome. I am an example of that. But I also know many people who have problems for years after their treatment. And there are feelings of anger, frustration, and fear for a variety of reasons. Unfortunately, many books aimed at cancer patients only focus on the good results and gloss over a vast population who have to deal with ongoing day-to-day problems. These books perpetuate a prejudice in society that only the happy and the healthy, the fighters and the winners are to be applauded, while pain and suffering are ugly and to be avoided at all costs. Therefore, people who don't get better think there's something wrong with them.

Grief and suffering are natural byproducts of something that has gone wrong, as are feelings of exhilaration and freedom when things go right. We must never be ashamed of having a full range of emotions, for that is our humanity. Out of these experiences, we develop compassion for others.

It is important to remember that the essence of the person is still inside of you. There is a creative person within you who wants to do the activities that he or she loves to do. These activities will anchor your old self in the face of all that is happening around you. Keep doing the things that you love and find inspiration in new things.

PART 2

Poems and Essays
by Family and Caregivers

BY VERA KROMS

History

Vera Kroms wrote "History" about her father as he was dying from brain can-
cer. Poetry allowed her to address his slow physical and intellectual decline, while
celebrating the complexity of his life at the same time. This poem appears in
The Cancer Poetry Project: Poems by Cancer Patients and Those Who Love
Them, *edited by Karin B. Miller. Kroms lives in Brighton, Massachusetts, and*
works as a computer programmer.

When a cell beneath this skull
began to multiply, devouring his life
backwards, English, his last mental feast,
started disappearing from his speech, word
by word, like coins dropping through a hole
in his tongue. At night, he woke to Berlin
toppling in the distance. Three women
who called him father kept visiting.
The slide rule, which had calibrated
his ascent from farm boy to professor
became, for him, an artifact
from a forgotten race. In the end,
he was spooned the softest food, his mouth
receiving what he understood.

BY LINDA

I No Longer Fear Death

Linda wrote this essay after the death of her daughter, Jamie. Jamie's story, including this essay, is published in the book, To Live until We Say Good-bye, *by Dr. Elisabeth Kübler-Ross and Mal Warshaw.*

In many ways, my life really began just before I learned that my daughter had a brain tumor. Most of my life before that followed a typical pattern. I went to college, taught for five years, married, became the mother of two children, and acquired a house in the suburbs. About a year before Jamie's tumor was diagnosed, I began to feel that I needed something more, something for myself. I became more involved in the parent-participating cooperative nursery school my son attended, joined a women's consciousness-raising group, and went into therapy. The growth and changes that came from these experiences may have helped to prepare me for the time ahead with Jamie but they also contributed to the end of my marriage. I was in the middle of divorce proceedings when I learned about Jamie's tumor. All of my excitement and plans for the future vanished at that moment. I knew that my own life would have to wait.

From the moment of her birth, for some reason Jamie and I shared a very special love. I knew that she would need me even more now, and I needed to be with her too. Learning about her illness began the most profound and emotionally intense time of my life. Everything that ever happened to me before belonged to another lifetime. All my energy was now centered on the fight for Jamie's life. There were moments when I resented the limitations Jamie's illness put on me, but if she was to die, I had to know I had done everything within my power for her.

I was told how serious Jamie's illness was from the beginning, as I had insisted on knowing the truth. Although chances were slim that she would survive, there was room for a little hope. However, at the beginning, I found it hard to hold onto that hope. We suddenly entered an unknown yet terrifying world. The staff at Babies' Hospital helped ease the transition somewhat, but it was difficult to watch Jamie go through the brain scans and the radiation treatments. Yet she accepted it all and gave me the strength I needed. I knew that, despite my despair, I had to make every moment precious for her.

Although I was no longer married, I was not entirely alone. Throughout Jamie's illness, I had the constant love and help of my parents and friends. Although they could not completely know the depth and complexity of my feelings, they were with me, for they too needed to do whatever they could to help Jamie, my son Rusty, and me. At times I found it difficult to relate to these people, as dear and wonderful as they were to me, precisely because this was happening to me, not to them. They could leave me and return to their "normal" lives while my world was shattered. Yet I know I could never have made it through Jamie's illness without them.

I experienced many moments of intense anger and bitterness. Despite the depth of my love for Jamie, there were times when I was so angry at her for putting me through this, for making me face the possibility of losing someone so precious to me, for depriving me of the chance to continue to love her and guide her and share in her growing up loved and loving. At the same time, I was aware of all she had given me in so short a time.

One of the things that made it so hard for me to face my life without Jamie was that I did not believe in any kind of life after death. I had always been terrified at the thought of my own death, believing it would mean the end of all consciousness, although I tried not to think about it and certainly never talked about it. Many of my friends do believe that there is life after death, but I rejected their attempts to talk to me about this. I did not think it would be at all comforting to me if I believed that a part of Jamie would survive death. I was more concerned with the tremendous loss I would have to cope with if she died.

Although part of me used a great deal of denial all through Jamie's illness, I also felt a need to try to prepare myself for her death. I began to read, beginning with Dr. Kübler-Ross's *On Death and Dying*. Perhaps my experience in a consciousness-raising group led to my desire to talk to other people who were going through a similar experience. Through Hospice of Rockland, I became part of a group of relatives of cancer patients. It was with these people that I could deal with the feelings and fears that I often pushed away.

It's also through a member of this group that I met Mal Warshaw and became part of *To Live until You Die*. I had been helped by so many people and I hoped that by sharing my experience, others would learn that they did not have to face alone the loss of their child.

I met Dr. Kübler-Ross just after I learned that Jamie's tumor was growing again and there was little that could be done for her. I was in the middle of my own investigation of possible future treatments. I could not give up, even though intellectually I knew Jamie was dying. Within a few minutes, Dr. Kübler-Ross knew exactly what I needed and, with Jamie's help, she gave it to me. She asked Jamie to draw a picture. It was Dr. Kübler-Ross's interpretation of this picture that was the first step for me in coming to accept the inevitability of Jamie's death and a change in my thinking about death itself. Among the many shapes on Jamie's pictures was a free-floating purple balloon. Dr. Kübler-Ross pointed out to me that this balloon's color, position on the page, and its lack of connection to any other shape indicated that Jamie knew what was happening to her and accepted without fear the transition she was about to make. I needed to know that the future would not be difficult for her.

Dr. Kübler-Ross also knew that I was not allowing my feelings of anger and despair to surface as much as they should. A few days after her visit, she sent me a piece of rubber hose to beat against some sturdy object when I needed to get those feelings out. I have used it and it works.

We talked about a possible way of setting up my house if Jamie were ever bedridden. That time did come. I had taken Jamie to the hospital for one last treatment. It did not help and her condition steadily worsened. She needed constant and complete care but she wanted to go home. Although I was very frightened, I decided to go along with Jamie's express desire. Dr. Kübler-Ross visited us again during Jamie's last three weeks at home and was so supportive of what I was doing. I came to realize how much I needed that time at home with Jamie. It made it possible for me to fully accept the fact that Jamie had to die. It also gave me a chance to do all that was left to be done for her – to make her comfortable, to provide her with familiar things, and most important, to surround her with the love of her family and friends. I too was surrounded. I could never have brought Jamie home without the love and help of so many people, my parents, my friends, especially Liz, Joan, Carol, Lois, and Lee as well as many others at Babies' Hospital. All of us, including my son, shared in caring for Jamie. It was especially important for Rusty to be part of this time. He had been shut out often when I was in the hospital with Jamie or taking her there for treatments. He has some beautiful memories from those last three weeks – reading to Jamie, polishing her nails, or just sitting with her on her bed and holding her hand.

I knew I had done the right thing in bringing Jamie home, but a few days before she died, I wavered briefly in my determination to keep her at home until the end. There were medical complications I was not sure I could handle. I called Dr. Kübler-Ross, and with only a few words she gave me the reassurance I needed. At that point, Jamie was in no pain and was rarely awake. Dr. Kübler-Ross strengthened my newly forming belief that Jamie's consciousness was focused elsewhere but she was still surrounded by love. I knew then that I would not take her back to the hospital. It helped me so much to know that I could turn to Dr. Kübler-Ross at any time with any problem and she would be there.

As Jamie's condition worsened, I tried to concentrate on the purple balloon and all it represented. I found myself wanting and needing to believe that part of Jamie would still exist somewhere, somehow, after her body died. During the week, despite episodes of respiratory distress, Jamie became very peaceful, and I no longer feared what was happening. I could almost see the purple balloon gently pulling on its string until at last it separated and floated away. I miss Jamie so much, but out of the pain has come much growth and learning. I no longer fear death, for as I held Jamie in my arms as she died, I saw nothing to fear. I no longer believe that death is an end. Even as I drove off from the cemetery, I had no feeling of having left my child there. She was with me as she has been many times since her death. In the midst of all the anguish are so many beautiful memories. Jamie's courage, her joy, her love will always be with me. She was truly a very precious gift.

BY BONNIE FELDMAN

Seth's Dream Come True

After the death of her son, Seth, Bonnie Feldman founded The Brain Tumor Society, a not-for-profit volunteer health organization based in Boston, Massachusetts. Seth was diagnosed with a glioblastoma multiforme at age fourteen and lived until his eighteenth birthday.

In August of 1985, my fourteen-year-old son, Seth, was diagnosed with a glioblastoma multiforme. Seth was an honor student, an avid skier, and a great fan of the British rock group, The Who. He played varsity tennis and football in high school, and was away at football camp when he became ill.

Told he had only eight months to live, Seth grappled with issues of life and death. He also concerned himself with typical teenage matters and worried that his illness would make it tough to catch up on his study of a new language, German.

Seth had surgery to remove as much of the tumor as possible. He then embarked on a six-week course of intensive chemotherapy, which required three hospitalizations, and five weeks of radiation treatments administered twice daily. When he felt bored and ready for a more normal challenge, we arranged for his German teacher to come to our home to tutor him. Following his surgery, Seth had become photophobic; he could not concentrate visually without much discomfort. He could not read or watch television, so he listened to comedy tapes to keep his spirits high.

Before long, we began reading books to Seth from his honors English class. We secured a tape recorder for the visually impaired, and eventually obtained most of the assigned books on tape. By December, Seth was able to attend school for one period a day. When his energy increased, he went for two classes, German and English. He was determined to begin his honors chemistry program after Christmas vacation.

Instead, Seth spent his next four weeks in the hospital. He suffered from massive edema as a result of his radiation treatments. The edema lead to tremendous muscle wasting from what his physician called "industrial doses" of Decadron, a drug used to reduce swelling in the brain. This set him back a few months.

Seth had many subsequent medical problems. Following a second surgery for recurrence, he had seizures, meningitis, and a twisted neck that required traction. He lost over twenty pounds in two weeks and came home from the hospital unable to walk or care for himself. With great determination and strenuous rehabilitation, Seth was able to attend his junior prom just five weeks later.

Unfortunately, the tumor recurred once again, affecting the strength on one side of Seth's body. Shortly after school ended, he began an experimental course of chemotherapy.

Every time Seth suffered a setback, he immediately started thinking about recovery. When he felt weak, he pushed himself to walk half a block. As his energy increased, he planned a half-day outing. Eventually he started lifting weights and going to rehab. He could not play his regular position in football, so he taught himself to be a kicker instead. And before long, he was back on the ski slopes; even though we had to drive him to the lift and carry his skis for him, he was able to take a few runs.

Seth used his remaining energy to speak on behalf of the institute that had treated him. He spoke on radiothons, at golf tournaments, and to groups of volunteers. He wanted to raise money for brain tumor research so that someday others would not have to experience what he was going through. One day, Seth asked me what I thought was the worst treatment for a brain tumor. I took my best guess: chemotherapy. His answer was, "No treatment at all."

Seth viewed his illness as a hurdle to be surmounted. He wanted only to be a normal teenager, and to fulfill his lifelong dream of attending Dartmouth College. Sapped of all energy, he managed to visit five colleges the summer before his senior year. He decided to apply to Dartmouth's early decision program. Passing his college board exams with flying colors, he got his early admission to Dartmouth.

Seth graduated with the other members of his high school class. As he accepted his diploma, he received a standing ovation. Seth attended his senior prom and prepared to set off for college. That summer, he retrained himself to read so that he would not need a special tape recorder or a reader at school. He plowed through nine novels, the first books he had read in three years. He felt the best he had since his ordeal began. His doctors wanted him to go back on chemotherapy, but he refused.

Seth loved every aspect of college life. Dartmouth exceeded his expectations. The school accommodated his every need to allow him as normal an experience as possible. But on Halloween of 1988, Seth's tumor recurred for the last time. He found himself a reader and managed, as best he could, to stay in school until final exams. In his mind, he had completed his first term of college. He regretted not having been able to spend more time at Dartmouth, where he had spent the happiest days of his life.

Seth passed away two weeks after he returned home, just days before his eighteenth birthday. He never lost his sense of humor or his indomitable spirit. His strength, his courage, and an abounding love of life are his legacy. Seth taught me that anything is possible when you set your mind to it.

Every parent who has a child with a brain tumor seems to draw strength from that child. There is nothing worse than watching a child undergo treatment for a life-threatening illness. We, as parents, are supposed to be able to make it all better. Teenagers present an unusual challenge. While their friends become increasingly independent, teens with a life-threatening illness must rely on their parents more than ever. That is why it is important to include them in the decision-making.

Inspired by Seth's determination, I researched brain tumor organizations, contacted their representatives, and learned about the objectives of each group. As there was no brain tumor organization east of Chicago or north of Atlanta, I established The Brain Tumor Society, a national organization based in Boston. I put together a board of directors with a deep commitment to the cause and expertise in a number of areas. I also recruited nationally recognized physicians to participate in the Medical Advisory Board. Our mission was clear: The Brain Tumor Society was committed to working toward a cure through research, education, and support.

The Society has accomplished a lot in the past twelve years. We have assisted thousands of patients and families throughout the country and beyond. We provide telephone counseling, disseminate educational information, and encourage the formation of brain tumor support groups throughout the country. For those who cannot attend support group meetings, we have established a patient-family telephone network.

The Society not only provides patients and their loved ones with up-to-date information concerning their specific tumor types and treatment options, but also contributes to continuing education for doctors and nurses. We sponsor numerous professional educational programs throughout the world. We also host symposia to provide patients and families an opportunity to interact with leading experts in the field of brain tumor treatment and research. In addition, we hold an annual meeting that is open to the public and attended by several hundred patients, family members, friends, and health professionals. During this meeting, we award The Brain Tumor Society Research Grants; to date, over $3.6 million has been allocated to more than sixty scientists, dramatically expanding the field of brain tumor research.

In February 1990, just months after The Brain Tumor Society was founded, the leaders of six independent brain tumor organizations met to share information and identify goals that they could accomplish as a group. In April 1991, these and other organizations from across the United States and Canada formed the North American Brain Tumor Coalition. Having organized the first informational and explorative meetings, I was given the honor of becoming the coalition's first chairperson. In May 1992, I testified before the United States House of Representatives Committee on Appropriations, Subcommittee on Labor, Health, Human Services, Education, and Related Agencies, as to the critical need for establishing brain tumor research centers. Later that year, it was announced that eight potential centers would be funded for three years at a total cost of $9.18 million.

In the years that followed, plans were drawn up to educate Congress and the National Institutes of Health on both the importance of brain tumor research and the critical need for increased funding. Brain Tumor Awareness Week was established. Encouraged by the coalition's increasing strength and outreach, the National Cancer Institute and the National Institute of Neurological Disorders and Stroke (NINDS) joined forces with leaders in the scientific and advocacy communities to determine the future focus of brain tumor research.

When Seth first left for college, I decided to volunteer my time and energy for the brain tumor cause. I felt, in some way, I was continuing his work. When he died, I felt an overwhelming need to create something positive from the loss of Seth and from this most devastating experience. Whenever I doubt my ability to face a particular challenge, I think of Seth, his courage, and his bravery.

It was Seth's dream that someday others would not have to go through what he had gone through. Those of us committed to finding a cure will continue to build on the work supported by my loving husband, Sid, our exceedingly generous donors and volunteers, and many caring, dedicated professionals.

Someday, Seth's dream will come true.

BY DARRYL FORSTNER

We Realized Many Things Too Late

Darryl's father was diagnosed with a glioblastoma and died four months later. Darryl Forstner is a fictional name for the author, who wishes to remain anonymous. He lives with his wife and children in Kansas, where he is a physician in private practice.

My dad recently died four months after he was diagnosed with a glioblastoma multiforme. I happen to be a doctor, which is somewhat relevant, as you'll see later. This story is less about my dad than about his family and his care. In retrospect, we realized many things too late, and they might have made our lives better.

My dad was admitted to University Hospital for a fever and confusion. He had a CT scan and an MRI. Our neurologist told us up until the morning of the surgery that he suspected cancer but still hoped that it might be a brain abscess. I later learned that the MRI had the classic appearance of a glioblastoma. I still cannot understand why a physician could not tell another physician what was really going on. My dad's neurosurgeon described my parents as philosophical. We were hardly in danger of falling apart.

The surgery was uneventful. The surgeon told us that the tumor was relatively small and in an accessible location, and that he had removed most of it. We were quite hopeful that my dad would be with us for some time.

While waiting for the biopsy results, my mom, my brother, and I began to talk to my dad about retiring. He had worked long enough as a lawyer.

He had always insisted that he could not stop working because he needed more money to retire on. Perhaps this was the result of having grown up poor during the Depression. He refused to consider closing his practice.

At the time it seemed that his stubbornness was due to denial. Looking back, we can see that his ability to reason had already been greatly affected by the tumor. We argued, and I finally left the hospital in disgust, flying home a day earlier than I had planned.

While I was in the cab to the airport, the neurosurgeon came to the room and gave my folks the worst news. He told them that the tumor was a glioblastoma, one of the most aggressive tumors. He later told my mom, but not my dad, that the average survival was twelve months. My dad knew that the news was bad. When I spoke to the neurosurgeon from the airport, he painted a rosy picture, saying that my father fell into a good prognostic group and would "be a good companion to my mom for perhaps three years."

I don't expect doctors to be able to tell the future. I don't expect to know exactly how long a patient will live. One always fears shortening a patient's survival with too gloomy an outlook; however, looking on the brightest side can really have its drawbacks.

We were told that my dad should have conventional radiation and chemotherapy, and that no experimental protocols could be considered without failing these standard treatments. In retrospect, I should have asked for all the different protocols that were being tried in the country; by the time patients are really sick, they can't fly to distant cities, or live in motels, or be cared for by their spouses unassisted. By the time someone fails the conventional therapy, as my dad did, it may be too late to consider other options.

We pursued the traditional therapy, hopeful that he would respond favorably. We hoped he would have a few months of decent life before he relapsed. I had planned to take the family on vacation in October, after he completed the radiation and recovered from its effects. He did well for six weeks, but, with two weeks of radiation left to go, his progress diminished rapidly.

Every day after this proved to be an ordeal for my mother. At first we ascribed his fatigue to the radiation therapy. But it was much more profound than this. He'd sleep for twenty hours every day, and it would take my mother hours of coaxing to get him ready for their daily trip for radiation therapy. He'd scream when anyone touched him. It was impossible to do much without his cooperation, which was nonexistent. He was incontinent. He'd stay for hours in the bathroom, unable to get off the toilet and unwilling to accept help. It would take a monumental effort to get him to eat or take his medication. Still, we believed that his behavior was a result of the radiation treatment.

Finally, the treatment was over. My family came to spend time with my parents, my brother, and my sister's family. The first night that we arrived, it took us three hours to get him out of a chair. The next day it took us three hours to get him into the car, but we could not get him out for five hours. He refused all help. Thinking that he was just being stubborn, we alternated coaxing, talking, then screaming and cursing at him, one person relieving another each time one of us got out of hand. We did not realize that the tumor was controlling his behavior. He just could not put together the many movements and decisions needed to get himself out of a car. He would start to move, then lose track of what he was doing.

We realized, on some level, that he had changed neurologically, but we didn't want to believe it. We still clung to the idea that it was the fatigue from the radiation. After several hours, my wife finally led him back into the house, knowing that this was really the end. Unfortunately, his physicians did not offer any explanation for what was happening. They increased his medication to decrease the intracranial pressure, which seemed to help a little.

The doctors never really saw how bad he was, because once my mother finally got him up and moving, often after many hours of struggling, he was always awake and a pretty good actor for his radiation treatments and other visits. My mom described his worsening symptoms to the doctors, only to be told that he was doing fine and was to be seen again in two weeks.

My mom, not willing to accept this assessment, took the neurologist physically by the arm and said, "Doctor, he is not all right. Look at him, he's much worse." He took her into the next room and told her that things were very bad, that the tumor was much larger on the MRI and had not responded to radiation and chemotherapy. He told her that my dad would die soon, and that we should get a doctor near us to take care of this stage of his illness. I heard this a few hours later.

My dad had five physicians: an internist, a neurologist, a neurosurgeon, a radiation oncologist, and a chemotherapy oncologist. What he needed was a doctor, someone who would contact the radiologist and then determine my dad's options from the neurosurgeon, neurologist, and chemotherapist. We needed someone who could answer questions such as whether it was worth the struggle to continue coming to the hospital for chemotherapy and blood tests. I was having trouble coordinating my dad's care even though I was a doctor and actually knew the system. I called and asked the radiation oncologist, who was a very open and honest man, if he would be "the doctor." He readily agreed. After consulting with my dad's physicians, we decided to stop all treatment. By this time, my dad could not communicate by phone, and he slept most of the time.

My dad's illness and his treatment were difficult for my mom. She was the sole caregiver and transporter. It was a difficult time because we had no idea what was going on eight weeks after the surgery. No one ever really told us my dad's prognosis; for a while, we hoped that he would recover. His partners called every day to ask for him, but he'd never take their calls. He forbade us to reveal his illness to them, and accused us of disloyalty when we did. After his radiation, he told me that he actually planned to go back to work. He was a very independent and stubborn person to the end.

My mom had to take care of him and deal with law partners who screamed at her almost daily. She was terrified of answering the phone in her own house. While he could still talk on the phone, our conversations would invariably end in arguments over his treatment of my mom. She tried to discuss his practice with him and persuade him to retire. She also tried to make him understand what she was going through.

As a result, all our interactions with my dad during the middle part of his illness were negative. We fought over getting ready for the daily treatments, eating, getting out of the bathroom, or physically caring for him. We argued about his law practice and the calls he was receiving. We never got a chance to deal positively with his illness, and we certainly never got a chance to really say goodbye. By the time we realized that he had no time left, he had regressed too much to communicate with us.

To add to her stress, my mom had to deal with all the details of my dad's practice after his death. She got a little help from her son-in-law, and she and I talked every night. However, she clearly shouldered most of the burden.

This condenses and in a way trivializes the emotional trials that we experienced. My dad maintained his defenses and a considerable amount of denial, until he became so disoriented that his illness probably was not much of an issue for him. But we had real problems as a result of not knowing why he acted the way he did, how his tumor was progressing, and when to step in and deal with his affairs. My mom feels tremendous guilt now about having put him through the ordeal of treatment when it obviously did no good.

We should have known that his problems were largely due to his tumor, and that he was using his remaining resources to cover and maintain a semblance of normalcy. Instead of arguing, we would have liked to spend the time he had in a more positive way.

BY KAREN LEAHY

Adagio for Ginny

Karen Leahy had written a poem after her father's death that her sister, Ginny, had framed for her home. Then, in October 1999, Ginny was diagnosed with an aggressive brain cancer – treatable, but not curable. She asked Karen to write a poem for her. A version of this poem appeared in The Cancer Poetry Project: Poems by Cancer Patients and Those Who Love Them, *edited by Karin B. Miller. Leahy lives in Great Neck, New York.*

When I see my brave, bald sister
stumble over stones of fear
on this hard path she did not choose,
I search my own heart for courage
and try to hold her steady.
I'd like to be for a day
the magical mother
who could kiss her on the brow
and make her brain all better.
Ginny deserves more years,
more dreams come true.
Oh Great Beating Heart of the Universe,
Keeper of Time and Tides,
slow the tempo of her days
until all her time swells

rich with melody and meaning.
Let her feel the sweet space of every minute,
the symphonic expanse of an hour.
And let her dreams bloom with beautiful abandon
like birdsongs filling the blue Ohio sky
along the paths of our childhood,
when cancer was a word related to
others, but not to us,
when our only concern,
walking back from piano lessons,
was for the hour before us:
spending our bus money on ice cream
and singing in harmony
all the way home.

BY RICHARD HAILE

I Could Hardly Say the Words, "My Daughter Has Cancer"

Richard's daughter, Leslie, was diagnosed with a ganglioneuroma. She had surgery, radiation, and chemotherapy. In the years since, Leslie has experienced a number of difficult symptoms and illnesses that may have been related to her treatment. He and his family live east of San Francisco.

I suppose that the most important part of solving any problem is to identify it, label it, and then outline a course of action. I remember in November 1984, the neurologist told us, "Your daughter has a deposit in the spinal ganglia of her brain. It could be a calcium deposit or maybe a cyst." He never uttered the word "tumor," as if we couldn't handle it. He was almost right.

I came home, back to my radiator and muffler shop, and called my banker. With tears in my eyes and a shaky voice, I asked him for enough money to run the business for six months; I knew that one of my little girls was going to need all of us by her side. My banker and the people of our small town were very supportive during this time.

It wasn't until early in 1985 that it finally hit me and I was able to say the words: "My daughter has cancer." I think that I did everything I could in the first two months to avoid uttering them. I kept my mind occupied with the problems, the many trips to San Francisco, the arrangements that had to be made, and our younger daughter Stephanie. I would occupy myself with almost anything to keep from saying, "Leslie has a brain tumor."

I'm pretty good at fixing things; however, it took me a long time to realize that her doctors couldn't just cut this thing out. They couldn't just fix it.

I started asking questions that any parent would ask: Why my child? Why us? I would tell myself that only those children who lived in big cities could get cancer. It couldn't happen to small-town folks like us. We lived simple, healthy lives. We ate fresh food. Leslie was a star athlete. She raced an 80KX Kawasaki. She was no wimp! But cancer just doesn't care about that.

As we progressed through Leslie's treatments, our family really became one. We asked our friends, extended family, and our church for their prayers. We believed that Leslie would beat the cancer; we grew as tough as she had become. Soon, radiation and chemotherapy were a part of dinner-table conversations.

We met other people from different parts of the state, country, and world who had problems far worse than ours. We thanked God for preserving us. I learned to accept that some of the kids I had met would not make it. But I always believed that my child would pull through.

Leslie did make it, and made it well. She was on the honor roll her entire sophomore year and also on the high school track team. Her special event was the low hurdles. She is currently Cotton Queen in our town. She is the past Honored Queen of Job's Daughters and does an excellent job in her memory work. She has spoken before such groups as the local Chamber of Commerce. When she graduated from eighth grade, she received the American Legion Award. She looked beautiful accepting the award, even though she had no hair. But I don't think that anybody noticed the lack of hair.

We're proud of both our daughters. We are thankful for their strong attitudes and amazing will to live. Leslie has a slight tremor on her right side. She has gone from being right-handed to being left-handed. Her memory is not as great as it once was. But she manages with notepads.

It is never easy to watch a child go through treatment for a serious illness. It is especially difficult for parents. When my daughter feels low, I remind her – and myself – of the motorcycle racers' motto, "When in doubt, gas it. You've got to go for it."

BY HARRY SMITH

Her Love Still Abides

Harry Smith lives in New York City, where he is a publisher and writer. He enjoys hiking, painting, and gardening. Harry's wife had surgery for a low-grade astrocytoma in 1977. After many complications and years of decline, she died peacefully on July 12, 1995. Says Harry, "She died the instant of my arrival that day, as if she had been waiting for me." Harry's poem, "Last Ode," was orig-inally published in Two Friends II, *by Harry Smith and Menke Katz.*

LAST ODE

The day they told me you were dying, the air was
oversexed with Spring,
the first full musky heat of Spring, and lovers
bloomed in every park
like lilacs, and lilacs sang like love, and the song of
lilacs smote me,
cut me open to the quick of love; lay open all the
years onto
such a day in a little park with lilacs: God! You
reeked of lilacs,
after having bathed in a tub of lilac water for the
Spring, for me!
And I sneezed and laughed and gave you lilacs.

The day they told me you were dying, Death's soft
lilac shadow bathed you
from our first Spring, renewing love,
and it was the first Spring heat of love,
filling us with each other, dispelling all the business
of the years,
returning us to full-time lover, and we called our
destiny a gift.
Finding in Death's infinite transparency all pleasures godly pure,
we called it lucky to be young for Death.

When you were missing from your place, I searched
for you in the labyrinth
deep in the hospital underground. And I was
Orpheus. Love has led me here
to these realms of silence and cold creation.
The lords of those terrible abodes
trembled at my sacred rage and let me pass,
hearing Orpheus ask,
"Where is my wife? What have you done with my wife?
I have come for my wife.
Which wheel can spin the thread that was her life?"

When they returned you to your place,
yet missing from yourself, pale, blighted
shadow, Death's grip graven on your brow, I learned
to envy Orpheus.
O lucky, lucky Orpheus! For love plucked in the full
of beauty,

for the starry lyre of lament and the consummation of death.
What if his Eurydice had followed from shadow into sunlight
yet stayed a shade forever lost beside him, without a
last farewell.
I make a lyre of lilacs for my wife.

I liken the loss of my wife to the legend of Orpheus, except that I envy Orpheus for losing his wife completely while everything was still beautiful. My Eurydice is in a nursing home several blocks away, alive but forever lost, like a ghost. She cannot talk, nor learn anything new. She cannot walk, and seems to have little awareness of her situation. I believe that she recognizes me and our children and a few old friends. She is somewhat responsive and can communicate pleasure or displeasure and affection through facial expressions. She is paralyzed on one side; she gestures with her good hand occasionally, usually to indicate irritation. She can also hold hands and reciprocate a kiss. The ability to love seems to abide after most of the other mental abilities are gone.

It is now about seventeen years since she was diagnosed as having a moderate left-frontal astrocytoma. Being alive, she is a statistical success, as nearly all the people who have been diagnosed with this affliction have died within the first five years, the majority dying within three years. She is a private patient at the nursing home and has a private companion who feeds and nurses her. She is in no pain, except when she aspirates. Because eating – even the mush that she must be given – is one of her few pleasures, I have not authorized the introduction of a feeding tube. Her impairment is due to injured and dead brain cells all across the frontal region, a product of high-level radiation therapy.

Ironically, she had frequently asked about the possibility of impairment from the treatment, and at every step we had been reassured that it was not a possibility to be feared, that the main danger was the progress of the tumor itself, which was effectively sterilized. Now, there is continuing necrosis of the brain cells, thus the possibility of more strokes (she had one three years after the radiation) and arterial occlusions. Had she known what would befall her, she never would have consented to the treatment.

In 1977, she was operated on by a neurosurgeon at a university hospital, who removed the ventricular blockage as best he could. Another doctor then administered the radiation. A couple of weeks after radiation therapy, the residual mass swelled, causing another blockage. She was in such severe pain that she remained in a fetal position, unable to move. The neurosurgeon operated again to install a shunt. She developed severe aphasia during the radiation treatment, which mostly disappeared several weeks later. Her hospitalization for the treatment lasted more than two months.

Before the diagnosis, she had been hospitalized for three weeks by a neurologist. Some kind of glioma had been suspected, but the type of the tumor was not determined until after the operation.

She had probably had the tumor for at least a year, possibly two, before the diagnosis was made. She had lacked most of the classic symptoms of a brain tumor – dropping things, stumbling, radical behavior changes. Looking back, I'm quite sure that she had stumbled a few times while hurrying, which I'd considered unusual because she was a graceful person, and her walking had slowed. She had always suffered from frequent headaches, but they gradually became worse and more frequent. One internist had treated her for sinusitis; then an ear, nose, and throat physician treated her for neuralgia. Only after her symptoms had escalated to include projectile vomiting, temporary blindness, and diplopia (double vision) did another doctor send her to a neurologist.

Before that, she'd considered going to a psychiatrist because she'd felt increasingly unable to cope with our children, the household, and her career opportunities. She had recently gone back to school, obtained an MA in psychology, and had a few courses toward a PhD. Then she stopped her studies and neglected to pursue a job that she had wanted.

In the few weeks between her diagnosis and her treatment (while we waited to see what the lesion would look like in a second CT scan), we had some of the best times of our lives. After the treatment, there were about three years when she was outwardly normal, able to walk and talk, even score well on an intelligence test. Yet she was very impaired. Her motivation itself was impaired. She no longer had the ability to decide where to go. She could not do anything on her own, and became totally dependent on me. She paid little attention to our three teenage children, and usually was confused about what they were doing. Her ability to retain new information was limited; thus, she became very forgetful, typically unable to recall daily events. Sometimes she even got lost.

Then she had a major stroke, again the result of the brain damage. At first, she was totally paralyzed on the left side and could not speak. She was hospitalized for about a month. With physical therapy, she learned how to walk again with a cane; most of her speech came back after some speech therapy. She stayed on that plateau for perhaps a year. A stair elevator had been installed in our brownstone, and I had hired a nursing aide, the same woman who cares for her now. She slowly declined thereafter. Confusion pervaded her speech, which gradually became less and less. About seven years ago, despite antiseizure drugs, she suffered a seizure lasting several days. As a result, she lost almost all of her speech and her ability to care for herself. She was subject to frequent seizures and swallowing problems from then on. It was no longer possible to care for her at home. At that time she became a resident of the Cobble Hill Nursing Home in Brooklyn.

In the years when she was an invalid at home, I took her for vacations in the Caribbean every winter and to Maine in the summers. She had to use a wheelchair. She still enjoyed traveling, but there were difficulties. For instance, I would have to ask strangers to help her in the restroom, and sometimes enter one myself if she fell. She was usually disoriented; sometimes, she would manage to hobble off by herself on some imaginary errand. In the absence of memory, any vagrant thought or dream seemed real to her.

In her current condition, she is serene. Like a slow child, she plays with stuffed animals; she has many plants in her room and looks at them often. Of course, she can no longer read, but she looks at pictures in magazines. She is apparently unaware of time, and, in some ways, at the age of fifty-six, she is remarkably untouched by time – no wrinkles, only a few streaks of gray in her dark brown hair. She is free of care and well cared for. Obviously, she is an easy patient and smiles beautifully at those who are kind. She is popular with the staff, and her regular private aide is very devoted.

I visit most days when I am in New York, but my absences have become longer. Now I go to Maine in all seasons and stay for the greater part of the summer at my country home. I travel more on business. Another woman became my companion several years ago. Nine years ago, when I turned forty-eight, the same age at which my father had died of a heart attack, I went through an intense middle-aged fool phase for a year. I dated dozens of women, even several very young women who had interned with me. I offered them "ideal nights," anything they wished for and anyplace they wanted to go.

I have not gone to any of the relatives' meetings at the nursing home, but I used to go to all such sessions when my wife was being treated at the university hospital. Rightly or wrongly – probably wrongly – there is a persistent belief among many relatives that their loved one's over-sensitivity to the stress of life and difficulties in personal relationships actually caused their malignant tumors. Many people, of course, feel guilt about not having been good enough to their loved ones before, and not being good enough to them during their illness, often even resenting them because of the hardships of the disease. I never had those problems.

I am bitter about our experience with the doctors, but I temper that with understanding of human fallibility. I tell myself that the average internist encounters only one or two brain tumor patients in a lifetime of practice, and their misdiagnoses probably make no difference in the long-term outcome. As to the tragic course of treatment, I have no doubt that the neurosurgeon thought he would succeed in giving her considerably more time of enjoyable life and did not foresee what would happen. He was very hard on the other doctors, but he had unlimited patience in answering questions from his patients and their relatives (not always correctly, as it turned out), and, despite being the busiest neurosurgeon in town, he always returned phone calls the same day.

However, when the chief resident asked him if he was going to install a ventricular shunt at the same time that he operated on the tumor, he said, "A human being is not a machine. . . . I think I can unblock her." That proved to be the wrong decision, but I think that he had not wished to mar her beauty. Strangely, her beauty was mentioned in the medical charts, which nurses told me was unprecedented.

Three years later, after the catastrophic stroke, the neurosurgeon would have nothing to do with her case. I can accept that people make mistakes, or that things don't always go exactly the way you intend them to, but we felt shoved aside afterward, and that was most painful.

I also felt that more could have been done with family members who visited in the hospital. It would have helped me to have something to do during the long months of daily visits, which often lasted six hours at a time. It would have helped to be a part of the rehabilitation process and be able to constructively help her when this was still possible.

BY GAIL LYNCH

To Believe

Gail Lynch is a licensed clinical social worker with a private practice in New Jersey. Her specialties include grief and loss as well as marital and relationship counseling. In March 1996, Gail's husband, Bob, was diagnosed with a grade-IV glioblastoma. He died in August 1996. This essay is adapted from Gail's mem-oir, In Sickness and in Health: One Woman's Story of Love, Loss, and Healing.

"Hi, baby," Bob said when I arrived at the hospital. "I missed you. Where've you been?"

"I just went home to sleep. Janet said she'd come by later this afternoon to visit. Has the doctor been here?"

"Yeah. He was here. We had a long talk. He's a good guy."

I turned on the TV for him. TWA Flight 800 had mysteriously crashed, and the news was full of airplane debris, weeping families, and airline officials.

"Aren't Mom and Roger supposed to be coming? I wish they didn't have to fly." I was surprised that he remembered his mother and brother were coming to visit. Roger and his wife, Janet, were attending to us in shifts so that they wouldn't have to leave their dogs with a sitter. I knew that the arrival of the rest of the family was important to him. He was afraid that they might die in a plane crash, though he would never acknowledge that he was dying himself.

The other event on TV was the summer Olympics. We watched for a while. Bob rolled it around on his tongue, "Olympics, 'Lympic, Limp Dick." He half-smiled. We hadn't made love since the first brain tumor symptoms. "Lovies or sleepies?" he used to ask, pulling me close. Now it was just sleepies, and not even enough of that. It saddened us both. We needed that intimacy more than ever. Sometimes after sex I would cry, not wanting to separate from Bob. That deep connection, that merging of spirit, body, and soul, should not have to be broken.

Each time Bob was in the hospital he invited me into his bed. "Come on in and lie down next to me, Shug. I need holdies." I needed holdies, too. I'd pull the curtain and peek around it to make sure no nurses were lurking. Then Bob would scoot way over to one side and I'd climb in next to him. It felt so illicit, like being a teenager and sneaking around in a parent's house with a boyfriend. A few times the nurses caught us and smiled.

I was glad it was the weekend and I could spend all day at the hospital. Janet and I took turns getting food. Lunch and dinner from McDonald's. Bob was delighted with his daily milkshake. Janet and I dreamed of real food, somewhere, sometime.

The next morning, Sunday, the phone rang. "Hi, Shuggy. I think I've been in an accident. There's blood all over my hat. I might be in the hospital. Can you come visit? The name of the hospital is St. Something or other. I think you might know the way but just in case you don't, remember to make a left at the restaurant. Okay?"

"I'll be there as soon as I can. It's 6:00 A.M., so it will take me a little time. I'll try to be there by 7:30." I didn't take him seriously about the accident – he was so confused about everything – and I knew where he had been all night. Besides, I needed a little time by myself, and a breakfast that wasn't from McDonald's.

When I got there, Bob was sitting up in bed with his hat on, blood all over it. I went to get the nurse. "What on earth happened?"

"Everything's okay. He pulled the IV out by mistake when he tried to get up to go to the bathroom. It was kind of a mess. But he's fine."

The next morning, Janet woke up with a stomach virus, or the consequences of too much fast-food. My friend and coworker, Marsha, came with me to the hospital after work. We went out for dinner after that. This was the first time I'd gone out with a friend in months.

"When do you give up hope?" I asked.

"Never," she said. Her husband had died of cancer when she was twenty-nine years old, leaving her to raise three small children alone. "You believe until the very end that there will be a miracle and your husband will not die."

"Thanks for going through this with me. You don't know how much I need to talk to you every day." I looked up and saw tears in her eyes. It surprised me. She took great pride in never crying about anything. The worst had happened years ago. Every other crisis paled in comparison.

"It's an honor," she said. Now we both had tears.

The waiter took one look at us and decided to return later. "He probably went back to the kitchen," I said, "and told his friends, 'I don't know what's wrong with them. I just told them the specials.'"

PART 3

Essays by Healthcare Professionals

BY ANATOLE BROYARD

Modern Fiction on the Couch: An Interview with a Retired Psychoanalyst

Anatole Broyard worked for many years as a book review editor for the New York Times. This excerpt was taken from "About Books: Fiction That Lies about Its Dreams," copyright © 1986 by The New York Times Company.

When Anatole Broyard, former book review editor of the New York Times questioned a retiring psychoanalyst on the difference between characters in fiction and his patients, he responded: "When I look back on them, it almost seems that my patients were more original – I'm tempted to say more talented – than people in many current novels.

"When someone tells me his story, he's fighting for his life, his happiness, his truth, if you like. He puts everything he has into his narrative . . . . Such pure need poured out of the people I saw, such beautiful sadness, such a reaching for the past or future, that I couldn't help loving them . . . . They may have felt that I alone understood them; I was the repository of their hopes and fears, their secrets. In a sense I was the mirror on the wall that enabled them to imagine for a moment that they were the fairest of them all, for there are times in analysis when nearly every patient takes on a great beauty, the beauty, you might say, of being the only creature who has to struggle with consciousness.

"Yet, I don't always feel this pressing toward clarification in novels. The characters don't talk with the same urgency. It's as if they haven't much faith in whomever they're performing for. Authors who aren't faithful to their characters remind me of people who lie about their dreams.

"One lets the men and women in a novel speak or act for themselves, and the situation in analysis is similar. Much of what I do is simply sit and wait while the patient shows himself to himself. Eventually, if we're lucky, something happens – something that he wants and needs and has been desperately waiting for. But in quite a few novels I read, I don't feel much wanting or needing, which baffles and frustrates me.

"One of the things that has always moved me in analysis was the patient's voice. No singer or composer could express all the changes of voice that an excited, grieving, or raging human being produces. But current fiction tends to be curiously dispassionate in its voice; I don't hear the break and tide of rhythm, the pulling for breath, the squawk or shriek of certain words, like bird or animal cries. And the images – those creatures from the black lagoon that used to haunt my consultation room – where are they?

"Then there were patients who would try to impress me with their brilliance or wit, as if to show that they didn't need me, didn't need anything. Certain authors are like that, and I want to ask them, Are you satisfied just to be amusing? What are you concealing?"

"Tell me," [Broyard] said, "What do you miss most? What did your patients give you that fiction doesn't?" [The therapist] thought a while. "Incongruity," he said. "Most of all I miss incongruity. A psychoanalyst, or at least this one, is constantly refreshed – even sustained – by the gorgeous incongruities that people produce under stress. Such a perspective is a measure of our range, our suppleness. Occasionally a patient will go through the kind of abrupt self-transcendence that's one of the glories of our species. Without transition, he'll leap from the disgusting to the sublime, from the petty or mundane to the wildest shores of human sensibility. These flashes of incongruity are like dying and going to heaven. If I wrote a novel, I would fill it with incongruities like kisses."

"Have you ever found any writers you envy because they came closer to the human soul than you did?" [Broyard] asked.

"Oh, yes. Indeed yes. There are certainly exceptions. Once in a while a novelist will raise a question and carry it to a height too exquisite to be described in any but ontological or theological terms. He'll develop his character's difficulty to a point where it dissolves into radiance and beatitude. It will have all the pathos of human fallibility, of original sin. It will identify our limits, and there's a consolation in this that only a few of us have the courage to appreciate. If a patient came to me with a complaint of such grandeur, I'd send him away. I'd tell him his difficulty is worth living for, worth suffering for, even worth dying for. I know this is romantic, but that's what psychoanalysis should be: a romance, or roman, an art form."

BY CHARLIE WILSON, MD

Focus on the Things You Can Control

Dr. Charles Wilson is former chairman of the Department of Neurosurgery at the University of California, San Francisco, and director of the Brain Tumor Research Center. He is originally from Missouri. In his spare time, he enjoys running and playing jazz piano. This essay was adapted from his speech given at the National Brain Tumor Foundation's Third Biannual Conference, March 10–13, 1994, and printed with the permission of NBTF and the author.

When you or someone close to you is diagnosed with a brain tumor, there are three immediate effects. One is practical – how will this affect your life? The second is physical – you may have some aftereffects from the tumor. The third, which I will discuss, is psychological.

First, the event itself can be traumatic. More importantly, there's your perception of the event and its effect on you and your loved ones, both immediately and in the future. It is perfectly normal at this time to have very deep emotions about such an event. They need to be acknowledged, and if they aren't acknowledged, they can prove to be very damaging. Some of the emotions you may feel include helplessness and hopelessness, and the two are very closely intermingled.

Second, you go through a period of bereavement, whether you are the patient or a member of the family. This was eloquently discussed by Dr. Elisabeth Kübler-Ross in her first book, *On Death and Dying*, where she described the various emotions: shock and denial, anger and rage, the deep depression – which, if prolonged, can be deeply damaging – and, finally, acceptance. Acceptance, however, is not resignation. Resignation is what I call the white flag; you're resigned to what you've heard, or even to what you may believe. To accept that you have a brain tumor and that things may not look too good is one thing, but to resign to its inevitable fate, I think, is quite another.

Science has tried to discover the mechanisms for the powerful effects that emotions have on our health, and this has given rise to terms such as *psycho-neuro-endocrine effects* and *psycho-neuro-immune effects.*

I'm often asked, "Does stress cause cancer?" I mean, who among us is not subjected to stress in some form. However, there is a basic hypothesis in science called the immune surveillance hypothesis. It states that every single day, something we eat or breathe carries in it something that may cause a cell to mutate and become a cancer cell, but we have this healthy immune system, and that particular cell is destroyed and never becomes a cancer.

It is unlikely that stress directly causes cancer, but I think it can unmask or certainly accelerate the appearance of cancer, a hypothesis supported by a hard-core scientist who, a few short years ago, thought this was nonsense. I believe also that stress can play a role in both the progression of disease and in the recurrence of a tumor.

Stress can become very powerful. It has to be harnessed so that it can be a positive power, and not something that has an erosive consequence.

In *Why Zebras Don't Get Ulcers,* Robert Sapolsky points out that stress is essential for us to react to a number of things in our lives. But, an appropriate five-minute response to stress becomes very destructive when those five minutes become five days, five weeks, and five months.

The highest court of science in this country is the National Institutes of Health, which has established a center for alternative medicine. In part, it's for scientific investigation. But, it also acknowledges that there are nonscientific factors that may impact disease, health, and survival.

In January of this year, the National Cancer Institute (NCI) held a symposium on the interaction of mind and body in disease. Bernie Siegel discussed the mind-body connection before a telecast of PBS's Bill Moyers "Healing and the Mind." From this, one could conclude that the mind is powerful, that this power can be developed and directed positively.

Who has not heard of spontaneous remission and spontaneous regression of cancer? It's been documented many times, particularly in tumors such as neuroblastomas, malignant melanomas, and lymphomas. Sometimes there is an explanation – an infection, for example. It's been known that if you had cancer of the lung and developed a complication, that is, a cancer in the pleural cavity where the tumor was removed, your chances of survival are much higher. It has been shown for a glioblastoma that a post-surgical infection is statistically significant for recovery.

There are other reasons for the basis of spontaneous remission: pregnancy, partial removal of the tumor, fever of a noninfectious sort. Usually, the basis for this remission involves the immune system, but often we simply do not know why.

There are ten very specific things that you can do, not in place of conventional medicine, but in addition to. There are certain things you can't control: you can't control that you have the tumor, and you can't control where it is. But there are things you can control. So, focus on things over which you do have some control. And I can assure you, there is real power in the things that are recommended here.

· · ·

First, seek psychological help. On the front page of today's *San Francisco Examiner* is a story about sports psychology called "Mind and Matter." It covers world-class athletes who often scoffed at the idea of needing any kind of psychological help. But you'd have to be pretty out of it not to recognize that sports psychology is a big thing. The Oakland A's have a full-time sports psychologist on staff.

103

There has to be a power within psychologically examining ourselves – who we are and what our strengths and weaknesses may be. This helps us in dealing with our lives and whatever life may bring us. More importantly, from your standpoint, psychological examination empowers people in a way that has been shown to increase their chances of survival and to have a profound effect on longevity. In other words, learn coping skills: how to manage stress. Whether you do this through meditation or breathing exercises, it is something you can learn to do that will give you some sense of having control over what's happening.

· · ·

Second: socialize, socialize, socialize. Visit your friends and your family. Dr. David Spiegel's work with breast cancer patients showed that those who became socially isolated had a mortality rate that was twice as high as those who were not socially isolated. This is a very impressive statistic. If a patient has at least one confidant, a person whom he can tell everything, his chances of surviving over any given period of time are approximately doubled. Some suggest that a pet has the same effect.

· · ·

Third, join a support group where you can go and express your fears, worries, and concerns. It is a place where you can laugh and bond with people who happen to end up in the same boat as you.

· · ·

Fourth, learn about your disease. Initially, it's very stressful. You read about brain tumors and you see what a scan looks like. You see your own scan. Your throat tightens and you feel sick to the stomach. But once you have learned something about your disease, you become a partner in the team of people who will determine your future treatment. And, over time, this improves your ability to cope. You have an understanding of your disease.

· · ·

Fifth, grieve. It's a terrible thing that has happened. Your family grieves, you grieve, and it's okay, it's natural.

. . .

Sixth, face your own mortality. This was the hardest one for me. As I look forward to my sixty-fifth birthday in a couple of months, I am finally in touch with my own mortality. I've always been too busy to think about it! I realize that life is finite. Life can be beautiful, but it's certainly not forever. A part of the end of life is dying, and it's okay to think about it. It's okay to wonder about it. It's okay to be a little bit afraid of it. But, it's not okay to just pretend it will never happen to you.

. . .

Seventh, try to learn something about visual imagery. There are many ways of doing that. Dr. Martin Rossman, of San Francisco, has introduced interactive guided imagery, which is just one form. I used to think this was not very important. But I am convinced now that it can be very powerful for some people.

. . .

Eighth, despite all that has happened, decide that you are going to develop some new interest or a new activity. Maybe you've always wanted to become a volunteer. Maybe you've always said you'd like to take a class in Greek mythology. Maybe you'd like to learn jazz saxophone, write a book, or learn to paint. Doing something that's different is compelling and will give you a new sense of accomplishment.

. . .

Ninth, exercise and eat properly. You might say to yourself, "I have a weak leg or arm" or "I don't have much energy." Well, if you want to be inspired, watch the Special Olympics or a wheelchair marathon. Exercise gives you a sense of discipline and control. It makes you feel better. Psychiatrists learned long ago that exercise is probably more effective for depression than the couch. You should be healthy. Having a brain tumor does not mean that the body harboring this tumor should not be maintained and improved.

. . .

Finally, get in touch with a higher being. It can be any form or spirit. This will give you strength. This will give you peace. Physicians are now learning that when religion matters to a patient, they should take it seriously. The mind can be a powerful determinant in healing and recovery. Believe that you can beat this disease against all odds. Focus on those things in your life that you can control, but, above all, put your trust in a higher being. The strength that you can find in a spiritual experience has power beyond your imagination.

. . .

It's a beautiful day today. It's the first day of the rest of your life, and I hope that my God, and your God, will bless you all.

BY JOHN WALKER, PhD

Every Tumor Has a Brain:
Assessing Neurological Changes

Dr. John Walker is assistant professor of neuropsychology in the Neurology Department and director of the Northern California Epilepsy Center at the University of California, San Francisco. He has worked with many brain tumor patients. Originally from Wisconsin, Dr. Walker now makes his home in San Rafael, California. This essay is dedicated to Stacy.

> *The human brain is a world consisting of a number of explored continents and great stretches of unknown territory.*
> *– Ramon Y. Cajal*

I have worked with a number of people with brain injuries in my career as a neuropsychologist. In each case I have tried to bring my knowledge of brain sciences, and my knowledge of human thinking and emotion, to help both the person and myself to understand what has occurred. Each person is unique, not only in such medical factors as the location, size, and type of tumor, but also in how it has affected that person's functionality, and how the person has responded to the illness.

Although each person's response is unique, there are some patterns that emerge across individuals. I want to share with you a review of those patterns, to guide you in evaluating whether you are relatively typical or relatively atypical of some known patterns that occur in people with brain tumors.

Each person who comes to me with a brain tumor has two things that I consider. First, I want to know something about the location, size, and type of tumor, as well as where the person is in his or her treatment. Second, I want to know how the tumor has affected the individual. I want to know whether there have been changes in perception, motor abilities, language, memory, and other aspects of thinking. I also want to know how the individual copes with the illness.

I'm aware that, for the patient, problems may be new and confusing. It is my job to help make sense of the symptoms. Usually this evaluation helps someone who is a long-term survivor of a brain tumor. Sometimes the effort is directed toward helping a person and family understand the changes that are happening as the tumor progresses. Both situations are important.

I use several guiding principles. First, I listen carefully to what the individual or the family has noticed so far. This gives me a good sense of strengths and weaknesses, of what has changed and what remains unchanged. I know that I will meet the person for only a short time, and many real-life problems may not be apparent in an office examination.

Second, I follow Walker's Law: "The customer is always right." I want to be clear about what the person or family thinks are the problems. However, I also believe, "The customer may be right, but for the wrong reason." That is, often people notice a problem, but may have the wrong explanation.

One of my favorite examples is a woman named Eileen who came to see me because she felt she had a bad memory. She told me that when people came up to her, saying hello, she would have no idea who the person was until there was enough said to finally trigger a memory. She found it very embarrassing not to recognize familiar faces. Eileen had had a brain tumor removed when she was a teenager, almost twenty years before I met her. There had been complications in her recovery.

In examining Eileen, I discovered that she was nearly blind, which she readily acknowledged. She had even attended the School for the Blind for rehabilitation. She could not see from her right eye. Her left eye allowed a very narrow, tunneled field of vision. Within this diminished field of vision, she usually ignored the left half of the image, favoring the right half of her visual world. Yet, the nature of her brain injury had left her feeling that her vision was perfectly intact. It wasn't surprising that she didn't recognize friends' faces – she got very little visual input, and it was only when they spoke long enough that she could place them. But her problem in this situation was due to vision, not memory.

The third part of my approach to understanding brain function is the Principle of Parsimony. It means we should favor simpler explanations over more complex interpretations. For example, vision is a simpler and earlier stage of information processing than memory. If a visually impaired patient complains of memory problems, it is likely that the visual problems are affecting memory. In other words, the defect is likely not with the memory, but with the vision. It's important to determine the cause of an impairment in order to overcome it. Often, understanding that the problem exists at a simpler level offers clues for how to work around the problem.

Several biological characteristics help to narrow the possible functional effects of a brain tumor. First, the left side of the brain controls most of the functions on the right side of the body, and vice versa. These functions include skin sensation and motor control, for example.

Other senses, such as vision and hearing, are more complex because of the partial anatomical crossover of nerves. For example, the left side of the brain monitors the right side of the visual world, taking inputs from each eye. A tumor affecting visual centers in the brain may make a person insensitive to one side of the visual world, even though each eye remains capable of vision. Tumors that affect visual pathways may selectively knock out only parts of the visual world, an important clue to the location of a tumor.

Speech is another example of a strong biological predictor. In most people, the ability to speak lies in the left side of the brain. A tumor in the left side of the brain is far more likely to cause some degree of language problem than the same tumor in the right side. However, about 10 percent of people have their speech center on the right side. This appears to be more likely if a person is left-handed, though most left-handers still have speech on the left side of the brain. Because speech is such an important function for humans, problems are often obvious.

Depending on the location of the tumor, an individual may experience problems with speech or understanding. Problems may be limited to reading, writing, spelling, or difficulty repeating words. Almost all people with language impairment will have problems finding the right word, an extreme version of the tip-of-the-tongue phenomenon that we all experience. A thorough evaluation of language strengths and weaknesses can be very helpful in these situations.

Once we get past such elementary functions as vision, hearing, skin sensation, motor control, and language, it is difficult to locate functions in particular spots in the brain. Studies of patients with brain tumors, as well as people with other kinds of brain injuries, suggest that some functions may be represented in both sides of the brain with one side being dominant over the other. For example, the right side of the brain probably has greater representation for visual-spatial analysis.

The back of the brain is primarily involved in high-level perceptual analysis, while the front part is primarily involved in evaluating and executing actions. Pathways in the temporal lobes are critical in receiving and storing new information, though they appear to be unimportant in retrieving that information once it has been learned. Previously learned information appears to be stored in multiple areas of the brain. Therefore, the total size of the injured tissue is closely tied to the impact of the injury.

In addition, an individual may have problems with intellectual or emotional control because of the distant effects of a brain tumor. For example, brain tumors grow and occupy space within a limited area inside the skull. This growth can lead to increased pressure on the brain and can be reflected in problems with concentration and the level of emotional arousal. The individual may feel more irritable or emotionally out of control. Some tumors affect the circulation of fluid inside the brain, leading to a buildup of fluid called hydrocephaly, thus increasing pressure inside the brain.

Some tumors, especially those affecting the connecting fibers of the brain (white matter), may block effective transmission from one area to another, even if the primary brain areas are intact. Some treatments for brain tumors can lead to temporary, diffuse problems with thinking skills. These are especially seen in chemotherapy or radiation treatments. In an effort to stop the tumor from growing, healthy brain cells are permanently damaged, often in the area near the tumor, and sometimes in more distant places.

Many people with brain tumors can benefit from a systematic evaluation of their intellectual strengths and weaknesses. There are hundreds, if not thousands, of tests that have been developed to test brain function. In general, a good neuropsychological evaluation should cover a variety of abilities that might be affected by a brain tumor. Such an assessment would include an evaluation of verbal and visual skills. It should also include tests for the ability to concentrate, and tests for motor speed and control. The total time devoted to such testing may vary from less than an hour to many hours, and should reflect the nature of the problem and any need for assistance. Sometimes, subtle problems require more evaluation than obvious problems.

A good evaluation should also be tied to more practical concerns. The same deficit may affect the lives of two individuals in very different ways. Language problems may affect a salesman very differently than a gardener. Similarly, two individuals with visual-spatial problems will be affected differently if one is a plumber and the other a clerical worker. It is not enough to define how an individual performs on a series of tests. Relevance to practical needs is essential.

An individual with a brain tumor does not exist in an emotional vacuum. Although some emotions may be the result of a particular type of brain injury, most emotions are a direct result of how that person reacts to the tumor and its effects. Depression is the usual result if an ability that the person considers essential to his life is impaired. It is common for an individual to go through various emotions, ranging from anxiety about the future, depression over losses, exhilaration at being alive, and determination to live. They don't necessarily occur in the same order for each person. For most people, emotions may even change from day to day, depending on the stage of the illness. It is important to understand that anxiety and depression may decrease cognitive function, and effective treatment may dramatically restore normal function.

I admire those individuals who are stubborn and don't let the tumor stop them. We can all strive to create a sense of realistic hopefulness based on acceptance of what has occurred. We can develop a positive attitude to strive for improvement in the future. We must also understand what is and is not possible concerning improved brain function.

It is imperative to find professionals who can help determine how the brain is functioning. Usually, the doctors most involved in treatment of brain tumors are neurosurgeons and neuro-oncologists. Although most are very knowledgeable, many do not have an extensive background in cognition or emotional evaluation. Other doctors, such as neurologists and psychiatrists, are often more knowledgeable of these concerns. Neuroscience nurses often have considerable, practical experience. Psychologists, especially neuropsychologists, are usually well prepared in evaluating cognitive and emotional consequences of a brain tumor. Other specialists, such as speech therapists, occupational therapists, and physical therapists, can also be of help.

A professional not only must have a knack for assessing performance, but also should understand how the evaluation translates into the real world and what kind of rehabilitation services are available to treat specific limitations. It's acceptable to push any of your doctors for as much information as you can get, and to ask them to refer you to the other specialists listed above. You and your family live with the consequences of the brain tumor every day, and you deserve the best insight possible about your brain's function.

BY KARYN REDDICK

What Is Faith? Reflections of a Hospital Chaplain

In 1988, Karyn Reddick wrote this story for Search, *while I was editor. Her husband, Bruce, was struggling with a brain tumor. They lived in Hawaii at the time. She moved to California after his death. She then studied theology and remarried. She is now director of pastoral care at Long Beach Memorial Medical Center in Long Beach, California.*

I come from a family of performers and achievers. People would come to us for advice and help. We were self-sufficient and we didn't need anyone. We were good at all we did. Bruce ran a successful company and played semi-professional soccer. I ran an advertising agency. We both sang lead roles in musicals, operas, and oratorios. Jim was a drum major and radio disk jockey at seventeen years of age. Debbie was an outstanding thespian as a freshman, winning many statewide talent and beauty contests. At four, Matthew was already playing soccer and winning baby contests. Our family sang together professionally. We thought there was nothing that we couldn't handle. We were active in church, but it was like a second job. We believed that God had specially blessed us.

There were challenges, though. My adopted mom, Tutu, was dying of cancer. I had been caring for her for several years. Her illness had overlapped her husband's. He had died in 1983 after suffering five heart attacks and three strokes. Tutu was now near death in Queens Hospital. I was working full-time, keeping house, taking care of the kids, and staying with her in the hospital each day, all without asking for any help. God had blessed me with strength. I was proud of my performance.

During that year, my husband, Bruce, had been acting strangely. He was a perfectionist, but things were not always getting done. He started to sleep instead of doing his chores. He had always been known for his calm personality, a thinker who didn't give in to much emotion. He had never raised his voice. But now he yelled at the kids, even used profanity. His customers complained of inefficiency. I thought our marriage was on the rocks. I believed he was working too hard in his business and just didn't have enough time and energy for us. I looked for psychological reasons for the changes. I even considered divorce.

Bruce was a pillar of the church. He was a Bible scholar and often preached and taught. One Sunday, a friend said, "Something happened to Bruce when we were together, maybe a seizure." He knew that Tutu was dying and didn't want to add to my grief, but felt he needed to let me know.

That night, in the dark, I confronted Bruce with the information. He cried and admitted that for several months his mind had not been doing what he wanted it to do. When he wanted to roll down the window in the car, he would reach for the radio. He couldn't always turn off the shower. He would have episodes where he would be unaware of his surroundings. He would still be awake and standing, but not functioning. He could tell when the "spells" were coming and warn people not to be alarmed. Later, clients and our young son told of times when he would just drive into intersections or stop in the midst of traffic. He hadn't wanted to bother me. He hadn't really wanted to face the fact that something serious was going on. We prayed together that God would take away our fear.

After three appointments with the neurologist, a CAT scan was ordered. He was diagnosed with a glioblastoma multiforme, grade IV. His doctors gave him two to six months to live. The day after his first surgery at Queens Hospital, Tutu died. I planned her funeral outside of the intensive care unit where my husband lay recovering from surgery.

I wanted so much just to sit and tell her all of this. How could this be happening to us? We did everything right. We were good Christians. We helped others. We read our Bible.

During a visit, our pastor asked us to change our way of thinking and not give in to the medical information. Our church members asked us to believe that God only gave perfection to God's children, all we had to do was believe it. We tried. . . .

Our daughter had joined a charismatic church. Her pastor told us that if we had "enough faith," the brain tumor would be healed. We prayed and asked for enough faith. It was hard to imagine just exactly what that would be. We wondered who was measuring and how we would know if we had enough.

It was a wonderful feeling to be surrounded by our community of faith. We felt God's presence and power. We believed that God was hearing us and would answer our prayers. There was so much more that we wanted to do.

Praying passively wasn't enough. After the initial shock, we actively gathered information at the medical library. It wasn't going to get us down. Ten days after the surgery, we opened as Captain von Trapp and Maria in the *Sound of Music*. We attended a Marriage Encounter weekend and sang the Hawaiian Wedding Song to the other couples, who were all in tears.

After six weeks of radiation, Bruce's tumor had all but disappeared. We were on track; all of the prayers were being answered. Then the chemo. Bruce did better than most, as we had expected. He was proud of his discipline. We spoke to groups about how we were living with his disease. We made radio and TV appearances. We spoke at Bruce's alma mater. We spoke about faith and determination. Years later, our older children told me how phony it had all seemed to them when they were so afraid. But fear was not part of our game plan.

The scan after the first month of chemotherapy revealed a tumor larger than before. How could this happen after all our prayers? People said we didn't have enough faith. Once again we asked, "What was enough faith?"

What about all the good we were doing for the community, our righteous and Christ-centered behavior? What about Bruce's healthy diet and visualization techniques? What was happening? Weren't we doing everything right? We were ashamed of the fear we felt in our hearts. We were too afraid to express it to each other or to people at church. We suspected now that we didn't have enough faith. God knew the truth, others didn't. Individually, we thought about all the unworthy things we had done and were ashamed.

There was a chance to participate in an experimental project. We flew to San Francisco for a radioactive implant. Bruce was excited about being a part of such a project. The researchers informed us that they would blow the tumor away. Bruce went through the procedure with flying colors, as we had expected. We were back on track.

We left the hospital on Christmas Eve to fly east, visit his relatives, and join our children, who were staying with family. Bruce got weaker with each passing day. Finally, I could hardly wake him. We flew back to San Francisco and he lost consciousness. He didn't recognize me. This wasn't in the plan. What was going wrong? What were we to do? Where was God? Was God listening? I remembered the Psalms in which the Israelites cried out to a God who they thought didn't hear.

Our minds could not solve this, and medicine did not have all the answers. We did not talk to anyone about our frustration. After all, who wants to hear someone who is not winning? After Bruce regained consciousness, he was paralyzed on his left side. We flew back to Hawaii in a more introspective mood.

On the plane, I promised God that since He had spared Bruce, I would do something to help other patients. Soon after our arrival we started a group called Cansurmount, with the help of the American Cancer Society, to bring together brain tumor families and patients. We discovered that we were not alone in our struggle. We were beginning to recognize just how important it was to have someone who could share our emotions and understand them.

Now our house was always filled with people. We learned to experience real friendship. We began to develop deeper relationships with our friends and with God. God was always part of my thought process, walking alongside.

The people in our church became part of our family. The other brain tumor families became our family. We saw God in their faces and deeds.

I began to read books on scripture, theology, spirituality, and psychology. Factoring our experience into these subjects expanded my understanding. I was humbled into handing my problems over to God when I couldn't fix them myself. It was time to listen to God, instead of trying to manipulate Him.

Bruce's brain tumor journey lasted over five years. During that time, he had four brain surgeries and one back surgery. Our family structure had eroded. We were all different. Our young son needed hospitalization for emotional support. We were all in therapy at one time or another. Our relationship with Bruce's parents became strained as we competed for his last months.

Bruce did not have a realistic opinion of what he could and couldn't do. It was hard to allow him to be independent and watch him from behind a door in case he fell. It was important to Bruce to remain active. Although he couldn't see, he remained active in soccer, listening from the sidelines. He helped to prepare church lessons.

I was not always as sensitive as I would have liked to be. I tried not to get angry. In the attempt, I shut down emotionally. I was in survival mode. It was so painful to lose my husband, bit by bit. I remember early in his disease being sorry that I now had to take out the garbage, the man's job. Eventually, there was nothing that I could ask him to do. But God was working in ways that I hadn't noticed. I had never been very sure of myself. Now, I was managing chronic crisis. I learned I could do more than I had ever imagined. I also learned that help was always there. Friends were nearby, ready to help.

Bruce died at home in 1989, paralyzed and blind. In the last two years of his illness, I had begun my master's courses in pastoral studies.

I interned as a chaplain in the same hospital where he had had his first surgery. I quickly knew that this was where God was calling me. With the support of my family and friends, I finished my degree the year after he died. I was ordained as a minister in the Church of the Disciples of Christ. My son Matthew and I moved to Loma Linda, where I continued my training. Currently, I serve as director of pastoral care at Long Beach Memorial Medical Center. Along with caring for patients, families, and staff, I also teach ministerial students.

Life will never be the same for any of us. We learned that real relationships come from a willingness to share our lives and our vulnerabilities, not just our accomplishments.

In God's hands, we are perfect in our woundedness. God's grace fills an empty cup, not a full one; it cannot be earned or manipulated. Walter Brueggemann wrote, "The upshot of faithfulness is not certitude, but precariousness – precariousness which requires a full repertoire of hoping, listening, and answering to life joyously. . . . Life does not consist of pleasant growth to well-being, but it consists of painful wrenching and surprising gifts. And over none of them do we preside."

I have led grief groups for almost ten years. I hear pieces of my own story repeated week after week by countless courageous people. The biggest joy in my life is the honor of being present as they tell their own stories. I hope and pray that as I move farther from my own pain and closer to theirs, I will continue to provide professional support. There is so much that we will never understand as we navigate through this strange land.

BY DEBRA JAN BIBEL, PhD

A Zen Approach

Dr. Debra Jan Bibel is author of Freeing the Goose in the Bottle: Discovering Zen through Science, Understanding Science through Zen.

Korean Zen master Seung Sahn visited a Zen center one evening, and offered to answer any questions about Buddhist teachings and practices. In a large audience of monks, students, and the generally curious laypeople, one man asked the master, "I have a friend who is dying of a brain tumor. What teachings can I give him?" Without a moment's hesitation, the master replied, "First, do not mention death or dying. Have your friend practice breathing in and out. With each inhalation, have him concentrate on the energy and clarity of his mind. With each exhalation, let him feel the expulsion of poisons. After your friend practices this for a while, tell him that his body has a tumor, but that his true self will not die. His true self also does not live. Ask him to find his true self with each breath."

BY WILLIAM BUCHOLZ, MD

Hope: The Generic Formula

Dr. William M. Bucholz wrote this essay for the Journal of the American Medical Association. *He has a practice in northern California. The style of the essay is a humorous parody of the written information disseminated by drug companies.*

DESCRIPTION: HOPE is what gets us out of bed in the morning.

CLINICAL PHARMACOLOGY: HOPE is a naturally occurring substance created by an individual's ability to project himself or herself into the future and imagine something better than what exists in the present. It serves as a cofactor for most purposeful behavior and is necessary for coping with fluctuating feelings of despair, depression, fear, anxiety, and uncertainty.

HOPE has three components: the individual's hoping; the projection into the future (expectation); and the object, event, or state desired.

Individuals experiencing HOPE vary with respect to the density and binding constants of HOPE receptors. There is both up-regulation and down-regulation of receptors depending on the danger of the circumstances, the individual's sense of vulnerability, and the support system available. Certain individuals have a pathological need for HOPE and are susceptible to False HOPE.

Expectation, comprising the subunits Credibility and Attainability, is conveniently measured as a vector having units of distance and difficulty.

Even if there is a strong belief that a goal is possible (Credibility), if the individual perceives it to be too difficult to attain, or that it is impossible to project himself or herself into the future, Expectation will be low. Both intellectual and emotional Expectancies must be above threshold levels for HOPE to be effective.

The Object Desired is the most visible aspect of HOPE and may be expressed concretely or implied (e.g., "I hope the surgery will cure the cancer" or "I hope everything turns out all right"). The strength of HOPE often depends on the meaning or importance (Preciousness) of the Object.

PHARMACOKINETICS: After administration either verbally or visually, HOPE enters cortical and thalamic pathways, where it is processed for Credibility and Attainability. If receptors are blocked by depression, anxiety, or distraction, there is no binding and HOPE dissipates immediately. Depending on the number and avidity of open receptors, there is an immediate effect that has a half-life of minutes to hours. Longer effects require repeated administration. Both sensitivity and tachyphylaxis can develop depending on how often the Desired Event occurs or does not occur.

INDICATIONS: HOPE is indicated in the treatment of HOPE Deficiency, Depression, and Anxiety and to increase Motivation and Compliance with treatment. It is useful in relieving fear, pessimism, and a sense of vulnerability. It increases energy and courage in all individuals, resulting in greater likelihood of difficult goals being accomplished.

HOPE should be given at the initial diagnosis of a potentially fatal disease, at any recurrence, and when the disease is terminal. It should also be used when dealing with chronic "benign" diseases such as arthritis, diabetes, and hypertension. It should be given whenever despair is anticipated.

HOPE Deficiency (Hopelessness) is a state of despair characterized by inability to anticipate any positive outcome. Patients are generally unable to act decisively, make decisions, have meaningful relationships, or experience joy or meaning. They are described as having "given up." The Will to Live is diminished in proportion to the degree of hopelessness.

CONTRAINDICATIONS: There are no known contraindications for giving HOPE.

MECHANISMS OF ACTION: Depression is characterized by the inability to imagine anything different from the present. HOPE, because of the component of Expectation, relieves the inability to project into the future. HOPE allows such individuals to create a possible future, thereby relieving the onus of living in the present. The anticipation of pleasure relieves pessimism. Anxiety, characterized by a sense of loss of control, is alleviated by predicting a desirable future event, thereby providing an anchor for the individual in the midst of free-floating anxiety. The sense of aloneness is relieved by anticipating allies or help. Fear, which consists of projecting into the future an undesirable event (helplessness, pain, etc.) is redirected by the expectancy of a positive rather than negative outcome. Motivation to accomplish goals and compliance with medical treatment are increased by a sense that the goal is attainable.

WARNINGS: False HOPE is the intentional or inadvertent creation of the expectancy that a low-probability outcome is likely. It is a violation of medical ethics to deceive a patient intentionally for the purposes of manipulating his or her behavior. Physicians and nurses generally try to avoid any appearance of False HOPE and may generate False Despair instead. Certain individuals, because of a high need for HOPE based on the seriousness of their condition or their premorbid personality characteristics, are prone to misinterpret information given and develop False HOPE or False Despair even though none is intended. Patients generally use False HOPE to diminish the full emotional impact of an intolerable situation.

False Despair is the intentional or inadvertent discrediting of any probability that a desired outcome is possible. To avoid any suggestion of False Hope, some medical professionals will purposely lower patient expectations to avoid any chance of disappointment. Patients likewise may avoid the disappointment of unrealized hopes by purposefully keeping the expectations low, feeling it is safer to expect the worst. It is a violation of compassion and the Hippocratic oath to purposely withhold HOPE of a low but finite probability outcome from those patients who desire it. It may be pointed out that even under the bleakest of circumstances, there are some survivors.

USAGE IN PREGNANCY AND CHILDREN: HOPE is safe during Pregnancy. It passes into the breast milk and is known to be safe for infants. HOPE may be used in the pediatric population, adjusting language, but not dosage, according to age. . . .

HOW SUPPLIED: There is no standard dose. Individual patient needs and individual personnel styles determine how HOPE should be given. Listening carefully to both verbal and nonverbal communication will often suggest the best preparation of HOPE to use. Sometimes it is pointing out that even though the chances are slender, there is at least a chance. Sometimes it is just being there, with a gentle smile and a promise not to abandon the patient. Sometimes the greatest challenge is keeping a sufficient supply on hand for the personnel dispensing it.

BY TESS SIERZANT

The Strength Inside

Tess Sierzant has over twenty-five years experience as a neuroscience nurse. Currently, she is neuroscience clinical nurse specialist and neuro-oncology program coordinator at the Minneapolis Neuroscience Institute, Abbott Northwestern Hospital. Tess is also past president of the American Association of Neuroscience Nurses.

As a nurse, I am humbled when I work with individuals diagnosed with brain tumors. Recently, I was talking with the wife of a gentleman who was diagnosed with glioblastoma multiforme. She asked me how I keep going day in and day out, supporting people who receive such awful news. I had to stop and think before I answered her, since I haven't experienced what they experience or haven't received awful news about myself or someone in my family.

My patients and I often discuss the many changes that have already taken place in their lives. They talk about missing work; when the children should come to see Dad after his surgery; why he had those seizures; will his hair grow back; and, will his personality ever be back to normal. We talk about chaos and the disruption to the patient's life and the lives of the family and friends.

We talk about the big questions that are out on the horizon. Patients hear many statistics about survival rates, then we talk about how no one can truly predict the future. Henri-Frederic Amiel once said, "Uncertainty is a refuge of hope." For many patients, not knowing what lies ahead is exactly what keeps them going. Samuel was a fifty-three-year-old carpenter and successful businessman when I met him. He had put his "blood, sweat, and tears" into his work and now it was finally paying off. He was married. With three children in their teens and twenties, he was looking forward to playing with his grandchildren someday. The tonoclonic seizure came out of the blue for Samuel. Neither he nor his family had ever seen one. The next few days were a whirlwind, going to the emergency department, the MRIs, the consultations with many doctors, being admitted to the hospital. He hadn't been in a hospital since the day he was born. He tried to be strong for his family, but he wasn't sure he was doing a good job.

The recommendation was surgery. His tests revealed a high grade oligodendroglioma. He wasn't sure what that meant exactly – he just knew that somehow his life would be different from then on.

I got to know Samuel very well in the ensuing months. He religiously went to treatment – radiation, chemotherapy, support group sessions, visits with his doctors, and follow-up MRIs. In knowing him, I discovered that all the "facts" about his tumor type were not important to him. What was important for him was all that he continued to do: he enjoyed his family, continued to build his business, and found time for a baseball game or some cribbage. He never really wanted to know "the numbers," as he called the oft-quoted statistics that health professionals would give. I think Samuel wanted to hold on to the life that he had always hoped for. Some called this denial, but I disagreed. I think Samuel very thoughtfully chose how he would travel the road that he did. Even as Samuel's situation worsened and those around him could see that the end was near, he held on to hope. Samuel taught me a great respect for hope and the uncertainty surrounding it.

When I work with newly diagnosed patients and families, I am often invited into a very intimate part of their lives. I hear about fears, regrets, and hopes. Over and over again I am amazed at what is inside each person: the desire to live this life as best as they can, the desire to love, and the desire to be loved. I think the reasons why I continue are the strength that I see in the human spirit and my desire to help others see that strength within themselves.

BY NICHOLAS DE TRIBOLET, MD

The Patient and Physician Must Fight Together

Dr. Nicholas de Tribolet is professor and chairman of neurosurgery at the Centre Hospitalier Universitaire Vaudois in Lausanne, Switzerland.

I remember very clearly the first patient on whom I had to operate on my own. He was twenty years old, a healthy mountaineer, and Swiss champion in wrestling. His brain tumor revealed itself through an epileptic seizure, but otherwise he was perfectly healthy. His younger sister had died two years earlier of a malignant brain tumor that her doctor had not even considered worth treating. His parents were desperate and ready to accept the worst. I removed a right frontal glioblastoma, the most malignant form of brain cancer.

After the operation, I had a long discussion with the family. I convinced him and his parents that he should have radiotherapy. Now, more than fifteen years later, he is married and the father of two lovely girls. He enjoys life and works full-time. This is rather unusual for someone who had a malignant brain tumor. It does not really fit in with the statistics.

I learned from this experience that each patient should be given the chance to be an exception, whatever his or her prognosis may be. The neurosurgeon must not only provide the technical skill and clinical competence for treatment, but also the psychological prowess to convince the patient that there is always a chance to survive, and that it is worthwhile to fight against the disease with all his or her energy. The patient and physician have to fight together. This is only possible when genuine human contact has been established between the two.

Afterword

Never underestimate yourself. From the beginning to the end, you will be taking small but courageous steps in learning about and dealing with your diagnosis, treatment, and recovery. In *Time and the Art of Living*, poet Robert Grudin writes: "We are like people climbing out of an immensely deep valley on a trail which only occasionally allows us glimpses of the geography below or the heights above."

Never forget that you may be an inspiration to someone else. Your bravery in facing your condition will affect those around you positively. Never underestimate your own inner-resources, strengths, creative abilities, and common sense. Never underestimate the love of your friends and family. Asking them for help gives them a gift: it gives them the opportunity to show you their love.

If you have lost a loved one, may these words by William Penn bring you some comfort: "They that love beyond the world cannot be separated by it. Death cannot kill what never dies. . . . Nor can spirits ever be divided that love and live in the same divine principle, the root and record of their friendship. Death is but crossing the world as friends do the seas; they live in one another. This is the comfort of friendship, that though they may be said to die, yet their friendship and society are, in the best sense, ever present because immortal."

No one says that this is an easy burden to bear or that there are any magical solutions. Life presents us with many challenges that we didn't ask for. We must find our own meaning in them, and go forward.

On behalf of all the authors who shared their stories, we wish you a future filled with joy, prosperity, and good health.

TRICIA ROLOFF

PART 4

Resources

A Million Decisions

It is hard to fathom the difficulties that some people face. Illness is devastating for the people who must live with its consequences. We, as bystanders, can only empathize with these people and learn from them. As one family member said of her mother's ordeal, "My mother is going through hell, and there's no other way to say that."

Some people find facing their own mortality ultimately invigorating. There is a newfound desire to live, and live better than before. It takes away all pretentiousness. Life becomes personally meaningful; the demands of society and the demands imposed by others are stripped away.

And yet, death is an unwelcome topic for many people in our society. No one really wants to talk about it. Medical personnel view it as a failure, rather than a natural event. But death, like life, is sacred. Whether or not we have been touched by illness, we need to learn how to prepare for death, both psychologically and spiritually, so that it is not feared but welcomed. And we must help our relatives and friends when their own end is near. We must make them feel loved and honored for their contributions in life, so that they may go with peace in their hearts, not loneliness or sadness.

In addition to a fear of death, one of the most common issues that brain tumor patients face is bewilderment over the years wasted in misdiagnoses, conflicting opinions, and general confusion over the complex details surrounding their condition. Many feel paralyzed while trying to decide what to do or whom to listen to.

Sometimes the situation is clear: we just know the right thing to do. One patient knew from the start that she wasn't going to have surgery, even though she had an aggressive tumor. Over the years, she controlled it with a multitude of alternative therapies. Her courage is inspirational. When asked what made her decide to forgo surgery, she replied, "I've just had this horrible gut feeling that if I go into surgery, I won't come out alive." She is living by her gut instinct.

Whether to have surgery, radiation, chemotherapy, or any other treatment is a personal decision that only you can make. You don't have to try every possible therapy if you don't want to. Of course, most people want to try something. Some who have exhausted conventional treatments have opted for more controversial therapies. Even if these treatments provide only a few more months where your quality of life is acceptable to you, it is your right to have this time.

Ultimately, extensive research is the best way to relieve fear. The answers to our questions lie not with one source, but with many. Libraries, physicians, friends, other patients, foundations, and so forth are all potential resources. Research is necessary to make informed decisions about treatment. Once you make a decision, know in your heart that it was your best choice. New techniques and advances in treatment are reported every day. Don't burden yourself with guilt if you find a different piece of information later down the road. There's no such thing as the "perfect decision," just what makes sense at the time. The following resources can help you in your search for answers.

TUMORS
Acoustic neuroma
Well-differentiated astrocytoma, called low-grade or grade I
Anaplastic astrocytoma, called mid-grade or grade II
Glioblastoma multiforme, called astrocytoma grade III
Brain stem glioma
Chordoma
Craniopharyngioma (near the pituitary; affects growth hormones)
Ependymoma
Ganglioneuroma
Juvenile pilocytic astrocytoma

Meduloblastoma

Meningioma

Oligodendroglioma

Optic nerve glioma

Pineal tumors

Pituitary tumors

- Prolactinoma: A tumor on the part of the pituitary gland that secretes prolactin.
- Acromegaly: A tumor on the part of the pituitary gland that secretes growth hormone.
- Cushing's disease: Outer shell of the adrenal glands secretes an excess of cortical hormones. (In children, pituitary disturbances most commonly cause growth retardation, delayed puberty, diabetes insipidus, and Cushing's syndrome.)

Primitive neuroectodermal tumors

Schwannoma

Vascular tumors

TREATMENTS

Surgery (microsurgery using the surgical microscope)

Radiation therapy: Interstitial irradiation, also called Brachytherapy, Radiosurgery, or Gamma Knife

Chemotherapy: A combination of various drugs, depending on the tumor

Bromocriptine (Parlodel): For pituitary tumors (sometimes used in conjunction with surgery)

Transphenoidal operation (through the nasal passage): For pituitary tumors

BRAIN TUMOR FOUNDATIONS AND ASSOCIATIONS

Note: Donations are used for research grants and patient services, such as information publications. Most organizations were started by a small group of people, or just one person, with the goal of providing patients and their families with information and support. Each group has a slightly different focus, such as research fundraising, support services, or written information. They are listed geographically.

An asterisk signifies a member of the North American Brain Tumor Coalition, a network of groups that share resources. The coalition also created the Brain Tumor Awareness Week. It meets in Washington, D.C., to organize speakers to address congressional meetings, increase awareness, and lobby for research funding. Patients and family members are encouraged to participate in this annual event.

> United States – East Coast

Acoustic Neuroma Association. 600 Peachtree Parkway, Suite 108, Cumming, Georgia 30041-6899. Tel: (707) 205-8211. Started in 1981. Targets benign cranio-nerve tumors including acoustic neuromas (eighth nerve tumors), and meningiomas. Resources include booklets and pamphlets for patients and a network of forty support groups around the country. Publishes a quarterly newsletter, *The Acoustic Neuroma Association Notes.* Holds a biannual national symposium. Internet: www.anausa.org. E-mail: anausa@aol.com.

*The Brain Tumor Foundation for Children, Inc. 1835 Savoy Dr. # 316, Atlanta, Georgia 30341. Tel: (770) 458-5554. Fax: (770) 458-5467. Started in 1984. Publishes a quarterly newsletter that includes a column in which physicians respond to medical questions. Formed a Teen Club to offer teenagers a source of peer support. Also initiated the Little Peoples Group, for ages six to twelve years. The foundation is affiliated with Emory University and Egleston Children's Hospital, for which it also raises funds, including funds for a pediatric research laboratory. Internet: www.btfcgainc.org. E-mail: btfc@bellsouth.net.

*The Brain Tumor Society. 124 Watertown Street, Suite 3H, Watertown,
Massachusetts 02472. Tel: (800) 770-8287. Fax: (617) 924-9998.
Started in 1989. Publishes the newsletter and resource guide, *Heads
Up.* Offers an award-winning Web site, support group information,
a patient/family telephone network, and individualized support
and information for brain tumor patients and families. Holds
educational symposia, sponsors professional meetings, and hosts
an annual meeting at which research grants are allocated. Internet:
www.tbts.org. E-mail: info@tbts.org.

*The Children's Brain Tumor Foundation. 274 Madison Avenue, Suite
1301, New York, New York 10016. Tel: (212) 448-9494. Fax: (212)
448-1022. Started in 1990 by a group of parents. Holds an annual
fundraiser, Big Apple Circus, in October. Publishes a free hundred-
page resource guide. Internet: www.cbtf.org. E-mail: cbtfny@aol.com.

*The Healing Exchange Brain Trust. 186 Hampshire Street, Cambridge,
Massachusetts 02139-1320. Tel: (617) 876-2002. A forum for
exchange of information and support. Deals with all kinds of brain
tumors. Internet: www.braintrust.org. E-mail: info@braintrust.org.

International Radiosurgery Support Association. P.O. Box 60950,
Harrisburg, Pennsylvania 17106-0950. Tel: (717) 671-1701.
Provides information on stereotactic radiosurgery (Gamma Knife).

*Pediatric Brain Tumor Foundation of the United States. 302 Ridgefield
Court, Ashville, North Carolina 28806. Tel: (828) 665-6891. To
contact a clinical nurse specialist for specific medical questions or
concerns, call 1-800-253-6530. Has a national program to help
families establish a support group in their area. Resources include
brain tumor literature and other publications. Internet:
www.ride4kids.org. E-mail: ride4kids@pbtfus.org.

> UNITED STATES – SOUTH

*The South Florida Brain Tumor Association. P.O. Box 770182, Coral Springs, Florida 33077-0182. Tel: (954) 755-4307. Started in 1991. Has organized two support groups in the area. Holds an annual conference in October on future research and treatment for healthcare professionals, patients, and families.

*Southeastern Brain Tumor Foundation. P.O. Box 422471, Atlanta, Georgia 30342. Tel: (404) 843-3700. Conducts fundraising for research. Support group meets monthly. Publishes a newsletter. Organizes patient programs. Internet: http://groups.accessatlanta.com/sbtf.

> UNITED STATES – MIDWEST

*American Brain Tumor Association. 2720 River Road, Suite 147, Des Plains, Illinois 60018. Tel: (800) 886-2282. Fax: (847) 827-9918. Publishes numerous detailed booklets on various aspects of brain tumor disease. Services include resource listings, information about support groups, social service referrals, Connections (a pen pal program), and a listing of physicians who offer investigational treatments for brain tumors in adults and children. Internet: http://www.abta.org. E-mail: info@abta.org.

Fairview-University Brain Tumor Center. 2450 Riverside Avenue, Minneapolis, Minnesota 55454. Tel: (800) 824-1953, (612) 672-7272. A regional referral center for the Upper Midwest and a national and international resource for brain tumor patients and their families. The center is a partnership of academic and community physicians and healthcare providers with the University of Minnesota Cancer Center. A multidisciplinary team combines research and patient care to provide the best possible outcomes. Internet: www.braintumor.fairview.org.

> United States – West

*National Brain Tumor Foundation. 414 Thirteenth Street, Suite 700, Oakland, California 94612. Tel: (510) 839-9777. Fax: (510) 839-9779. Patient support information line: (800) 934-CURE (2873). Publishes a quarterly newsletter, *Search;* a booklet listing all support groups in the United States and Canada; and a resource guide for patients and families. The first copy of these items is free. Holds a biannual three-day conference. Copies of lectures given at previous conferences are available from CAL Tapes of Menlo Park, California. Tel: (800) 360-1145. Internet: www.braintumor.org. E-mail: nbtf@braintumor.org.

The Pituitary Network Association. P.O. Box 1958, Thousand Oaks, California 91358. Tel: (805) 496-4932. Fax: (805) 557-1161. Formed in 1993. Publishes the *Pituitary Patient Resource Guide,* 2nd Edition, and *The Emotional Aspects of Pituitary Disease.* Has biannual patient conferences and an online bookstore. Internet: www.pituitary.org.

> England

The Brain Tumour Foundation. P.O. Box 162, New Malden, Surrey KT3 3YN, England. Tel/Fax: 0181 336-2020. Started in 1994 by several family members of brain tumor patients. Publishes the newsletter *Brainbox,* conducts fundraising for research, and offers patient literature. E-mail: btf.uk@virgin.net.

> Canada

Acoustic Neuroma Association of Canada. P.O. Box 369, Edmonton, Alberta T5J 2J6. Tel: (780) 428-3384, in Canada (800) 561-2622. Started in 1984 by four patients. Publishes the quarterly newsletter *Connections.* Provides booklets and video brochures, support, patient networking, and information on physical and facial neuromuscular rehabilitation and postsurgical problems. Internet: www.anac.ca. E-mail: anac@compusmart.ab.ca.

*Brain Tumor Foundation of Canada. 650 Waterloo Street, Suite 100, London, Ontario N6B 2R4. Tel: (519) 642-7755. Fax (519) 642-7192. Started in 1982. Publishes the quarterly newsletter *Brainstorm,* the *Adult Brain Tumor Patient Resource Handbook, and* the *Pediatric Brain Tumor Handbook* (for parents and teachers). Developed and maintains the Kelly Northey Memorial Library to provide educational materials to patients, families, and physicians. Holds an annual information day in October. Can assist with support group formation. Internet: www.btfc.org. E-mail: btfc@btfc.org.

> OTHER SERVICES AND INFORMATION

Brain Tumor Support Group on the Internet (BRAINTMR): To join, send a message from your e-mail account to: listserv@mitva.mit. edu. The text of your message should read: Subscribe BRAINTMR (your name). For example: Subscribe BRAINTMR John Taylor

MEDICAL LIBRARIES

The National Library of Medicine (NLM). The world's largest research library is a resource for all United States health science libraries. Medical Literature Analysis and Retrieval System (MEDLARS) is a computerized system of more than thirty databases and databanks offered by the NLM. Databases include MEDLINE, which cites international biomedical sources, and DIRLINE, a directory of information resources. Access is available at Internet: www.medscape.com.

In the public library you will also find programs such as Books in Print and Forthcoming Books in Print. These will list all the published books on brain tumors under the subject title, "brain tumor."

Brain Surgery Information on the Internet

The Web site http://www.brainsurgery.com provides information on
brain surgery and brain tumors.

The Web site http://www.virtualtrials.com lists all current experimental
protocols at universities for brain tumor patients.

Consumer Health Information

Institute for Health and Healing Library (formerly Planetree) of the
California Pacific Medical Center, San Francisco. Tel: (415) 600-
3681. The library is nationally known and highly respected for its
collection of consumer health information. It has resources for
compiling an information packet on a specific topic and can also
fax individual articles for a nominal fee.

Transportation, Financial Assistance, and Equipment

American Cancer Society (ACS). Most chapters of the ACS will direct
brain tumor inquiries to the brain tumor foundations listed above;
however, other important services they can provide are: (1) local
transportation, (2) equipment, such as wheelchairs and canes, (3)
emergency financial assistance, and (4) the Angel Flight Program,
which offers assistance with commercial flights for out-of-state
treatments. These services are provided through each ACS chapter.
For more information, contact your local chapter.

Aircare Alliance. Uses private pilots who donate their time to transport
those in financial need. Internet: www.aircareall.org

Mercy Medical Airlift: Volunteer pilots offer long-distance travel
assistance to low income families. Internet:
http://mercymedical.org.

MEDICAL CONSULTATION

Cancer Consultation Service in San Francisco. Tel: (415) 775-9956. A panel
of specialists studies medical records and biopsy reports. Provides second opinions on diagnosis and treatment. Chapters of the American
Cancer Society may have information on similar services in your area.

> WRITTEN AND VERBAL CONSULTATION ON CANCER

National Cancer Institute (NCI). Through the National Institutes of
Health, the NCI publishes excellent self-help booklets. The Cancer
Information Service (CIS) of the NCI answers questions from the
public. To get single copies of their publications or direct phone
assistance, call 1-800-4-CANCER. This number can also assist you
in clinical trial searches. Internet: www.nci.nih.gov,
www.cancernet.nci.nih.gov.

Cancer patient education databases. Internet: www.chid.nih.gov.

United States Department of Health and Human Services. The site
provides links to related agencies. Internet: www.healthfinder.gov.

> NEUROSCIENCE REHABILITATION CENTERS

Brain Injury Association. 105 North Alfred Street, Alexandria, Virginia
22314. Tel: (800) 444-6443 or (703) 236-6000. Fax: (703) 236-6001
Provides resources and referrals to rehabilitation facilities. Has
branches in each state, a catalog of reference books, and a quarterly
newsletter, *TBI Challenge*. Check with this group for specific rehabilitation centers for brain tumor patients. Internet: www.biausa.org.

> CANCER RETREATS, ALTERNATIVE THERAPIES, AND HOSPICES

Children's Hospice International. 901 North Pitt Street, Suite 230,
Alexandria, Virginia 22314. Tel: (800) 24-CHILD. Lists hospice
centers specifically designed for children and their caregivers.
Internet: www.chionline.org.

Commonweal. P.O. Box 316, Bolinas, California 94924. Tel: (415) 868-
0970. Information line for alternative treatment. A well-known
retreat for people with cancer. Michael Lerner, founder of
Commonweal, publishes *Choices in Healing: Integrating the Best of
Conventional and Complementary Approaches to Cancer.* This
publication provides the most current information on cancer
therapies and alternate healing practices. Internet:
www.commonweal.org.

The Compassionate Friends, Inc. P.O. Box 3696, Oak Brook, Illinois
60522-3696. Tel: (630) 990-0010. Organization of support groups
for bereaved parents and siblings. Focuses on self-help. Publishes
pamphlets, newsletters, and a listing of books. Organizes chapters
around the country. Internet: www.compassionatefriends.org.

National Hospice and Palliative Care Organization. 1700 Diagonal Road,
Suite 300, Arlington, Virginia 22314. Tel: (703) 243-5900. Hospice
provides specialized services and assistance to terminally ill patients
and their caregivers. Provides nursing, counseling, and volunteer
services. Can assist with locating a hospice near you. Call (800)
658-8898 for a general information packet. Internet:
www.nhpco.org.

Office of Alternative Medicine Clearinghouse. National Institutes of
Health, P.O. Box 8218, Silver Spring, Maryland 20907-8218. Tel:
(888) 644-6226. The clearinghouse will send out information
packets to patients and caregivers. Internet: www.nccam.nih.gov.

The Wellness Community. 2716 Ocean Park Boulevard, Suite 1040, Santa
Monica, California 90405. Tel: (310) 314-2565. Has developed a
network of wellness communities around the country. Focuses on
alternative healing practices and therapies. Harold Benjamin, PhD,
one of the founders, is the author of *The Wellness Community
Guide to Fighting for Recovery: From Victim to Victor.* Internet:
www.wellness-community.org/facilities.html.

www.pitt.edu/~cbw/altm.html. Provides extensive information on
  different alternative therapies for cancer.

FINANCIAL ASSISTANCE

Cancer Care, Inc. 275 Seventh Avenue, New York, New York 10001. Tel:
  (800) 813-HOPE. Internet: www.cancercare.org.
Cancer Fund of America. 2901 Breezewood Lane, Knoxville, Texas
  37921-1009. Tel: (865) 938-5281. Provides assistance with medical
  equipment. Internet: www.cfoa.org.

PHARMACEUTICALS

Pharmaceutical Manufacturers Association. (800) 762-4636. Provides
  medication assistance to low-income families. Internet:
  www.phrma.org.

THERAPISTS

Ask your hospital social worker or clinic staff for referrals to reputable
and well-liked counselors. Some may be on staff at the same hospital. Or,
call the local chapters of professional associations for a listing of therapists
in your area. Look through your local telephone directory. Also ask friends.

Hospitals usually have chaplain services. Other assistance may be found
at local religious facilities.

CREATIVITY AND THE ARTS

Art and writing are therapeutic tools that express our innermost needs
and wants. You might keep a daily journal of thoughts, feelings, desires, and
conflicts; write poetry or short stories; keep a dream journal; or draw, paint,
make pottery – anything that helps you communicate on a different level.
Check with your local community college for classes on creative writing and
other arts. There are also retreats specifically for writing. Ask the college English
department about these programs.

Legal and Financial Planning

> Disability, job discrimination, and insurance

The National Coalition for Cancer Survivorship (NCCS). Tel: (301) 650-9127. The coalition will help you with discrimination cases either in your job or with insurance companies. It publishes *What Cancer Survivors Need to Know about Health Insurance,* by Irene C. Card of the NCCS. Internet: www.cansearch.org.

The American Association of Retired Persons (AARP). 601 E Street NW, Washington, D.C., 20049. Tel: (800) 424-3410. AARP has a wealth of information on retirement issues. Internet: www.aarp.org

The Information and Referral (I and R) Program can direct you to help agencies. Contact your local United Way for information.

The National Organization on Disability. Tel: (202) 293-5960. Based in Washington, D.C., the organization can help with issues of benefit eligibility, filing for benefits, and incidents of discrimination. Internet: www.nod.org.

Social Security Administration. City and state offices are listed in the phone book under "government offices." The Social Security Administration handles state disability insurance claims.

> Financial planners

Partnership for Caring. 1620 Eye Street NW, Washington, D.C., 20007. Tel: (202) 296-8071. Fax: (202) 296-8352. Nonprofit group that provides information and current forms for living wills and durable powers of medical attorney. Internet: www.partnershipforcaring.org.

Institute of Certified Financial Planners (ICFP), 3801 E. Florida Avenue, Suite 708, Denver, Colorado 80210. Tel: (800) 322-4237 (information services). Provides a list of planners by area. Internet: www.fpanet.org.

National Association of Personal Financial Advisors. 355 West Dundee
Road, Suite 200, Buffalo Grove, Illinois 60089. (800) 366-2732. A
small group of "fee only" planners. Provides a list of full-time
planners in your area. Internet: www.napfa.org.

> LEGAL COMPUTER SOFTWARE

Family Lawyer and Estate Planner. Published by The Learning Company.
Tel: (800) 223-6925.

Willmaker. Focuses on wills, living wills, and documents for final
arrangements. Discusses federal and state estate taxes and proxy
requirements for healthcare directives. Published by Nolo Press.
Tel: (800) 992-6656.

BRAIN TUMOR BOOKSHELF

> BOOKS FOR BRAIN TUMOR PATIENTS

Epstein, Fred J., and Elaine Shimberg. *Gifts of Time.* New York: Berkley,
1994.

Ferruci, Toni, and Chris Gilson. *Worst Fear: One Woman's Story of Brain
Surgery and Survival.* Los Altos, CA: Rising Star Press, 1997.

Gunther, John. *Death Be Not Proud.* New York: Harper & Row, 1971.

Libutti, Rebecca. *That's Unacceptable: Surviving a Brain Tumor –
My Personal Story.* Martinsville, NJ: Krystal Publishing, 2001.

Nolan, Patrick, Patricia Nolan, and Michele Nolan. *Against the Odds: The
True Story of Michele, A Cancer Survivor.* Tel: (800) 831-3082.
Internet: www.whidbey.com/nolan/.

Priebe, Sandy. *Alex's Journey: Story of a Child with a Brain Tumor.*
Chicago: American Brain Tumor Association, 1994.

Rosenberg, Doris. *The Talking Lady Presents Having a Brain Tumor.*
Toronto: Talking Lady Press, 1996. For children ages four to twelve
years. Tel: (888) 512-TALK. Internet: www.talkinglady.com. E-mail:
ellierose45@yahoo.ca.

Smith, Gregory W., and Steven Naifeh. *Making Miracles Happen.* Edited
by Fredrica S. Friedman. Boston: Little Brown & Company, 1997.

> BOOKS ON CANCER

Harpham, Wendy S. *After Cancer: A Guide to Your New Life.* New York:
Harper, 1995.

McKay, Judith, and Nancee Hirano. *The Chemotherapy and Radiation
Therapy Survival Guide.* Second edition. Oakland, CA: New
Harbinger Publications, 1998.

O'Regan, Brendan, and Caryle Hirshberg. *Spontaneous Remission: An
Annotated Bibliography.* Institute of Noetic Sciences, 1995.

Pelton, Ross. *Alternatives in Cancer Therapy: The Complete Guide to Non-
Traditional Treatments.* New York: Fireside, 1994.

Rosenbaum, Ernest. *Everyone's Guide to Cancer Therapy.* Third edition.
Edited by Malin Dollinger. Kansas City: Andrews McMeel
Publishing, 1998.

> FOR WOMEN

Jackson, Carole. *Color Me Beautiful.* New York: Ballantine Books, 1987.

Noyes, Diane Doan. *Beauty and Cancer: Looking and Feeling Your Best.*
Dallas: Taylor Publishing, 1992.

> ON DEATH, LOSS, AND RECOVERY

Cousins, Norman. *Anatomy of an Illness As Perceived by the Patient.* New
York: Bantam Doubleday Dell, 1991.

"Facing Death: It's Inevitable, It's Difficult, and It Just Might Transform
Your Life." *Utne Reader* 47 (September/October 1991): 65-88.
Tel: (612) 338-5040.

Fairview Health Services. *The Family Handbook of Hospice Care.*
Minneapolis: Fairview Press, 1999.

Fairview Press, ed. *Holiday Hope: Remembering Loved Ones During Special Times of the Year.* Minneapolis: Fairview Press, 1998.

Felber, Marta. *Finding Your Way after Your Spouse Dies.* Notre Dame: Ave Maria Press, 2000.

Fiore, Neil A. *The Road Back to Health: Coping with the Emotional Aspects of Cancer.* Berkeley, CA: Celestial Arts, 1990.

Heinlein, Susan, et al., eds. *When a Lifemate Dies: Stories of Love, Loss, and Healing.* Minneapolis: Fairview Press, 1997.

Kennedy, Alexandra. *Losing a Parent: Passage to a New Way of Living.* San Francisco: Harper, 1991.

Krementz, Jill. *How It Feels When a Parent Dies.* New York: Knopf, 1996.

Kübler-Ross, Elisabeth. *Living with Death and Dying.* MacMillan Publishing, 1997.

———. *On Children and Death: How Children and Their Parents Can and Do Cope with Death.* New York: Scribner, 1997.

———. *On Death and Dying.* New York: Scribner, 1997.

———. *Questions and Answers on Death and Dying.* New York: Simon & Schuster, 1997.

———. *To Live until We Say Good-bye.* Prentice Hall, 1997.

Levang, Elizabeth. *When Men Grieve: Why Men Grieve Differently and How You Can Help.* Minneapolis: Fairview Press, 1998.

Levang, Elizabeth, and Sherokee Ilse. *Remembering with Love.* Minneapolis: Fairview Press, 1992.

Pitzele, Sefra K. *We Are Not Alone: Learning to Live with Chronic Illness.* New York: Workman Publishing, 1986.

Register, Cheri. *The Chronic Illness Experience: Embracing the Imperfect Life.* City Center, MN: Hazelden, 1999.

Silverman, Janis. *Help Me Say Goodbye: Activities for Helping Kids Cope When a Special Person Dies.* Minneapolis: Fairview Press, 1999.

Simonton, O. Carl, et al. *Getting Well Again.* New York: Bantam, 1992.

Sterns, Ann Kaiser. *Living through Personal Crisis.* New York: Ballantine, 1992.

Viorst, Judith. *Necessary Losses: The Loves, Illusions, Dependencies, and Impossible Expectations That All of Us Have to Give Up in Order to Grow.* New York: Fireside, 1998.

> CREATIVITY, INSPIRATION, AND POETRY

Beck, Charlotte Joko. *Everyday Zen: Love and Work.* Edited by Steve Smith. San Francisco: Harper, 1989.

Cameron, Julia. *The Artists Way: A Spiritual Path to Higher Creativity.* Tarcher, 1992.

Carson, Richard. *Taming Your Gremlin: A Guide to Enjoying Yourself.* New York: HarperCollins, 1986.

Dreher, Diane. *The Tao of Inner Peace: A Guide to Inner Peace.* New York: Plume, 2000.

Gibran, Khalil. *The Prophet.* New York: Knopf, 1999.

Goleman, Daniel, Paul Kaufman, and Michael Ray. *The Creative Spirit.* New York: Plume, 1993.

Grudin, Robert. *The Grace of Great Things: Creativity and Innovation.* New York: Ticknor & Fields, 1997.

———. *Time and the Art of Living.* New York: Houghton Mifflin, 1997.

Hayes, Helen. *Gathering of Hope.* New York: Walker & Company, 1985.

James, Elliott. *Living a Balanced Life: Applying Timeless Spiritual Teachings to Your Everyday Life.* Atlanta: Dhamma Books, 1990.

Miller, Karin B., ed. *The Cancer Poetry Project: Poems by Cancer Patients and Those Who Love Them.* Minneapolis: Fairview Press, 2001.

Samples, Pat. *Daily Comforts for Caregivers.* Minneapolis: Fairview Press, 1999.

Stoddard, Alexandra. *Making Choices: Discover the Joy in Living the Life You Want to Lead.* New York: Avon Books, 1995.

> MONEY

Domiguez, Joe, and Vicki Robin. *Your Money or Your Life: Transforming Your Relationship with Money and Achieving Financial Independence.* New York: Penguin, 1999.

CATALOG BOOK SERVICES

> LEGAL

Nolo Press is a self-help legal publishing company in Berkeley, California. It publishes books and software on all aspects of the legal system. Catalog available at (800) 992-6656.

> MIND/BODY MEDICINE

A-R-E Press (Association for Research and Enlightenment). Publishes a catalog of new-age books and videos. Tel: (800) 723-1112.

The Institute for the Study of Human Knowledge, run by David S. Sobel, MD, and Robert Ornstein, MD, author of *The Healing Brain,* has a book/tape service called Mental Medicine. It publishes a newsletter, *Mind/Body Health News* ($10/year), and also provides the most current books on mind/body medicine. Tel: (800) 222-4745. Internet: www.ishkbooks.com.

Acknowledgment for Previously Published Work

"Modern Fiction on the Couch: An Interview with a Retired Psychoanalyst" by Anatole Broyard, copyright © 1986 by The New York Times Company, reprinted by permission. "Hope: The Generic Formula" by William Bucholz, MD, adapted from an article published in the *Journal of the American Medical Association,* used with permission. "I Could Hardly Say the Words, 'My Daughter Has Cancer'" by Richard Haile, adapted from an article published in *Search,* used with permission. "I Can Do Everything I Dreamed I Could" by Norman Kornsand, adapted from an article published in *Search,* used with permission. "Why Me? Why Not Me?" by Linda Kendall, adapted from an article published in *Search,* used with permission. "History" by Vera Kroms, first published in *The Cancer Poetry Project: Poems by Cancer Patients and Those Who Love Them,* used with permission. "I No Longer Fear Death" by Linda, first published in *To Live until We Say Good-bye,* by Elisabeth Kübler-Ross, MD, copyright © 1978 by Ross Medical Associates, S.C., and Mal Warshaw, reprinted by permission of the publisher, Prentice Hall/A Division of Simon & Schuster, Englewood Cliffs, N.J. "Adagio for Ginny" by Karen Leahy, first published in *The Cancer Poetry Project: Poems by Cancer Patients and Those Who Love Them,* used with permission. "To Believe," by Gail Lynch, adapted from *In Sickness and in Health,* used with permission. "Excerpts from *Magic and Loss*" by Gregory Raver-Lampman, first published in *Magic and Loss,* used with permission. "What Is Faith? Reflections of a Hospital Chaplain" by Karyn Reddick, adapted from an article published in *Search,* used with permission. "Last Ode" by Harry Smith, first published in *Two Friends II,* used with permission. "Focus on the Things You Can Control" by Charlie Wilson, MD, adapted from a speech given at the National Brain Tumor Foundation's Third Biannual Conference, March 10–13, 1994, and printed with the permission of NBTF and the author.

Index

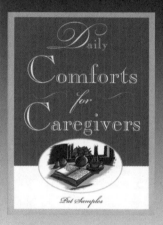